GROWING UP
WITH
TELEVISION

GROWING UP

WITH

TELEVISION

EVERYDAY LEARNING

AMONG YOUNG

ADOLESCENTS

JoEllen Fisherkeller

Temple University Press
PHILADELPHIA

Temple University Press, Philadelphia 19122
Copyright © 2002 by JoEllen Fisherkeller
All rights reserved
Published 2002
Printed in the United States of America

Library of Congress Cataloging-in-Publication Data

Fisherkeller, JoEllen, 1952–
    Growing up with television : everyday learning among young adolescents / JoEllen Fisherkeller.
        p. cm.
    Includes bibliographical references and index.
    ISBN 1-56639-952-1 (alk. paper) — ISBN 1-56639-953-X (pbk. : alk. paper)
    1. Television and youth—United States.   2. Youth—United States—Attitudes.
3. Popular culture—United States.   I. Title.

    HQ799.2.T4 F57 2002
    302.23'45'0385—dc21

                                                                    2001054250

In memory of Peggy and John,
who guided me from day one

Contents

Acknowledgments

lthough I am its author, this book was written by many. These sentences cannot thank all those people adequately for the contributions they have made to this work and my life. But these words are a public note of genuine appreciation.

I am forever indebted to the young participants in my study and to their families and teachers for the time and insights they gave to me. I wish Marina, Christopher, and Samantha only the best in life and hope that my rendering of their experiences contributes to their well-being and to that of other young people.

When I was a graduate student, Anne Haas Dyson helped to focus my attention on individuals and their complex relationships to language, literacy, and different means of cultural representation. I am continually awed by the integrity with which Dyson approaches children and their learning experiences and am honored to have her as a mentor and friend. Don Hansen and many others at the University of California, Berkeley, developed my ideas about culture, identity, learning, and interpretive research. But I must thank Don in particular for introducing me to Ron Lembo, whose name appears often in this book. Lembo's work on TV viewing culture and contemporary social experience has provided inspiration and perspective. I am deeply grateful that he is generous with his feedback, support, and friendship.

I cite David Buckingham often because his research on youth, media, and education sets a standard. I consider myself lucky to have his many writings as models and to be working with him to examine issues of multimedia education and cross-cultural communication. I am fortunate to know his British colleagues Cary Bazelgette, Julian Sefton-Greene, and Jenny Grahame, who also contribute to my ideas. On this side of the Atlantic, Kathleen Tyner expertly guides my thoughts and questions about multiple literacies and schools, while Steve Goodman shows me the reality of kids' learning through media. They help me laugh, too—a healthy way to keep going.

I have received support from New York University in many ways. The university and the School of Education both provided me with Research Challenge Grants to develop the manuscript and to conduct follow-up interviews with the focal participants. Many in NYU's Department of Culture and Communication encouraged and mentored me, especially Neil Postman, Christine Nystrom, and Deborah Borisoff. Robin Means-Coleman has been a steadfast compeer whose work is exemplary and whose collegiality is admired. My writing has been stimulated and strengthened by exchanges with Niobe Way, Robert Cohen, and members of the faculty writing group in the New York University School of Education. Although all of my students end up teaching me about my work, several graduate students deserve mention for their assistance on this project, including Julie Jackolat, Jill Steinberg, and Brian Cogan. Special thanks to Allison Butler and Emilie Zaslow, who proofread diligently and contributed in many ways. They are bright spirits.

Micah Kleit at Temple University Press has been an enthusiastic, reliable, and intelligent editor whose recommendations have made this work more readable. I am grateful to others at the press for their assistance, accessibility, and friendliness, including Jennifer French, Tamika Hughes, and editor-in-chief Janet Francendese. I also thank Carole LeFaivre-Rochester and Susan Maier of Berliner, Inc. And thanks to Torrance York for her talent in producing the photograph incorporated into the press's cover design, and Lisa Conrad and Kellon Innocent for helping with the photo shoot.

Many colleagues and friends move my work and ideas forward and make life worth living. Sara Dickey first taught me about anthropology and symbolic interactions; now she and her son Daniel remind me that playing is important, too. Karla Hackstaff is always there with thoughtful questions and full-fledged empathy, professional and personal. Kathleen Hogan shows me how to be a rigorous investigator into kids' learning and thinking—and a happy gardener. I rely on Cyndy Greenleaf and Melissa Phillips to talk about what matters for children and adolescents, whether in schools, their own homes, or via multiple media. I am grateful to teachers from days past who became friends and supporters, including Carol Padden, Susan Davis, Dan Schiller, Michael Schudsen, and Herb Schiller, whom we sorely miss. I depend on all of them, near and far, for their good humor and goodwill.

Chris Elder is a soul sister whose everyday experiences working with youth help ground my ideas; her energy buoys me. My biological sisters, Mary Sue, Betsy, and Patty, give me a sense of history and belonging like no others, and their children—Mallory, Rachel, and Michael—enrich and inform my sense of purpose. David, who has lived through many years of my stress and neglect of him, deserves a medal and a trip to someplace far away from his piles of stuff and lists of things to do. But he'll need a TV and VCR, CD player, and potatoes.

GROWING UP
WITH
TELEVISION

Introduction

I think the message [*Beverly Hills 90210*[1]] tries to give [is] don't be so provocative, 'cause it might get you into trouble. But it does not necessarily have to be like that. Just because a guy see a girl looking sexy and with tight things does not necessarily mean that she wants to get raped.... People have their freedom, and you know that's wrong for other people to violate it like that.

—Marina,[2] Dominican American,[3] age 12

I'm gonna make my own movies and put 'em on [my own cable station, named Silver Screen]. Then I'm gonna have, like, a talk show, with famous people on it. And I'll have Silver Screen specials, like, shows about topics in the news that have to deal with family matters, like drugs and alcohol and playing with guns and AIDS and, uh, pregnancy and that stuff. Like two hour-specials on that.... [And] world news, like CNN.... It's gonna be a long newscast. It'll, like, be an intermission between movies.... I'm gonna have one movie that I play maybe every other week, not every day, I'm gonna have so many movies that I won't have time to play another movie over again.

—Christopher, African American, age 12

[Oprah Winfrey] gets on my nerves. 'Cause when she has, like, a victim up there, it's very disturbing. And ... the person is up there crying, instead of, like, going for a break or something, she'll go, "Tell me more, tell me more. Come on, come on, tell me more." And it's just, like, you know, enough is enough.... It's kind of disturbing to see someone, like, so insensitive and so uncaring. For her to just be like, 'Come on, go on— it's OK if you cry and break down. Actually, that's what I want; it will get me ratings. Come on.' You know? It's just, I don't like her.

—Samantha, Irish–Jewish American, age 12

Why talk with young people about TV? It is important to talk *with* children and adolescents to counter the nature of much public discourse that talks *about* them and their interactions with popular media such as television. For even though cultural and media studies now conceive of audiences as active meaning-makers at some level, most often adults refer to youth as passive receivers of media messages and images. At the same time, marketers and advertisers profile youth as consumers to be targeted and manipulated into making lifelong commitments to product brands and styles. Relatedly, news coverage reports that children and adolescents are troubled or in trouble, even though those who are engaged in high-risk behaviors are in the statistical minority. Thus, for the most part, adults talk about young people as duped, a demographic, and in danger. Youth are very seldom given opportunities to distinguish themselves as diverse individuals who have thoughtful and intriguing insights into television, trends of commercial culture, or troubles in life. In this book, some very distinct individuals speak for themselves and have illuminating things to say about these matters.

Yet these young people's words alone are not enough. Their words make sense only when they are placed in social and cultural contexts, and when the speakers are located historically, socially, and materially. Marina's, Christopher's, and Samantha's particular situations at home, at school, and with peers have something to do with the words they say and have a great deal to do with what their words mean. And their situations at home, at school, and with peers have something to do with how they interact with television and have a great deal to do with what their TV interactions mean.

Why focus on television when digital communications systems and cyber-networks dominate discussions about life at the beginning of the twenty-first century? Desktop computers and online systems do not have the reach and scope of television. In the United States, only about half of poor and working-class households have access to desktop computers and online networks; their access often comes through school and work rather than from home. However, poor and working-class households have at least one television set, often more, and frequently have cable and satellite hookups, a videocassette recorder, and TV-based gaming systems. And most young people still watch television for more hours each day than they use desktop computers and online networks (Roberts 2000).

But this book is not about the presence of TV and related technology in young people's houses; it is about young people growing up in television *culture*. Television culture is a phenomenon that exists both on and off the screen, like it or not, although most viewers, like me, understand that the "reality" of on-screen life is different from the reality of off-screen life (Davies 1996; Lembo 2000). When I talk with young people about television, I do so as an anthropologist who wants to understand how young people learn to live in a world where corporate media systems such as television represent, as well as constitute, contemporary existence. How do youths make sense of themselves in a world permeated by corporate media such as TV? How do youths learn how to be successful and powerful members of TV culture? These are focal questions of this study.

How did these questions come about? The first emerged in response to claims about how TV and other commercial media make it difficult for young people to have an authentic identity or a solid sense of self. Such claims are rooted in conventional worries about the nature of TV and about youths' susceptibility to TV messages and images. Scores of studies show that television stories contain stereotypes of all kinds and that both news and entertainment programs present limited points of view. Critics argue that young viewers are seduced by biased and superficial TV realities and so develop selves that are mere collages of style—or disjointed identities without a genuine core or sense of coherence.[4] Such individuals can be easily swayed and do not necessarily have allegiances to a common set of ideas or values. In short, kids are growing up to be flakes and fakes.

If this is the case, it is a problem, because democratic societies value individuals who can think and act for themselves, look critically and reflectively at the world around them, and create change when and where needed. Democratic citizens are not superficial but substantially informed. They do not shift constantly according to trends; they are loyal to agreed-upon principles of society.

These concerns about youth development, however, are based largely on analyses of media content and forms and on theories about culture and society. They are not based on studies of actual people and their own sense of themselves. Thus, I ask the first question of my research—How do youths make sense of themselves in a world permeated by corporate media such as TV?—to examine how particular young people actually develop in the current environment and to discuss whether, and how, their development is problematic in these ways.

I ask the second question—How do youths learn how to be successful and powerful members of TV culture?—because of the powerful roles commercial television (and other media) systems play in contemporary societies, particularly in the United States, and increasingly the world. Media producers currently operate from within huge mega-mergered corporate institutions that strive to maintain market control on a global scale.[5] These corporate media have stepped up the pace of advertising and program delivery and have accentuated glossy and sensational styles. Because of steady increases in cable and network programming and consumer "zapping" via remote and pointer controls, they now compete fiercely for consumers' attention—especially that of young consumers. In addition, multitudes of music recordings, video games, box-office movies, rental films, computer software, and online environments both compete with and promote one another. To capture and maintain consumers' attention, and ultimately their product and brand loyalty,[6] creators are forced to deliver media goods that are formulaic and cheap.[7]

Yet the U.S. and world commercial media are more than economic systems of industries, competitive markets, and mass-produced products. Commercial media, especially television media, constitute a public sphere, providing communication spaces in which people of all kinds encounter symbolic realities "out there," or worlds of issues and problems common to many (though not all). The issues and problems that young people encounter in the media lie in the realm of official politics as well as in the domain of everyday life and social relations, which are not without their own sense of politics. That is, news, documentaries, political campaigns, and public-service announcements all present contemporary audiences, young and old, with information and perspectives on current issues of the state, policies, and governance—however biased. In addition, situation comedies (sitcoms), dramas, variety shows, advertisements, sports broadcasts, and many other entertainment-based media provide young audiences with stories about who is successful and powerful in the world, and why. Madonna is known to many as a star, media mogul, and provocateur, doing whatever is necessary—given the system—to be popular while advancing the cause of female sexuality (however problematic). Bill Cosby is known as a creator of family programs that show how parents, Black and White, can gain authority over their children, as well as how Blacks can become lawyers, doctors, and other successful professionals in a world that discriminates against non-White and poor people in general. Murphy Brown is known as a TV character who speaks strongly about being an independent, assertive woman while belonging to a team of fictional journalists who strive, albeit comically, to get at "the truth" in the name of freedom of the press. Thus, TV stories, nonfiction and fiction, represent ideas about worlds of power and success.

While encountering TV as a commercial system and as a representation of worlds of power "out there," adolescents are wondering who they are and who they will be. They are intensely engaged in imagining and learning—indeed, "playing with"—what adulthood entails and what they might do in the future as adults. TV culture gives them material for figuring out how to feel powerful as adults in the future. TV culture shows them successes they might strive for, as workers in corporate industries and as citizens of contemporary publics. But exactly how do particular young adolescents come to understand adult worlds? How do different individuals imagine they might become powerful and successful as workers and as citizens? And how do everyday experiences with formulaic, commercially biased TV culture actually figure into young people's imagination and learning about being adults and participating in contemporary public realms? Posing these questions directly to adolescents helps us to arrive at the answers that are the central concern of this book.

I come to this book with my own memories of growing up in TV culture. As a young adolescent girl, I tingled with awe when, standing in our Midwestern suburban living room, I heard the voices of the astronauts as they landed on the moon. I was also devastated by John F. Kennedy's assassination, then Dr. Martin Luther King's, then Robert Kennedy's. The televised Civil Rights demonstrations, Vietnam war protests, and environmental activism of the 1960s and 1970s galvanized my emerging political awareness.

A variety of programs and personae connect me with trends and styles of a particular era and with my family. I laughed at comedians such as Carol Burnett, Phyllis Diller, Richard Pryor, and the young Bill Cosby. I swooned over Richard Chamberlain, the star of *Dr. Kildare*, and thrilled when I saw The Supremes, The Temptations, and The Beatles perform their music on TV. Science-fiction episodes of *The Twilight Zone* and *Outer Limits* gave me the creeps. I watched *The Wizard of Oz*, *The Mary Tyler Moore Show*, and *Laugh-In* while huddled with my sisters; talked to my mom about Victor Borge's being a silly but stunning piano player; and learned about the game of football by watching with my dad. The television of my youth serves as a kind of scrapbook in my mind, connecting me to the larger situations of those days and to the people who shared my time, space, and life.

TV memories remind me that I watched a great deal of television because, as a young adolescent, I was not involved in many extracurricular activities. That came later. Also, when I entered a private school outside my all-White, middle-class neighborhood, I could no longer walk to visit my few friends or play on the school grounds after school. Childhood games were no longer "cool," anyway. As a quiet, introverted girl, I felt awkward socially, and as a tomboy, I did not know what to make of the changes taking place with my body. So besides doing homework and household chores, watching TV at home filled many of my afternoon and evening hours; interacting with TV people and with my family during TV viewing was familiar and comfortable.

My uses of television are not unusual. They are similar to how TV is used sometimes by Marina, Christopher, Samantha, and their peers, even though their situations and circumstances are different from mine. Like these young people, I found meaning in specific TV characters and stories that helped me work through identity dilemmas of my adolescence. Like Marina, who admires Madonna because she perseveres in the face of criticism about her appearance and performances, I looked to TV women who struggled with issues of women's sexuality. Like Christopher, who admires Bill Cosby in his 1980s show because he reinforces the teachings of Christopher's father, I looked to TV figures who complemented what some of the authority figures in my family had to say about getting along in the face of adversity. Like Samantha, who admires *Murphy Brown* because the main character knows how to act assertively and get public attention, I looked to characters in shows who would help me express my point of view with confidence and assurance.

My background in performance gives me a unique perspective on growing up in TV culture. As a teen, I got involved in theater arts, working behind the scenes as well as on-stage in different capacities and many genres. As a young adult, I joined with a group of friends to create parodies of popular culture. We combined music, comedy, and theater to make fun of everything on TV. Thus, I moved from being an adolescent consumer of television to a young adult producer of TV satires, though what my performance group created on-stage never made it to any mainstream screens. What is pertinent about this, with respect to this study, is that my group members and I were not formally taught to send up TV culture except by TV culture itself.

I bring my informally learned "inside view" of TV culture and my formally acquired academic approaches and methods (see the Appendix) to bear on my understandings of the youths in this study. I found these youths to be aware of the "insides" of TV and critical of TV in their own ways. As noted earlier, for example, Christopher hatched a plan to create his own cable company and adjust the programming to suit viewers like him, revealing his sense of television's supply-and-demand processes. Samantha held a negative view of the behavior of a talk-show host who, to her, seems to be crassly motivated by the TV ratings system, revealing her perception of television as a marketing enterprise rather than as a public service. These young people developed their awareness of TV constructions and TV critiques by watching regularly and talking about television casually with family, friends, and peers. In other words, they have learned about TV culture from TV culture itself.

These young people also have learned how to create TV culture. Sometimes they imagine themselves appearing before others as if on television; sometimes they actually perform before others as if they were a TV image. They can see that the creation of imagery is a valued activity in the United States and in the larger world. Thus, young people's seeing themselves as images or creating themselves as images before an audience should be expected; it is problematic only if their imaginations are not given legitimate forums for expression as well as critical reflection.

Yet self-as-image processes have not replaced processes of self-formation associated with life off the screen. These young people's experiences with real people in their homes, at school, and with peers give them identities that are grounded and solid though sometimes at odds with each other. For example, Marina proudly identifies herself as the daughter of an immigrant from the Dominican Republic who came to the United States as a single mother to make a better life for her children. Marina's mother, who makes a meager living as a child-care worker, has motivated Marina to make a better life for herself and for her future children, as well. To accomplish this, Marina recognizes that she must finish school, go to college, and establish a career before having children. This means that Marina must go against the traditions established for women of her home country and, instead, adopt the expectations of middle-class America. As will be shown in the Epilogue, Marina feels this struggle of identities most acutely when she goes away to a small private college as a scholarship student. There she is regarded by classmates as "ethnic," and she describes herself as "loud" and "a clown" among her college peers. Yet her mother and sisters back home ask her why she is so quiet and serious, and she worries that she has become "whitewashed."

Most youth have to negotiate multiple senses of self that do not always fit neatly together (Amit-Talai 1995). Perhaps life today and the nature of power and success in TV culture present youth with new kinds of challenges. This book aims to let real young people bring their struggles and challenges, and their ways of negotiating them, to life and discuss what this suggests about learning and development in postmodern times.

1

Coming to Terms with TV Culture and Everyday Learning

[TV is] for when you don't have anything to do, or when you're lonely, or something. It's for you to learn, things and stuff. You learn about the programs and about the plots and stuff, the stories.... You have a lot of choices, to choose from to watch ... you can always turn it on and everything.... I usually put it on for light or whatever, just to see, just for company, I don't know. I'm alone, I don't like to leave the TV off, unless I'm getting ready to go to sleep or something. I turn out all the lights. . . and then I leave it on. I go to my room and watch videos. I just like it.

—TeniyaSerita, Puerto Rican American, age 12

TeniyaSerita's comments seem to capture, in a broad sense, some of the complex nature of our experiences with television. TV has multiple uses and a variety of features, and a good deal of "ambivalent pleasure" is associated with this fixture of contemporary life. What exactly is this thing to which she is referring? A reliable companion? A teacher? A warehouse full of stories and "stuff"? A night-light? As almost anyone who watches TV knows, it is all of these things, and it is not, and it is more.

What do these comments mean about TeniyaSerita and youths like her? What is she learning about TV "plots and stuff, the stories"? What kinds of choices does she make when she watches for "company"? Should we be worried about how young adolescents like her are learning and making choices in TV culture?

Coping with a Vexing Commodity

Television is difficult to talk about because it is so much a part of our world that it seems like the air we breathe. Also, because so much has already been said about TV, it is difficult to say anything that is new or that is not obvious, and perhaps inane. Since the decade of television's initial distribution to U.S. consumers, it has been the subject of debates, gossip, hype, research, policymaking, and promotions. Some of this discourse goes undocumented in people's everyday exchanges; some is taking up ample space in libraries, bookstores, private collections, cybermedia, and the daily press; and some is found in the medium itself and in its sibling media, film and radio. Reports about the convergence of technology and media such as TV, computers, and online networks make discussions of "television culture" seem quaint or behind the times. But the history and nature of TV is anything but quaint, and the role it plays in contemporary life is still worth talking about.

Like many types of modern communications technology, television was first widely used as a defense tool.[1] Television technology was useful in that it transmitted images as well as sound immediately from one source to multiple receivers in different locations—like radio with pictures. This capability enhanced the Allied forces' communications and surveillance strategies during World War II. After the war, when industry and government needed to convert to peacetime production and policymaking, debates ensued about the best use of this audiovisual tool. Some argued that the technology should, with government support, be made available for public use and provide educational, civic, and cultural programming. Then TV could be like a "people's university" (Barnouw 1978: 12), giving all citizens access both to the information they need to participate in democracy, such as news and lectures, and to aesthetic experiences that could enrich their lives, such as theater, music, and other arts. Others, however, argued that TV technology should be part of the world of commerce and governed by the laws of the free-enterprise system. Then TV could not only transmit cultural,

civic, and educational fare; it could also provide information about consumer products and services—the staples and symbols of the "good life"
in capitalist America.

The arguments over television's place in society then and now are primarily about different senses of the public sphere and the role communications media play, or should play, in creating and upholding that
sphere. What forces should be responsible for supporting the principles of democracy and humanity, which hold that all people should have
equal opportunities to participate in society and culture and equal access
to the means of participation? What constitutes participation, and how
should our governmental and economic systems encourage and maintain equal participation? These questions remain important, for in
answering them we work out nothing less than our ideas and values associated with freedom, justice, and the pursuit of happiness. And nothing
less than young people's dreams and possibilities are at stake.

But back in the late 1940s, commercial forces basically won the
struggle over TV's purpose and ownership. Today almost all television
systems in the United States are mass-communications industries that
operate according to corporate capitalist principles. Even the Public
Broadcasting System, which receives government funding, now draws
the bulk of its support from corporate foundations and private sources
that advertise their image by associating with PBS programming. And
the Federal Communications Commission, the only government
agency directly involved with the media, has been stripped of its reg-
ulatory role and powers largely via massive budget cuts and personnel
reductions (Schiller 1989). Thus, over the years, corporate marketers
have shaped television as a vehicle for product promotions (Barnouw
1978; Kellner 1990).

Yet how the TV system works as a promotion vehicle is not a simple matter. Corporations are interested in having their products
exposed to the largest audiences possible, and they want to buy airtime
supporting shows that will be seen by the maximum numbers of viewers. To get such advertising support, programmers need to create and
deliver shows that will appeal to the broadest of audience sensibilities.
But as programmers compete with one another for advertising support,
and as different products have different audience value, programmers
vie for airtime when the largest number of target audiences for specific kinds of products are available. Recently, cable stations and new
networks have increased the number of airtime choices a viewer can

make; intensive niche marketing via TV has been developed, as well. Encouraged by principles of free enterprise and by democratic ideals in the United States, consumers' having abundant choices is part of the ethos of commercial television (Miller 1988).

In this highly competitive atmosphere, one strategy for "marking off" territory is product differentiation. Using this strategy, programmers have created and developed a wide variety of program categories. Many genres, formats, styles, topics, and events are offered to the viewing public, including (not exhaustively) different kinds of sitcoms, dramas, soap operas, talk shows, music programming, game shows, sports, cartoons, "infomercials," home shopping, comedy–variety, live concerts, documentaries, movies, and news coverage.

Because of this abundance of program types, and because they are competing for advertisers, programmers conduct extensive market research on audiences to figure out when and how to create and sell program products that will appeal to specific masses of consumers at the right times. That is, programmers try to figure out how to "grab the most eyeballs" at any given point in time, better known as earning ratings shares via the Nielsen system.

While marketers and programmers work to get their products delivered to specific mass audiences, commercial programming is single-minded in its underlying objective: to increase audience ratings for its shows and thereby increase advertising revenues. The survival of a program thus depends ultimately on the producers' giving both audiences and advertisers what they want. From this middle-person position, most programmers choose to produce material that is "just entertainment" and not offensive or provocative on overt moral and political levels. As G. Comstock (1980: 20) puts it: "Popularity does not simply rule entertainment—it makes entertainment the principal dimension of commercial television." Even many contemporary news and documentary programs have adopted the styles and tone of entertainment, giving us so-called info-tainment and edu-tainment programs.

Entertainment material is imbued with mainstream ideologies because, to appeal to the most people without offending them, the ideas and values of programs need to align generally with those of mainstream audiences. In corporate capitalist terms, this means aligning with audiences who have disposable incomes and thus fall into the middle and upper classes. And although mainstream audiences as markets have power as the consumers of TV programming, their power extends only as far as their remote controls and spending decisions. The institutions of TV production and distribution are more powerful in that they set the agendas and define the categories or frameworks for the programming that audiences receive and choose (Gitlin 1985 [1983]; Hall 1980; Morley 1989; Schiller 1989). Thus, the ideas and values of corporate capitalist commerce inform the structures and practices of television production and delivery and shape the kinds of symbolic material that programmers create and transmit.

Learning and Developing in Postmodern Times

Many adults think that TV shapes young people's values and ideas in a negative manner by telling the wrong stories about culture and by teaching bad manners (see, for example, Postman 1985). In the past, movies, comics, and novels were seen in this way (Barker 1984; Blumer 1933; Buckingham 2000); now toys, video games, computers, and online environments are the subject of these concerns (Clark 1998; Kinder 1999; Sefton-Green 1998; Steinberg and Kincheloe 1997). Most people would prefer that children and youths learn about culture and how to be part of it from their real lives and from real people.

Everyday practices, rituals, and institutional activities—such as family dinners, school-ground play, television viewing, and e-mail messaging—do organize and shape people's sense of culture (Pitman et al. 1989; Wolcott 1982). But people do not learn all that culture presents to them, and different individuals do not learn from culture in the same way (Eisenhart 1995; Geertz 1983). Learning in TV culture is no different. Individuals in different situations have access to different kinds of television, and they make different decisions about what to view. They also vary in how they participate in viewing rituals and in how they interpret their viewing experiences (Ang 1990; Lembo 1997; McRobbie 1992; Morley 1992).

Viewers interpret all media from within a structure of identifications, such as gender, age group, family, class, race or ethnicity, and nation (Hartley 1983). When eleven-year-old Kelly watches *Beverly Hills 90210*, she is "inside" her multiple identities. She uses her experiences as a White, middle-class girl living in New York City and attending a small alternative middle school to compare with the shows' White, upper-middle-class girls and boys living in a famously rich Southern California suburb and attending a large, traditional high school.

However, gender, race and ethnicity, class, and other identities should not be seen as fixed categories (Buckingham 1993; Lembo 2000). Kelly might have values and ideas that are similar to those of the characters on *Beverly Hills 90210* (and perhaps those of the actors portraying them) because they are all White and live in large U.S. metropolitan areas. But the particular ways in which Kelly and the *90210* characters experience being White urban-dwellers cannot be known through these labels alone. They live in different regions with different climates, have different personalities, and come from different families and communities with different occupations, structures, and backgrounds. And because the *90210* characters are fictional, their experiences are constructed to be dramatically different from the everyday life Kelly knows.

My own work regards labels such as gender, race and ethnicity, and class as aspects of identity projects. "Identity projects" refers to the essential work in which a self engages to make sense of her or his particular social positions and life circumstances (Mead 1962 [1934]). As babies grow, their self-concept grows progressively more complex because they encounter more and different people and their social worlds (Berger and Luckman 1967 [1966]). Identity projects are lifelong and have age-related challenges and resolutions (Erikson 1980 [1959]; Honess and Yardley 1987; Winnicott 1990 [1971]). The identities discussed in this study are complex and changing by nature; they are fixed only by virtue of my reporting on them in this stationary document.

Young adolescents are faced with identity projects that are particular to their biological age (Csikszentmihalyi and Larson 1984) and social status in the United States. Going through puberty, they have to negotiate their sense of sexual identity, which is linked strongly to gender identity. Young adolescents in the United States also have to negotiate a sense of themselves as "almost adults," fashioning identities of the future as well as of the past (Feldman and Elliot, 1990; Hansen 1993). Youths have a sense that their own self-composition can move forward if: 1) they have learned from others through past experiences that their way of being in the world is somehow successful or powerful; and 2) their version of reality gives them powerful yet attainable visions of futures for themselves.

Power Relations and New Challenges

Identity projects are linked to power relations, or the dynamics of authority and control, which are an intrinsic aspect of all social relationships and institutional activities (Hall 1980). No matter what their situation or circumstances, young people are learning about where power lies and the nature of power. They are sorting out their own power within the realities of their lives and are dreaming of the power they hope to acquire as they move forward.

In the past several decades, feminists, civil-rights groups, and other social critics have challenged the inequities and injustices of power that are demonstrated through sexism, racism, and classism, among others. These challenges have brought about both ideological and practical changes in people's interactions and in their expectations. For example, schools such as the one in this study concentrate specifically on correcting gender biases by examining sexism in literature and history and by encouraging girls and boys to participate equally in traditionally gender-segregated activities, such as sports. Compared to females in past generations, more girls can now expect to work in the paid workforce and to put off child-rearing—if they choose to have children at all—until later in their lives. Yet, although such changes have occurred, dominant forces manage to maintain the status quo and create backlashes against such changes (Faludi 1991).

At the same time, changes in global economies, international politics, and technological capabilities have destabilized many societies' traditions. Corporate conglomerates move goods, services, and whole factories into and out of countries, looking for new markets and higher profits, practices that call into question national and regional loyalties and job security for local entrepreneurs and workers (Schiller 1989). The worldwide spread of mass media and computer communications brings more and more distant cultures into virtual contact with one another on a daily, if not hourly, basis—interactions that can foster new perspectives as well as alter the integrity of local customs and values.

Some argue that these kinds of changes have created decentered sensibilities, fragmented identities, and an overall sense of social insecurity—all signs of postmodernism (Gergen 1991; Giddens 1991). Modernist notions define the developed self as coherent around, and unified by, a central set of values and ideas provided by religion, family, local community, and civic ideals (Jagtenberg 1994; McRobbie 1992). In a postmodern world, selves are unmoored, responsive to the unpredictability of new situations and to the sensational gratification of consumerism and popular culture (Jameson 1991 [1983]). Indeed, advertising and commercialism are seen as part and parcel of such sensibilities.

Products and services are marketed as the fulfillment of human needs for social acceptance, desirability, and achievement (Kellner 1990). Ads suggest that using the right hair-care products will bring love and romance and that wearing the right brand of clothing will lead to popularity and success. Entertainment programs are fashioned as spectacularly pleasing packages for such consumer goods, reflecting corporate capitalists' intention to sell goods and services endlessly and repeatedly. Theoretically, people who construct themselves with and through commercial media and consumer products are superficial, ever-changing sensation-seekers.

Yet, people who are highly engaged with media and consumer culture may perceive their own identities as multiple and adaptive but not necessarily as unstable or fragmented (Lembo 1997; Turkle 1995). Perhaps people like TeniyaSerita appreciate all of their choices in television culture but also involve themselves thoroughly in traditions of home, community, and school. What is actually going on with real people? Do youths themselves feel decentered or solid? How do they experience the flux of social power relations, shifts in political economies, and globalized communication? What do they imagine for themselves in the future, growing up in a world saturated with the messages and images of corporate capitalist systems? To answer these questions, we need more than theoretical speculation; we need grounded insights.

Everyday Spaces of Young Adolescent Time

What young people "do" with and learn from television culture depends on who they are, their social situations and economic circumstances, and their interpretations of life experiences, which includes TV. We need to describe many contexts and levels of activity to understand how they select and use, find meaning and pleasure in, and learn from everyday television. This is a task I take up extensively in the individual studies that are at the core of this book. To understand these in-depth case studies in relation to broader scenarios, this section details young New York adolescents' general experiences of home, school, peer life, and television.

The Worlds of Home

"There are a lot of people, a lot of crime, a lot of buildings, a lot of pollution, it's loud." So TeniyaSerita, age 12, describes her hometown, New York City. It is one of the most heavily populated cities in the United

States, densely packed into five boroughs filled with tall structures. Yet how polluted, "loud," and crime-ridden is the city? The presence of many people and many industries in New York City results in a lot of noxious emissions and waste, and the busy streets and thoroughfares of the "city that never sleeps" can be noisy, sometimes day and night. And crime does have a presence there, especially in those areas that are most economically depressed. In some neighborhoods, lives are endangered or lost because of organized crime and drug trafficking.

But these problems are only part of the city's reality, and sometimes they are overblown and turned into a "stereotype," as Samantha suggested. New York City is one of the nation's major centers of cultural production and creativity in the arts; it teems with theaters, museums, galleries, libraries, and media agencies. The number of festivals, concerts, performances, exhibitions, and special events that happen each day boggles the mind. New York City is also home to people of almost every nationality and ethnicity on the planet. This demographic fact can be seen and heard at many public cultural activities and while riding subways, walking the streets, sitting in classrooms, playing in parks, and shopping at the markets and stores. As one of the renowned gateways into the land of the American dream, New York City invites immigrants. Everyday multicultural encounters give New York youths a wide range of norms, conventions, and ideas that they can compare with those they have acquired from their own diverse families.

Like other New Yorkers, adolescents such as Christopher recognize that "some parts [of New York] are cleaner and safer" than others. They know that some neighborhoods are better protected, with building doormen or private security guards. They see this when they take day trips with their schools or when their families have the resources to make excursions to museums, parks, and beaches, or to visit relatives and friends in other neighborhoods. To accomplish such excursions, these young adolescents and their families can use one of the most extensive public-transportation networks in the United States. According to Samantha, who has relatives in the suburbs, "it's easier to travel" in the city.

Samantha and her peers might be called streetwise, as they are generally savvy about their environment. They know how to use the subway and bus systems to get around. They know not to walk on certain streets, because there might be "a lot of people around there who drink and stuff, at night," TeniyaSerita says. And they know to stay on streets with a lot of stores, "so, let's say someone's following you or something, you [can] go in."

These New Yorkers also know that the city is not the only location that has advantages and disadvantages. Some have lived in other places, in conditions that are better or worse, economically and politically. Many of the immigrant families came to New York to escape extremely impoverished circumstances or oppressive political situations. And whether they are immigrants or relocated citizens, they may have left extended family or friends whom they miss and about whom they worry because of the social and economic problems in those places.

The neighborhoods these young people inhabit are mostly adjacent to or near the school they attend, although some of the students come from neighborhoods farther away (see the section "The Worlds of School"). These home communities consist of large buildings that contain rental units and, perhaps, some co-op units for purchase. Almost none of the students live in separate structures known as houses. The buildings and streets they call home are often residential, although those that are located on busier thoroughfares may offer food markets, delicatessens, pizza parlors, sundry stores, or other small-scale businesses at the ground level.

Most New York City apartments are small, especially those in price ranges that working-class and poor families can afford. Most of the young adolescents in this study live in such dwellings, because their parents' jobs (clerical work, food services, maintenance, security, child care, teaching, transportation, delivery, construction, and other labor positions) are lower in status than the professional and managerial positions held by the well-heeled folk of the area—and depicted glamorously on television. Many of these youths' family incomes qualify them for subsidies such as free school lunches, food stamps, Medicaid, and—seldom but sometimes—welfare income. This means that the furnishings and decor in their homes are basic, although they do not lack personal flourishes that express their tastes and backgrounds.

Living in small dwellings with no common areas besides halls and stairways, these young adolescents and their families often turn to local parks, playgrounds, eateries, shops, and street corners to talk and play with friends, relatives, and local folk. However, their choice of locations for these activities depends on weather, finances, and various policies.

First, gathering in any of the available outdoor locations is constrained by weather, which in the New York region can include rain, as well as extreme cold, snow, and sometimes ice storms during the winter months, and oppressive heat and humidity in the summer months. Second, gathering in eateries and shops assumes that some money will be spent; many of these families economize by avoiding eating out and shopping unless necessary or for a special occasions. Of course, they might know the eatery or shop owners and workers—or they might even *be* the owners or workers—in which case friends and family "hanging out" in such places may be encouraged or, at least, tolerated. Third, the policies of small local businesses and of city parks and playgrounds affect who may use these locations to gather at various times, and how the locations may be used. I will elaborate on this later, in the section on peers and leisure, as young people are often most affected by such policies. For example, adolescents are often discouraged from hanging out in stores, as they are seen to be potential troublemakers who may drive away customers (Chin 1993).

The Worlds of School

Like most eleven-to-fourteen year olds, the young adolescents in this study spent about a third of their day at school. They all attended the same alternative public middle school, which had opened five months before the study began (see Appendix). Alternative Middle School (AMS) was a small charter-school project sharing space with a traditional elementary school in a large, old public-school building. Many aspects of the building structure were in disrepair, and the furnishings and materials were an eclectic mix of scavenged and donated items, as one finds in many public schools that use old buildings and that do not have adequate budgets for maintenance and materials.

By design, AMS included a multicultural group of sixth-, seventh-, and eighth-graders. Students had to submit applications to attend. The faculty's selection criteria gave priority to those groups—mainly Blacks and Latinos—who are at a disadvantage in the private schools and public "magnet-school" systems in New York City.[2] The faculty hoped to counter the system of privilege that they knew benefited White and some Asian students (Ogbu 1985) the most. AMS had sixty students in the first year of my study (1990–91) and ninety students in the second year (1991–92). African and Caribbean Americans, Puerto Rican and Dominican Americans, and White European Americans were almost evenly represented. There was just a handful of Asian Americans.[3] In both years, the proportion of girls and boys was almost equal.

The faculty was also diverse. The director was a White woman who had worked for many years as a teacher in the public schools and was familiar with the education-reform movements that emphasized small-scale schools and theme- and project-based curricula. Six faculty members were female and four were male; they had varying degrees of experience and different areas of specialization, including language arts, social studies, science, mathematics, and the visual and performing arts. Two of the women were African American, two of the women were Latina, and two of the men were Latino.

In this and other ways, AMS expressed a progressive and innovative philosophy. Having been influenced by the successes of model programs in New York City at the time, the director and her diverse faculty and staff had developed the curriculum to be pertinent and relevant for young adolescents. In social studies, students were looking at the history of North American peoples—indigenous, immigrant, and enslaved. In language arts, students were writing their own autobiographies and reading fiction and nonfiction stories about young people with diverse backgrounds and situations. In science, students were studying the workings of their own body systems. With grants and donations, the school had purchased a handful of low-end computers for students to learn word-processing, and two portable videocameras to encourage the students to document events audiovisually, as the faculty believed that this technology would assist the students' success in the contemporary environment.

All students attended small-group advisories in which ten to twelve students met with the same faculty member four times a week to discuss social issues and problems, whether immediate or global. For many of the students, this was an important and valuable aspect of their school experience. Marina, for example, said that AMS was better than the school she had attended the previous year, "'cause it's, like, less kids, and all the teachers there ... make a big deal out of everything. Like, if there's an argument, they spend like about three hours to figure it out, just talking it out." Likewise, Samantha said that at other schools, she had felt as if she was "just ... a pupil, [not] actually a person. You were just like a member of something." But at AMS, "it's different, because it's a lot smaller, and it seems like people care more."

As the name indicates, middle school (also called "junior high" in some systems) falls between elementary and secondary school in the United States, and many changes occur in this phase. Students start changing classrooms for different courses instead of staying in one room with a single, all-subject teacher. Students have to learn to keep track of their assigned schedules and which rooms to go to at specific times. They have to carry their books and papers with them and mind their personal belongings, rather than keep them in one desk in one room. These changes, which are a preparation for high school and college, can be disorienting for eleven and twelve year olds. Many of the teachers at AMS commented that it took several weeks for the incoming students to learn these new responsibilities and that some struggled with these shifts for months, even years.

In elementary school, students stay in one classroom and get to know one primary teacher and one room full of students. In middle school, students get to know many teachers and may travel to different classes in such a way that they can be with different sets of cohorts during the day and week. These kinds of changes can be challenging. Different teachers have different expectations and different styles of interacting, a situation that can benefit some students some or all of the time, but may cause some to suffer academically overall, or in those specific subjects where the teacher–student interactions are strained (Hansen 1986). In addition, middle-school students have more peers to get to know. This can be an advantage in terms of finding friends and acquaintances, as there are more to choose from. But it can also mean there are more peers with whom students can experience conflicts or problems. I discuss this further in the next section.

Middle-grade students are generally expected to do more homework than elementary-grade students and to engage with more complex subject matter and abstract concepts. These students are told that they need to get more serious and consistent in doing their work, because secondary school will be even harder than middle school. If they want to go to one of the more highly rated high schools in the city, they need to achieve high scores on standardized tests and develop portfolios of exemplary work. The middle-school agenda prompts these students to confront anew their sense of themselves as a type of student or classmate (e.g., "smart," "lazy," "reliable," or "talented"). They also newly consider their prospects as college material and as workers and professionals of various kinds (Fine et al. 1990).

Most students today understand that they need to finish high school, and go to college, to have a successful career (Way 1998). These young adolescents are at the very beginning of a move away from dependence on school and family structures, as they dream of the independence that comes when they earn income from work. Yet adult worlds of work are still distant for youths of this age. Some may help their families at home or in a restaurant or store. But such work, even if it is paid, does not figure into the careers toward which they aspire or that the school emphasizes as ideal possibilities.

The Worlds of Peers and Leisure

Eleven-to-fourteen-year-olds in general appear to hang out with larger groups of peers more often than do younger cohorts (Cole and Cole 1993). However, the size and socioeconomic circumstances of a school or community influence the particular makeup and activity of peer groups. How young adolescents behave in response to, and find meaning in, their peer groups is associated with a variety of dimensions and factors, such as personality, ethnicity, family systems, and other life situations (Brown 1990).

Research indicates that most young adolescents desire to and do maintain fairly strong connections with their families at this time; if they do not, they are more likely to get into trouble with substance abuse and other problematic activities (Steinberg 1990; Way 1998). Yet because of puberty and related identity shifts, young adolescents redefine their relationships with their families. These processes of interaction vary greatly across different cultures and families. The diversity found in norms of child-rearing, approaches to caregiver authority, and attitudes about "coming of age" make it difficult to generalize about young adolescents and their move toward autonomy and away from care-giver governance.

Nevertheless, being with peers was highly valued by the young adolescents in this study. Friends and social life were important reasons for going to school everyday, and outside school a favorite activity was spending time with friends from school and home, including cousins. I witnessed teachers executing many directives and behavioral strategies intended to stop students from talking and playing with others in class. Energy and noise burst forth during breaks between classes and at assemblies, gym classes, and social events organized by the school.

The onset of puberty and associated body changes can create tensions and stress among peers. TeniyaSerita described fights at school that are

> about girl stuff. Like, who has more than me ... more body parts than the other.... The more bigger you are, that's how you're considered. 'Cause they tease you. You know, 'cause like, you know, usually in the summer, that's

when you start? You know, growing and stuff? And then when you go back to school, everybody is different from the last time you saw them. And then, let's say, you're more or less the same? You feel bad.

What the body is becoming poses problems, especially for girls (Thorne 1993). This will be seen in the portrait of Marina, whose body is "more bigger" than those of many of the other girls (see Chapter 2). Body changes for boys are different in that their gains in height and muscle bulk are not so readily linked to sexual maturation. However, because sports performance is important among male peers, being behind in physical development or having an out-of-shape body can prompt teasing and keep some boys from participating in popular activities. This will be seen in the case of Christopher (see Chapter 3).

Physical maturation, along with peer pressure (Thorne 1993), also prompts young adolescents to think about dating and romantic interactions with peers. As TeniyaSerita says, "You start getting boys into your mind and stuff like that. . . . [You] wanna have boyfriends." Samantha describes how the nature of play takes on a different meaning, as, "You know, you walk down the hall, and you see guys teasing girls, and girls chasing guys, all the time. And the one who's being chased always has a big smile. You know? And the chaser even has a bigger smile." According to these youths, being romantically involved entails hanging out with each other during breaks and after school, calling each other at home (if allowed), and "just basically [having] a name over your head," says Samantha. A date, according to Allen, means going to a fast-food restaurant after school. Such romantic relationships may last only a few days or perhaps a few weeks or months.

Friendship groups were generally more stable, as were cohort groups (both age- and grade-based and daily-schedule-based) and groups connected by activities such as basketball and jump rope. Friendship groups for these students were primarily composed of a single gender, but the romances of the day, week, or month prompted some mixing. These groupings also tended to be divided along racial and ethnic lines, with Blacks and Latinos/as mixing in groups more readily than Whites. As Samantha (who had non-White friends and for a while "dated" an African American boy) explains, "People fall into categories, because people like to be with people who are similar to them." Yet what constitutes being "similar to" another can vary, so that race and ethnicity might constitute less salient means of categorizing when compared with personality, popularity status, sports ability, and the like. I observed friendship groupings shift and change throughout the months of my study, and cross-race, cross-ethnicity friendships were evident (observations that were verified by faculty and students).

Having romantic friends, and interacting with friends and acquaintances in general, could be difficult for these students, both inside and outside school. Further, these difficulties could be psychological as well as practical in nature. TeniyaSerita says:

> I can't wait 'til I'm sixteen, though. . . . I just, I don't know, not hurry up and grow up, but I just wanna have my own freedom. Do whatever I want. You know, right now I'm like, 'Oh, my mother's. . . .' I can't hang out with boys; I mean, I can hang out with boys, but I can't have a boyfriend, or something like that. Which is sort of true. My mother tells me I'm too young, but I just wanna see how it is. [When I'm finished with school], I can do whatever I want. I can work; I can get married; I can do whatever I want. Nobody could tell me anything, I have my own choice. No one's responsible for me.

Christopher, age 12, expresses similar frustrations about his lack of freedom and choice, even though he seemed to be uninterested in romantic interactions at the time. I launched the following exchange after he suggested that when he gets older, he would not have much fun:

> *JoEllen:* Is there any way to have fun when you're older?
> *Christopher:* Not by yourself. [You need other people to] ride with you, or friends or something.
> *JoEllen:* What if you had some people to hang out with more? [At the time of the interview, he had not yet established friendships at his new school or in his new neighborhood.]
> *Christopher:* But where could you go? There's nothing to do in Manhattan; there's nothing for like children who are twelve and thirteen years old.
> *JoEllen:* What do you do when you're older for fun?
> *Christopher:* Go to movies, go driving, go to parties and nightclubs, go to, like, shows or premier things and stuff. The beach or the pool, barbecue; there's lots of things. [But] everything is, you have to be fifteen; you have to be sixteen.

Christopher's comments point to the constraints he and his peers experienced. Although caregivers acknowledged the advancing maturity of their children by, for example, allowing them to stay up later, buy clothing for themselves, or get themselves to school unaccompanied, most caregivers assumed that their children needed some kind of adult supervision most of the time. Yet the caregivers' work schedules often made them unavailable to supervise gatherings of friends during after-school hours and on weekends. And because these students' homes were cramped, having friends over was difficult.

There were limited spaces for these youth to gather outside their homes and schools. Some streets, parks, and playgrounds can be unsafe. For five to six months out of the year, the weather is cold, and there is less daylight—it starts to get dark around four-thirty in the afternoon in the dead of winter in New York City. Some schools and community centers offer subsidized after-school and weekend programs that provide young people from lower-income situations with safe, comfortable, and reliable places to go and be with friends. But during my research period, such opportunities were extremely scarce. Budget crises are a regular occurrence in the city's education and youth-service divisions, and extracurricular and community-support programs are typically the first to go.[4]

Many AMS students did not want to leave the building after classes were over; they wanted to stay and play with their peers. The first year in which the school was open, some of the faculty volunteered to play basketball and hang out with students after school four days a week. The second year, the director obtained a small grant to set up a limited after-school program, offering the students opportunities to play on a basketball team, perform in small theater and song groups, study languages, and make videos. But not every student had something to do every day of the week, and some could not get into the project they preferred because of space limits. The lack of community programs for youths is not particular to these students, or to New York City—indeed S. B. Heath and M. W. McLaughlin (1993) report limited youth services nationwide.

Although many of these young adolescent New Yorkers figure out how to cope in difficult circumstances, they would prefer to feel less wary and guarded and to have safe places to go away from home. People from the outside seem to think that "New York is such a cool place [because] of all of the department stores and stuff, all the people, all the companies," Kelly notes, but given a choice, she would rather live in Florida, where she has cousins. "There's just a lot more things to do there," she says. "We go to the mall everyday, eat our lunch there, and we go to the video arcade there, and there are a lot of stores and stuff ... and we get to go swimming and stuff."[5] Kelly is fortunate in that she is able to leave the city occasionally. Many of her peers cannot make regular visits to family and friends where there is more "stuff" to do.

However, TV culture is there, providing many different kinds of opportunities and options.

TV Activity Among Young Adolescent New Yorkers

To get a sense of the general television-viewing routines, preferences,
and experiences of the group of young adolescents in this study, I surveyed their school. I asked students about household viewing rituals and
rules, the programs they viewed on a regular basis and which they
favored, video-game playing, and the presence of other media technology in their home (see Appendix). Fifty students responded to the survey, and here I report and discuss the results. I also report on my observations and casual talks with students at school, on the playground and
during break times, and during special school functions. I noted and followed up on all activities that were associated with TV (such as talking
about a TV person or program; telling jokes derived from TV; and
singing and dancing to popular-music TV fare). I also elicited discussions of television with two small groups of students after school.

Household Media Situations

Although these students' families are mostly in lower income brackets,
many of their homes contained several types of media technology. All
of the homes had TV sets—indeed, 68 percent had two or three TVs,
and 24 percent had four or more. Seventy-six percent of the students
even had their own TV sets, presumably in their rooms. Although they
might share the set with siblings, this may mean that they did not have
to negotiate viewing choices with adults. And if they were the oldest sibling, they very likely had the power to decide (Lull 1982; Morley 1988
[1986]). Sixty-two percent of the homes received cable television; 90
percent had videocassette players or recorders; and 86 percent had
video-game systems of some kind. Only two households had a desktop
computer. These proportions of technology's presence in homes with
children are comparable to national averages around the time of this
study (Comstock 1993; Provenzo 1991).

One might assume that a lower income would be associated with a
limited presence of technology in these homes. Yet the costs of TVs,
VCRs, and video-game systems (hardware and software) have decreased
steadily since their introduction, a consequence of corporate interests

working to saturate media markets. Also, in many sections of New York City, concentrations of tall buildings make it necessary for households to have either cable or satellite hookups just to receive network and local programming.

The parents and some of the teachers I talked with saw TV and related technology as necessary, given the conditions of living in New York described earlier and given the circumstances of their own households and neighborhoods. One couple said that, because their work schedules do not allow them to be at home in the afternoons, they rely on television to occupy their child's time until they go home to have dinner and do homework together. Although they did not like to rely on television (by which they also meant video games and rented movies played on the VCR), they appreciated knowing that their child was safely at home. In some households, students who care for younger siblings while parents are at work use television as an accessible activity. Having limited financial resources, they depend on television, video games and rented movies to entertain themselves and their children inexpensively in a protected location.

About half of these students reported that, like in most households, they watched television in a common room with other people present, mostly family members (Lull 1990). Less than one-fourth report that they watched alone on a regular basis. One fourth of the students reported that they watched alone and with others variably.

About half of the students said that there were no rules in their house about TV, and about half of the students reported a diverse array of rules. These included doing homework first; doing homework without the TV on; reading before watching; no watching beyond a certain hour or a set amount of time; no watching certain kinds of shows (e.g., sexually explicit material and programs with excessive violence); no watching as punishment; and various "courtesy" rules, such as keeping the volume down, checking with others before changing the channel, and giving certain viewing seats to adults.

Regular Program Selections

I asked the students to list the programs they watched regularly, day by day. The range of program types and titles they listed for any one day ran almost the full gamut of available programming. But some kinds of programs were selected more frequently than others. During weekday after-school and early-evening periods, starting at about 3:30

and running until 6 or 7 P.M., the students can select from a variety of game and talk shows, soap operas, music programming, cartoons, educational programs, and situation comedies. Although at least one or more of the students selected each of those genres of programs, comedic programs were selected by more students more often. Each day, about twelve to fourteen different situation comedies (current and rerun) were being watched by one to four people; cartoons, which generally were not given titles but listed as a type, were watched regularly by eight to ten students per day.

Students also viewed a large variety of programs during weeknight prime times (7–10 P.M.) and late-night periods (after 10 P.M.), but certain types of programs were more popular than others. Again, the students were drawn largely to situation comedies and other humorous fare. Some students also listed episodic dramas, news and information-oriented programs, sports events, and TV movie specials. Yet each night, twenty to thirty of the students watched two or three sitcoms regularly. Late-night talk shows, sitcoms, and movie specials were seldom listed, in part reflecting the restrictions and regulations of bedtime for these young adolescents.

From Friday night through Sunday, student viewing of programs besides sitcoms appeared to increase. The students listed more types and titles of programs viewed on weekends within the following categories: sports, music programming, adventure-style dramas, and specialty variety shows featuring comedians or humorously contrived situations. Viewing of these other kinds of programs most likely increased because students had more time to watch TV over the weekend. Also, programmers provide more viewing options for youths and for other family members over the weekends. Programmers make it their business to know the schedules of their target audiences so that they can capture their attention.

Throughout all of the viewing periods accessible to these students (weekday afternoons and evenings; prime times and late nights; weekends), according to the survey responses, the majority of the students were watching humorous programs most of the time. Many different daily and weekly sitcoms, cartoons, and comical variety shows were viewed regularly by most of the students. The two shows listed most often by the most students—*Fresh Prince of Bel Air* and *In Living Color*—are comedies. Also, the majority of students listed comedy fare when asked about their favorite show and movie rentals.

Choosing Programs to "Re-create"

The students' regularly selecting comedies and humorous programming is consistent with the findings of studies of children and other young adolescents (Medrich et al. 1982). Young people typically choose lighthearted fare, as they (like adult viewers) generally use television to entertain themselves. Also, many lack recreational alternatives. Comparative studies of time use have shown that television largely displaces other activities meant for relaxation and enjoyment, such as sports, dancing, and parties (Williams and Boyes 1986).

Relaxation and enjoyment through TV are valued after six-and-a-half hours of school. As noted earlier, middle-school students must begin thinking about more complex topics; deal with heightened teacher expectations and new responsibilities; and ponder their high-school and college futures. They are also contending with changing body images, the consequences of sexuality, and the transition from childhood to adulthood. Watching TV gives them time to "chill."

Notably, the leisure activities that TV displaces are social events: They involve people gathering to interact with one another; to move around, talk, and have fun. Watching TV for "company" fulfills a need to be social. Most students told me that they preferred engaging in social activities to watching TV—that they would rather be with friends, talk on the phone, or go somewhere with their peers or families. And as will be seen in Chapter 3, Christopher's television viewing dropped off in his second year at AMS because he had made new friends and joined the school's basketball team.

Watching TV also contributes to the students' socializing at school. Christopher and Marina talked with their peers about basketball games on TV—who had won, who should have won, and who played the best. Marina reported that she and her friends talked about the shows that they like, such as *In Living Color*, music programming, and various sitcoms. These students acted out scenes and relived the moments they liked best. "Did you see the . . . ?" "What about where they . . . ?" and "Yeah, and then they . . . ?" were segues for recalling funny lines, cool dance moves, silly situations, and "dope" (i.e., very cool) rap lyrics. Kelly said that sometimes she and her friends just "start singing for no reason, or just do really weird things," such as dancing to the song from a movie musical they have seen. These situations are not unlike those described by A. H. Dyson (1994), who found that young children learning to write in an urban primary school acted out scenes from TV; they also used this peer play to write stories. Likewise, P. Palmer (1986) found children in Australia using a TV show as a framework for playground games.

Because the students often could not play with one another away from school, and because they were often stranded at home without peers, they viewed programming that was popular and therefore exchangeable at school. The students watched shows that contain meaningful bits of symbolic material that they "lift" and "transport" to school to share, such as a toy or comic superhero cards (which some of the students actually exchange). Notably, the two shows watched by the most students—*Fresh Prince of Bel Air* and *In Living Color*—present young people who rap, tell jokes and funny stories, and dance in styles that are hip to young urban tastes and sensibilities. This heightened their exchange value among the students.

P. Willis (1990) views young peoples' use of "cultural commodities" (e.g., television, music, fashion, and dance) in everyday social play as "symbolic work." He and others have studied how young people appropriate, adapt, and re-create commercial media resources to express themselves as individual identities and as members of their preferred social groups (Buckingham and Sefton-Green 1994; Frith 1981; Giroux and Simon 1989; Hebdige 1979; Lewis 1990; McRobbie 1994). Indeed, when these students play together using TV material, they make statements about themselves and the kinds of programming they appreciate individually. They also claim membership in like-minded groups of peers.

Not only comedies are used for symbolic work. The students also talked about TV sports events, talk shows, and music videos. One group of girls at AMS, all Spanish- and English-speaking due to their family heritages, regularly watched the Spanish-language soap opera *Pasionara* and talked about it at school. In fact, like fans of other programs who refashion their favorite media (Jenkins 1992), one girl, Colette,[6] has better ideas about how the characters should act and the plots should advance, so she writes her own versions of the program in English. After showing her scripts—which are mostly dialogues and scene descriptions—to her fellow soap fans, a group of six then gave her more ideas for scenes and characters verbally or in their own writings. At one point, the girls had more than one hundred handwritten pages of alternative soap-opera scripts, which they proudly displayed for me. These girls are engaged explicitly in symbolic work, quite consciously re-creating TV material to express themselves while negotiating their social connections with one another.[7]

Young Urban Adolescents Living in TV Culture

It is not necessarily illuminating to report that the young adolescents in this study used TV to relax and enjoy themselves at home, as well as to connect playfully and creatively with their friends at school. According to general ratings, common-sense knowledge, and some research into TV and everyday life (Kubey and Csikszentmihalyi 1990), these young people are like many viewers in the United States, young and old; rich and poor; urban, suburban, and rural.

But given general views of the nature of television, it is a wonder that these youths (and adults) can enjoy their TV entertainment at all. The "boob tube" is accused relentlessly of turning our minds to mush and of creating badly behaved and morally corrupt youngsters, in particular. Mass-produced culture has always been regarded as low in quality and based on elite standards for cultural fare; the popular culture of the "folk" might be considered exotic or quaint, but it is rarely regarded as uplifting (DiMaggio 1991).

Certainly, a fair amount of TV programming contains negative messages and images that deserve criticism. Yet despite decades of critique, the TV industry regularly claims that it is giving people what they want and continues to use the bottom line to judge its programs' appeal. As the TV medium increasingly competes with newer commercial media, it works ever more intensively to capture youths as consumers, to win their brand loyalty for years to come (Fabrikant 1996; Kline 1993; Seiter 1993; Steinberg and Kincheloe 1997). Programmers continue to produce material that responds to the demands of corporate capitalism over the needs of democracy or an interest in cultural enrichment.

And despite decades of studies on the influence of commercial television—many of which have yielded confounded and contingency-laden results (Anderson and Collins 1988)—exactly what audiences get from TV is still at issue. The dynamic and complex nature of people's everyday experiences in culture have a bearing on how audiences interact with and interpret television, which then shapes the nature of television's influence.

Thus, I found that the young adolescents in this study use television in ways that accommodate and reflect the realities of their diverse lives.

But while generalities can be made about this group of young people and their common uses of TV in everyday contexts, it is unclear exactly what they are learning through their interactions with TV about themselves and about the world outside their immediate surroundings. How do they regard the material and social situations shown on TV as compared with their daily lives? Do TV stereotypes, sensationalism, and negative ideologies of culture figure into their thinking about their identities or about the worlds of power in society? If so, in what ways? And how do they reconcile (or fail to reconcile) the immense popularity of television and its usefulness in their daily lives with its equally negative reputation as a standard-bearer of low culture and fragmentation? Such questions need to be addressed by finding out how individuals think and feel about the television they experience and how this relates to how they think and feel about themselves and their lives. That is what the next three chapters are all about.

2

Marina

*Composing Images of Popularity
and Sexual Power*

welve-year-old Marina takes pride in her size, her strength, and a unique feature, which she described in a sixth-grade autobiography assignment:

> In the hospital, my father thought I was a boy 'cause of the way I cried. . . . I was born with eleven pounds. I was so strong I knocked down the basin they washed me up in. After that, the doctor took me all around the hospital to show me around, because I was born with a tooth. After a month, it fell out.

Marina is tall and physically mature, with a strong, full-figured body that makes her look older than twelve. Her face has dramatic features, including piercing brown eyes and voluptuous lips. Her hair is dark, thick, and long, usually pulled back into a braid or ponytail but sometimes styled in sculptured waves. She walks at a jazzy pace and looks straight ahead, with determination. She has an intense and fiery look, a bold presence.

I selected Marina as a portrait because of her presence and because she looked right at me and asked what I was doing at her school. She was polite but reasonably suspicious: She wanted to see what I was writing as I sat and observed activities in her classroom.

I also selected her because of her reputation at the school as a leader and as a self-assured girl. Some faculty noted these qualities as unusual for a Latina, yet they were qualities the school wanted to encourage and support. I was intrigued to find out how Marina might see herself, given how the faculty and others viewed her.

Finally, I selected Marina because she listed TV as a favorite thing to do at home (in her autobiography); she intermittently broke out in rap phrases, such as "I'm gonna take the world by storm" (MC Hammer); and she wrote a brief statement about wanting to grow up and be "like Madonna or Marilyn" in a writing assignment.

Focusing on Marina, I came to understand that she is very proud of her strong and mature body and that she wants to display it in ways that are considered provocative. I also learned how she plans to escape her difficult socioeconomic circumstances and have a "better life"—as seen on TV. Marina's desire to present her body in a strong and sexy fashion is linked to her plans for a better life, as well as to a wish to be creative and well liked. She is figuring out how to compose herself as alluring and competent, and she finds meanings in television culture that help her imagine herself as a sexy, successful woman. In the following sections, I detail what I learned about Marina's life and her experience of television culture.

Locating Marina at Home, at School, and with Peers

Marina lived in a Manhattan neighborhood that is diversely populated, although many people of Latin and African heritage live in the surrounding blocks. Marina had to cross one street going to and from school where drugs were actively dealt, and just one block away from her,

> there are a lot of shootouts and things like that, and there's always a problem around here.... My mother don't like me going to that block.... Every time I'm there, she don't like me going over there.

Yet despite her mother's worries, Marina said, she does not feel unsafe in the neighborhood. She knew a lot of people, and she hung out in a nearby park when the weather permitted with her cousins and sister, who "are my best friends.... We fight once in a while, but we love each other.... We always challenge each other ... but we have the same mind."

Marina's small but neat apartment was in an old building that showed years of wear. Her apartment walls held Christian religious pictures and photographs of family members; fabric and paper flowers adorned tables, along with picture frames and TV and stereo equipment. Marina shared a bed with her fifteen-year-old sister, Gabriella; their mother had the apartment's other, tiny bedroom.

Marina did not always live with her mother. For four years, Marina and her two older sisters (the oldest was living elsewhere at the time of the story) were raised by an aunt and their grandparents in the Dominican Republic while their mother came to the United States to work, leaving an abusive husband. In New York, Marina's mother made money by caring for other people's children and selling beauty products on the side; she also drew on public assistance. Rosa Fernandez was known as a *curandera* in Latin culture—a traditional healer who uses herbs.

Marina acknowledged in a writing assignment the power that her mother had in her life as her protector and provider, both physically and emotionally. But the authority of her mother and of other adults bothered her, too. Adults on whom she depended controlled her life while acting in their roles as caregivers. "They don't mind their own business," Marina said. "They be all in your business, and if something happens in my house, everybody else knows from the family. I don't like that. And the first one is my mother."

Marina's frustration with her mother was a matter of negotiating control, a struggle between a girl on the cusp of womanhood and her adult protector. The importance of personal control is evident in Marina's autobiographical statement that the "fun" part of living with her sister and mother is their being out of the house often because of their work schedules. "So I get to have the house all for myself and I be putting music real loud and I do whatever I want," she said. "I love my home, because I feel free to do anything I want at anytime I want."

Although Marina did not like her mother "being all in [her] business," she eventually came to understand her mother's reasons for telling her what to do and what not to do. In our second interview, Marina said, "I'm putting myself in her position, and I know what she don't want me to do. . . . We don't have to discuss many things, you know?"

The faculty members at AMS were impressed by Marina's academic ability. Her social-studies teacher said that her "intelligence is very clear, from her *Roots* worksheets to her participation in class discussions." The reading and writing teacher dubbed Marina "quite an independent writer [because] she comes up with her own topics and completes all her assignments without seeking help. . . . Marina is a bright and thoughtful student." Her science and math teachers said that she was "working well in the investigation group and in class. She shows a grasp of concepts, [and she] did a fantastic job learning fractions."

Marina described her own academic nature:

> I like challenges. . . . I look forward to new things. . . . I love reading textbooks and actual facts. I also love to find new things, and I love discoveries. In another words am too intrepid to stay too long on something I have to challenge my mind [*sic*].

Marina is curious about current events and social issues, such as AIDS, pregnancy prevention, and drugs, that relate to her emerging identity as an adolescent. She speaks her mind energetically and expects others to do the same, as shown by a letter she wrote to *Seventeen* magazine:

> I want to know more about what's going on in the real world. What we need to hear about is not only fun things, but things that are happening in our environment—not in the world of movies or celebrities. You know people are getting killed out there. This magazine lives in a fantasy world.

Marina's intelligent expressiveness is a characteristic that faculty members admire and want to encourage. But her tendency to speak her mind also challenges their institutional norms and standards for order. They commented often in her seasonal reports that she talks too much to others, "talks back," and does not follow the rules.

Similarly, Marina challenges the norms and standards for order among her school peers and does not follow some of their rules for gendered and sexual behavior. Marina can be seen with the boys more than most other girls. She is one of the three or four girls who regularly play basketball, which is male-dominated (including teachers). Marina is also known to slug the boys and chase them when they tease girls by trying to grab their bottoms and their breasts. But her angry retaliations do not seem to reassure many girls that Marina is on their side. Instead, many of the girls talk about her as a "bitch." She really does not understand why the girls see her this way and considers this behavior on their part as "stupid."

> [The girls at school,] they hypocrites. . . . Like, they be nice in front of your face, but then they be talking about you. They be talking about me, and I don't even talk to them, I don't pay attention to them. It's because of the boys, mostly. . . . You always see me with the boys, right? 'Cause I like to talk with them. . . . [We're just] friends, like if I was one of the boys. . . . What's the big deal about the kids at school, the guys? They aren't that cute or anything. [The girls] don't have to be fighting over them.

Marina is crossing a gendered boundary simply by hanging out with the boys. In *Gender Play* (1993), Barrie Thorne found that boys and girls at school actively construct the meaning of gender identity through social interactions that function to mark or identify gender boundaries, and thus define "them" and "us." In her study of sexuality and adolescent girls, *Sugar and Spice* (1993), S. Lees also describes gender-marking processes in which girls marginalize other girls who interact with boys on anything less than an official dating level. Girls who try to be friends with boys casually are called names and stigmatized. Thus, female sexual identity is defined by girls' availability as sex partners to boys. According to Lees's and Thorne's studies, Marina's female peers are telling her not to cross their boundaries of gender and sexual identity.

Marina also challenges sexual boundaries that are connected to how a young adolescent girl should display her body. Although she wears jeans and T-shirts—the standard fare of her peers—most of the time, she sometimes wears clothing that accentuates her mature and voluptuous features, such as mini-skirts; short, tight pants; and tight-fitting tops. She also often wears red lipstick. In addition, for one of the school's all-school meetings, she and her friends dance the merengue, a dance they learned in the Dominican Republic, to celebrate Dominican Independence Day. The dance calls for rapid torso and hip rotations that mimic the action of a whisk beating egg whites into a meringue—thus, the name.[1]

Marina's style of dress, the lipstick she wears, and her dancing the merengue draw attention to her female sexuality. In Dominican culture her sexuality may be less noted, because clothing styles and body movements that are boldly expressive are a cultural norm.[2] But here, at a U.S. middle school, she is looking and acting in ways that are typically linked to being available sexually, which for her age is socially inappropriate. Her peers' assumptions that she is "loose" seem only to be confirmed by her dance behavior and appearance.

In sum, Marina is intelligent, outspoken, inquisitive, talkative, spirited, determined, and socially sensitive. These words, along with "female," "young adolescent," "Latina," "low socioeconomic status," "urban," and "first-generation immigrant" help identify and situate her socially. Within different contexts, some labels or descriptions are more salient. Sometimes Marina is primarily an immigrant daughter and sister with a vital Dominican heritage. Sometimes she is an enthusiastic and competent student, searching for new "actual facts" to learn. And sometimes she is a boldly expressive young adolescent challenging norms and standards of school discipline and female sexuality.

Marina's Use and Evaluation of Television

TV as a Means of Control

Whenever possible, Marina prefers to be with her cousins and friends, out and away from access to TV. Especially in the summer, she watches very little, because most of the time she is outside at the park two blocks from her building. But in the winter, when it is dark early and the weather is too cold or rainy, or when she cannot visit her cousins or hang out with peers after school and in the evenings, Marina watches TV.

Sometimes she watches with her cousins or her sister in the living room, even though they have their own TV in their bedroom, as does their mother. Marina's shared bedroom is small, so it is more comfortable to sit on the couch in the main room, trading off the use of the remote control. Marina does not watch TV with her mother, who mostly watches Spanish-language soap operas.

TV is a home activity that Marina likes, followed by eating or sleeping and listening to music. Her least favorite activity is chores. One reason she likes TV is that "it's exciting. You don't know what's gonna happen. Some things are funny; sometimes it's scary." Marina appreciates unpredictability and adventure, variety, and emotional movements. This makes her not unlike many other viewers who seek stimulation and adventure in their leisure moments.

Marina also likes TV is because it is "fast." Reading takes too long, she says; books are boring because "they're not fast enough." (Later, her sister will persuade her that romance novels are worth reading.) This interest in an activity's being fast is like Marina's interest in getting her work done fast in school and not wanting to "stay too long on something." Work and leisure activities must move along at a brisk pace for her. Television moves briskly, especially since the advent of remote controls that let people "zap" through channels.

A final reason Marina likes TV as an activity is that, when she is on her own, she can watch whatever she chooses, turn it up loud, and not be concerned about other people's needs or wants. While watching TV at home alone, she is in control.

Rejecting the "Same Thing Always"

Television can bore Marina when it is too predictable or when programs are too similar. She "hates" repeats and will not watch them unless she likes a program "a lot." This connects with her wish to be challenged as a learner and not to "stay too long on something."

> Some (non-rerun) programs are "the same." *Wonder Years* is the same thing, always. His father misunderstands him, his mother doesn't understand him, his brother is stupid, and his sister is stupid, too, you understand? And then, he likes his girl, but his girl don't like him, and his friend Paul, it's like every episode is the same thing.

Marina has deemed this show "not funny" because of this sameness she sees in every show, a sameness that R. Lembo (2000) identifies as recognizing formulas of TV. When viewers can identify a particular pattern to the plot of a program, or a repetitive strategy that is part of the structure or themes of a program, then they are recognizing the formula of television construction. Marina recognizes the formula not only in *The Wonder Years* but also in programs she likes. She acknowledges that the "same thing could happen in *Roseanne*, as like in another show, sometimes the shows are the same."

Clearly, many programs apply formulas to their construction, and indeed are recognizable as distinct genres because they contain specific formulaic elements. Like most students her age, Marina watches mostly situation comedies, as well as video music programming and movie channels, genres that have distinctive and repetitive formats, settings, themes, or styles. Marina can see that formulas can be applied across programs as well as within a single series. She is thus accepting some formulas while rejecting others based on other kinds of judgments.

Seeking the Real Along with the Potentially Real

Even though "sometimes the shows are the same," Marina likes *Roseanne* because the show is "about real things." The "real things" that Marina likes about this program, compared with *The Wonder Years*, are a recognizable time period and a situation that is somewhat like hers in terms of family makeup and economic circumstances. Like many viewers, Marina evaluates program reality based on her own standards of familiarity or plausibility. Lembo (1997) claims that viewers find certain programs to be "realistic" if the story, characters, or style of representation are believable, or plausible, given their own situation and circumstances.

The Wonder Years represents life in a U.S. suburb in the 1960s, as seen through the eyes of a middle-class boy who has an older sister and brother. Marina is too young to be familiar with life in this country in the 1960s; she has lived in the United States only since she was four years old. *Roseanne* presents life in a working-class home in contemporary times, and the family has two sisters—Becky and Darlene—around adolescent age, a situation that is more familiar to Marina. The story setting of *Roseanne* carries "real" meaning for Marina because of her present-day working class identity and her status as a daughter who is close in age to the Becky and Darlene characters.

Marina also finds a kind of "wishful plausibility" in *Roseanne*'s characters and family activity. In our first interview, Marina said that she preferred the parenting style of the Roseanne character to that of her own mother:

> *Marina:* In my family, we don't play around like [they do on *Roseanne*], but maybe, you know, some people do play around. Like the way she and Dan play? And the way they play with their kids and things like that? I wish my mother was like that. . . . [Roseanne's] fair. I don't know how to put it. She's not like just a regular mother; she's . . . she understand her kids. [But my mother], sometimes she be acting stupid. . . . She's. I don't know, like, I love her and everything. . . .
> *JoEllen:* She's worried about too many things?
> *Marina:* Yes. Very much. [And] you cannot talk to her ever. That's the one thing I don't like about her. You cannot talk to my mother about anything.

Marina assumes that the way the characters Roseanne and Dan Connor "play with their kids and things like that" is the way some people play around, even though her family is not like that. Marina finds Roseanne to be "not just a regular" mother because she is "fair" with her children, "she understands her kids." It is intriguing that Marina assumes that Roseanne's style of parenting is "not regular" at the same time she assumes it is "real" and "fair." What Marina knows about mothers is that they are controlling, and "you cannot talk to [them] about anything." That is, "regular" mothers are not fair and not playful.

It is likely that Marina believes Roseanne to be "real" even though she is not "regular" because Roseanne is an extremely popular television parent. And because she is popular, she represents a fictional "standard parent" in the United States. During my data gathering, *Roseanne* was among the top-ten prime-time network programs for many months, according to the Neilson Ratings (see Carter 1992a). Although Marina may be unaware of ratings, she is aware of what is popular. But the idea that Marina wants her "regular" mother to be like a fictional TV mother whom Marina finds to be real suggests that Marina is judging reality based on wishful believability.[3]

Evaluating the "Normal"

The opposite of programming about "real things" is programming that is "fake." Marina explained what qualifies as fake for her in our first interview:

> Sometimes it's very fake. . . . Like the show *Diff'rent Strokes.* Some things are fake, like things that wouldn't really happen. . . . An example, like Arnold [a character on the show] had the chance to do sex, and he did it, and, like, what kid in real life, like, normal guys wouldn't do that. And the cartoons, you know. Some things are stupid, too. . . . *Get a Life*—that show is dumb. Stupid. How could, like, how old is he? Twenty-six or something like that? A grown man doing like. . . . His job is, he's a paper boy. That's a dumb show.

For Marina, "fake" things on TV fall into two types. The first encompass those activities that are not possible in the realm of the social norms that she knows but are represented by the program style as possible. The character on *Diff'rent Strokes* having sex at an early age is not "normal," according to Marina, even though she is thoroughly aware that it is physically possible. She qualifies this act as fake because it is not socially appropriate, given what she considers should "really" happen in life. As with the young viewers in M. M. Davies's study *Fake Fact and Fantasy* (1996), Marina's sense of real life provides the basis for judging TV reality.

The second kind of fake shows are those that present activities that also are not possible in the realm of social norms but are represented as outlandish situations that are marked stylistically, or formally, as unreal—as in the case of cartoons. Some shows are technically the opposite of cartoons yet contain cartoonlike qualities. Real people or scenes can be shown on the screen, but the situations and circumstances can be outlandish and unrealistic.

Marina, who recognizes cartoons as "fake," refers to the sitcom *Get a Life* as "dumb" and "stupid" because it uses actors instead of drawings in outlandish situations: A grown man would not be riding a bicycle to deliver newspapers in a surrealistically rosy suburb. Marina does not like TV to represent behavior or situations that are not socially normal, and *Get a Life*'s stylistic markers, used to excuse its outlandish situation, cannot persuade her to accept it.

"Real things" on TV fall within Marina's present-day family life, actual and wishful. Fake things on TV lie outside Marina's ethical sense of experience (sex at too young an age) and outside of her reasonable sense of experience (a grown man having the job of a boy).

The Appeal of "The Morals of Things"

When Marina expresses distaste for what she sees as socially unreal, she is verifying her preference to find out about real, "actual facts." She is also supporting her belief that television has a purpose beyond entertainment. She states that television exists to entertain, but it also has an informative and social responsibility. In our first interview, I asked the question: What do you think TV is for?

> *Marina:* To entertain you. . . . To let you know things, like the news, and other things, like those shows, always at the end they have a moral, right? . . . I like the morals of things. . . . There's another thing, too. Like to maybe help people prevent things, too. It gives you messages, too, the shows.
>
> *JoEllen:* What kinds of things does it help you with?
>
> *Marina:* Like, drunk driving [and] things like that. Seeing movies about it, seeing TV shows about it. And about AIDS and things like that. And about drugs.

Marina's experiences living in a troubled city neighborhood doubtless have given her a heightened awareness of dangers to avoid and problems to solve. She can see drug activity everyday, and her adolescent status makes her newly sensitive to issues associated with her age and emerging sexuality, such as drunk driving and AIDS. These and other topics pertinent to urban youths' experience have been brought up at the school in the students' advisory groups.

Marina believes that television messages should be, and are, helping people to know about such dangers and problems in the world and ways to avoid them. TV has a responsibility to let its viewing public know about things that are going on, the same responsibility that *Seventeen* magazine has: to tell people about "not only fun things, but things that are happening in our environment."

Marina says that television's role is to be outspoken, like her. She thus positions television in the public sphere, as part of a larger social interaction. She seems to recognize that being part of the public sphere and of larger social interactions carries responsibilities. As she writes in a self-evaluation at school, she is "like a politician" when she expresses her opinions and ideas. To her, this is the responsibility of a leader or a politician: to express ideas and opinions to the public, to challenge people. Likewise, television should challenge viewers with its presentations of the "real" world; TV should play a political role in society.

The Challenge of Seeing "Your Conscience . . . Divided Up"

Marina watches *Herman's Head,* a prime-time situation comedy in which the lead character, Herman, deals with everyday situations with the help of four imaginary characters, who portray different aspects of his self. When Herman encounters a problem or something new, or when he is trying to make a decision, these characters appear on-screen in a separate frame, like a thought bubble or comic aside. Visually, they are displayed as within his mind, talking and discussing the situation, often arguing and wreaking havoc on Herman's interactions outside his mind, out in the "real" world. The program has made a comedy out of the chaos and turmoil of the voices of human consciousness.

Marina likes *Herman's Head.* It has made her realize the complexity of her own thinking and feeling:

> *Marina:* I like it, because, you know, . . . I never thought about . . . your conscience is divided up into many things. Like, you know, what makes you scared, what makes you feel, you know, sexual, whatever. And what makes you want a guy or something like that. Or what makes you cry, or your anxiety, things like that. Or what makes you sensitive. . . . It's like four people have to make his decisions. And then they don't all agree, and then, you know, it's like, I don't know how to explain it, but it's a nice show. It's different, very different from the others. I mean, you gradually see what he's thinking and what he's gonna do, and that's divided up in four people.
>
> *JoEllen:* I saw that happen. Does that ever happen inside your head? Do you disagree with . . .
>
> *Marina:* Myself? . . . Yeah, I do.
>
> *JoEllen:* You do? What does it sound like?
>
> *Marina:* Like one side is telling you something; other side is telling you another thing.
>
> *JoEllen:* What kind of thing would you disagree about?
>
> *Marina:* Like, um, in class, you have to, let me see, you have to debate somebody. Against something. But then, I'm debating my own self, because I agree and disagree. Like, with abortions. Something like that. Let's suppose I agree with it, but I also disagree with it. Yeah, so, you're debating your own self.
>
> *JoEllen:* What do you think about abortion? Can you tell me?
>
> *Marina:* I think that, you know, that it's somebody's business to have their abortion, like if they cannot afford the baby. Or if they don't want it, I

think that they should have an abortion. But I don't think they should, because in the first place if you wouldn't have wanted to get pregnant, you could have used a condom, or, you know, something else, birth control. But you just start doing that. And, and, why kill somebody, a baby, if you would have liked to be mother to it? So, there's like two sides to everything.

JoEllen: Yeah, those are hard choices.

It is significant that Marina brings up the issue of abortion in her illustration of a debate that she might have with herself. It is telling of her concerns as a young woman who now has to think about the possibility of having sex, getting pregnant, and the situated consequences of both. Her choice of this topic reveals once again her concern with "real-life" issues related to her gendered, sexual, social-class, and age identities. "Um, a couple of friends of mine, you know, they are having sex and things like that," she says. "So, it just make me think, and makes me make decisions about certain things, and how I want my life to be. And how I want people to see me as." She is becoming familiar with the dilemmas of becoming a sexually active female.

At the same time, she is watching a program that prompts her to think about these dilemmas as a dialogue in her mind. Marina has learned from the format and premise of a television show that she can think about herself as "divided up into many things" that can compete within herself.

Watching Programs to Play and "Talk About It" with Friends

Marina prefers that programming be about real life and deal with the real world—external and internal—by providing helpful messages and useful information. But primarily she watches sitcoms, as well as cable and network movies and music programming, which contain various unreal aspects. Although she prefers that the substance of programs be representative of a real, and often serious, world, the style or aesthetic of shows may not resemble any reality that Marina is familiar with on a day-to-day basis. Her family does not "play around" like the family in *Roseanne*, and unlike the character Angela on the sitcom *Who's the Boss?*, Marina's mother does not have a live-in male housekeeper. Remember that Marina's first response to "What is TV for?" was, "To entertain you." So although TV needs to be about real and serious things for Marina, it also needs to present this substance in a style that allows her to enjoy herself, to "play," to some extent. Although most sitcoms and some music programming have stories and themes that are "real," they are aesthetically playful in ways that are not like actual life. This allows Marina to escape her actual circumstances, which sometimes are far from lighthearted.

Marina also watches playful fare so she can play with her friends. She lists *In Living Color* as a program that she watches and enjoys. *In Living Color* is a comedy–variety program that presents sketches that parody and spoof many aspects of contemporary culture in a style that is vaudevillian and bawdy, or outrageously outlandish and "unrealistic." By her own aesthetic standards, Marina should regard this show as dumb or stupid, like *Get a Life*. But she does not. Her peer group plays a role in her enjoyment of *In Living Color*.

Marina does not watch TV with her school friends, but she knows what they like. On the survey that I gave to her and her classmates at AMS, she reported watching several popular early-evening and prime-time programs, including *Blossom, Coach, Doogie Howser, Family Matters, Fresh Prince of Bel Air, Growing Pains, Married . . . with Children, Perfect Strangers, True Colors,* and *In Living Color*. Most of these programs are watched regularly by at least a third of the students; *In Living Color* is watched by the largest number of students in this group.

I observed that the students talked about these programs often, especially the day after they were broadcast. The programs served as "ice breakers" for conversation and created common ground. Marina confirmed my observations:

> *Marina:* We talk about it, like, the shows—*In Living Color* and things like that—and mostly everybody says the same things. . . . We mention the funny things and the most important things that happened, . . . things that they should have done in the show or something like that.
>
> *JoEllen:* Have you ever gotten into arguments or disagreed about stuff that you've seen?
>
> *Marina:* Yep, like basketball games, football games, things like that.

By watching the most popular shows, and by bringing her TV experiences to school to talk, laugh, and act out scenes with her peers, or argue about the outcome of a sports game, Marina is able to participate in a symbolic-exchange activity at her school.

Acceptance by her peers is important to Marina—indeed, her conflicted relationship with the girls at school has made her sensitive about expressing herself. She wants to be part of a popular crowd; she wants to have people like her. "It's better than having people dislike you," she says. Marina chooses to watch and "play" with comedies such as *In Living Color* so she can play with her friends, using these popular shows to interact and, perhaps, be liked.

Marina uses television broadly and diversely. She is discriminating, yet she describes a wide range of tastes and judgments, indicating an eclectic sensibility in her choices and preferences. She wants to have fun by herself and with others; she wants to learn about the world and herself; and she wants to view realities that she recognizes and that she hopes for. A close look at Marina's interpretations of television further illuminate her sense of herself and of her life.

Reflections of Marina Through the Screen

The brief writing below, which I was shown by Marina's adviser, Ms. Ariza, clinched my decision to select Marina as a focal participant:

> When I grow up I would like to be like Madonna or Marilyn. I want to be an actress and a dancer. I would also like to be president of an advertising agency or a lawyer or an undercover narcotics police woman.
>   May my wishes and other's come true.

Marina hopes that when she is older, she will be like two extremely popular celebrity figures, media personae who are famous—or, perhaps, infamous—for their sexual image. What is the appeal of these particular media figures for Marina? And how do her other aspirations relate to her admiration for these media figures, if at all?

Moving Up

In our first interview, I asked Marina about getting older, about what she looks forward to and what she will do when she is older. What she looks forward to is "being able to go to clubs and having a boyfriend." She asks what I mean by what she will "do," and I specify "getting to be an adult, getting a job, stuff like that." So she tells me:

> After I go to college, and things like that? You mean the job I'm gonna have someday? . . . Get an apartment for myself, or if I have a boyfriend, I'll help him. Or maybe I'm gonna be a mom or something like that. Or maybe, I'm gonna be a model to get a job, or an advertiser.

Certainly, these statements suggest a degree of uncertainty, which is reasonable at Marina's age. She hopes for a relationship, and maybe a family. The only thing she seems sure of is going to college, which she states as a given. The idea that college should be pursued has been strongly emphasized by the school as a ticket to a successful future, and Marina doubtless has been made aware of the importance of a college degree through other sources, including television. One of the programs she watches regularly and enjoys is *A Different World*, a sitcom produced by Bill Cosby featuring young adults attending a Black college.

The importance of college as a means of moving up and being successful is suggested in Marina's talk about escaping the world that surrounds her. In our second interview, Marina said that she has changed in seventh grade; she now has to "think a lot . . . about what life is about." She continued:

> Like experiences that happen to me, some make me think a lot, and the world around me. . . . I'm growing, you know, my mind and my body. . . . I don't like the world around me, that what I live in is drug dealers, you know, people, girls having babies, from drug dealers, and getting nowhere except for the drug dealers end up in jail, or dead, or the girls be ending up with their mothers, and their babies, and they're only like fifteen, fourteen years old, and they don't graduate from school. . . . It made me think: I don't want this kind of life. . . . I wanna do something for myself. Different than get myself a guy, get pregnant, and stay here. . . . I wanna be successful, you know, do something good for myself. To have a very good, smart man. I want to go to college, graduate, get myself a career that pays well, move from around here, and when I have kids, I don't want them to have nothing to do with this. Yeah.

Marina has taken stock and gained a sense that she is fighting against certain odds that are stacked against her as a young woman and as a resident of a troubled urban environment. She imagines a future career and family life that will allow her to provide an upbringing that is very different from her own. Her dreams are not unlike those of most people in the United States, the imagined land of opportunity and fortune for all. Marina has acquired some ideas for her future from television, which will be discussed in the next section. But Marina may well be dreaming like her mother, who also wanted a better life for herself and her children; she came to this country to work and must have said, in her own way, "I don't want this kind of life."

Making Something of Yourself and "Coming Up with Ideas for Things"

Marina says that Angela Bower, one of the lead characters on the sitcom *Who's the Boss?* has given her the idea of running an advertising business:

> I be seeing people on TV, like, Angela Bower, she, you know, she made some-
> thing of herself. And people like that. It made me think: I don't want this kind
> of life, I want that kind of life. I wanna do something for myself.... Get
> myself a career that pays well.... I wanna be able to buy anything I want, to
> be successful, you know, to do something good for myself.

Angela Bower is successful in her TV sitcom world. Marina sees Angela
as a person who has accomplished her success self-consciously—"she
made something of herself." This is an important aspect of success to
Marina. She needs to be in charge of her own life rather than just accept
the life that seems to surround her—"different than get myself a guy,
get pregnant, and stay here." Angela Bower is a character who offers
Marina an image of what it is like to escape her surroundings and create a different kind of life.

But what does Angela Bower represent compared with other characters who have the "good life" on TV? Marina likes being able to speak
out, to express opinions, and debate. If she were a lawyer, she could capitalize on her outspoken nature. How would advertising suit Marina?

Angela Bower portrays an advertising-campaign marketer, and
Marina shows an appreciation for the nature of this work. She likes
advertising because the work involves "coming up with ideas for
things"—that is, creativity is associated with the work. This creativity
can be just for fun or it can be done in the service of delivering serious
messages, such as Public Service Announcements. Marina talks about
messages in explaining why advertising appeals to her:

> You see advertisements, like, you know, that really strike people, you know?
> Gets their attention. And you think, like, Oh, my god: How could that per-
> son think of that? ... Like commercials, let me see which one.... Like there's
> one, she suffers from a serious drinking problem. How could the baby suf-
> fer from a drinking problem? It's that the mother used to drink alcohol. Or
> like the one in, the one that a man, have you seen it? At the bus stop? That
> man is with a gun, pointing to his nostrils? ... And it's talking about cocaine,
> cocaine kills ... and it's like if you're putting a gun through your nose.

To Marina, these advertisements present images and convey messages
that "really strike people" because they confront the viewer with harsh
realities, such as the consequences of drug and alcohol intake. Marina
may envision that if she were to do the work of advertising she would
have another means of speaking her mind, or, in her words, "being like
a politician." She could express her opinions and ideas through ads and,
at the same time, "get a career that pays well." She sees Angela Bower

wearing nice clothes and living in a big home with many amenities, including a housekeeper.

Marina also expresses appreciation for the lighter side of ads. She talks about several comedic TV commercials and how "it's funny how people come up with things like that." Here she is noting not only the content of the ads but also their constructed nature and the role of those who make them. Angela Bower, who makes fictional ads on TV, helps Marina acknowledge the work of constructing ads.

"You Have to Think About How You Want People to See You As"

Marina indicates that, in addition to the appeal of "coming up with ideas for things" in advertising, she wants to come up with ideas for herself, to create an image of herself that expresses her own sense of success and power. I see this interest reflected in her talk about modeling and clothes. She has modeled before: A photographer took pictures of her and her cousin, and as a result, her cousin got her picture in a department-store catalogue. But Marina really wants to do more active kinds of modeling. She wants to be on video and in TV commercials; she wants to act and dance, not just stand still. This falls in line with Marina's energetic presence. But what is it about modeling that appeals to Marina? In our second interview, she talked about going to France to be around some of the images and activity that appeal to her:

Marina: I have this friend, she's like twenty-three years old now, and my mother been taking care of her little girl for two years. And babies.... She's from France, and she tells me it's really really nice, and she's gonna take my sister. And I'll probably go there for vacation.... And I love it because of fashion.... [My friend] tells me about her cousin; her cousin is a model. And in all the magazines you see that the fashion will come from Paris. London and France, England. And things like that. I love the fashion from there. And it's like here you have to dress with sneakers and jeans, you know, 'cause that what's in style right here. So, yeah, if I wear something like that, you know, the fashions from there, people [here] they'll think: She's crazy! Yeah, so I really love the way they dress.... I like the language, too, with the way that she is. And she tells me it's really, really nice.

JoEllen: What is it that you like about that kind of fashion, compared with, you know, this [T-shirt and jeans]?

Marina: That it's, um, I think, erotic, weird, and very, let's see, how can I put it into words? Oh, different from here, it's exciting, I don't know, I just like the look. It's expensive, too.... Yeah, 'cause that's exactly—it's the way that you feel about yourself, that, you know, people see you as the way that you see yourself. Like, let's suppose a fat person, they wear their clothes and everything so they feel sloppy. So people see you as a sloppy, fat person. But then you know you're overweight, but then you feel skinnier than what you are, and you know, you be wearing nice clothing—people won't really see you as a large person, understand?

JoEllen: Yeah, I do

Marina: Like if you walk through the streets with this air that you think that you're all it, and the model and everything, people see you as, like: Look, that girl looks like a model. But if you walk down the street, like all bummy and thinking the other way, they go: What's wrong with that person? Yeah, so, you have to think about how you want people to see you as.

In this conversation, Marina is expressing her tastes in clothing, describing an interest in the "expensive," "erotic," and "weird" clothes she says can be found in France and England, and not at school and around where she lives. But she is also explaining how to act and behave in clothes, how to project a sense of self through the clothes that you wear and through the movements you make with your body just walking through the streets. For Marina, creating your own image is not just a matter of donning clothes or having a title. Self-image for Marina does not exist in the mere surfaces of things; it is not something to copy or mimic. Marina cannot go to the store and buy an image or superficially adopt a way of being. Creating an image involves actively deciding "how do you want people to see you" and projecting a sense of yourself from within your clothes, using your body and ways of acting to express your attitudes, directly and strongly.

Perhaps Marina is concerned with how she presents her self through clothes and with her body because of how she has been perceived and treated by others. In her first year at AMS, the girls thought she was a "bitch" because she hung out and talked with the boys and played with them physically, putting her arms around their shoulders and engaging in sports. She did not understand why the girls thought bad things about her just because she liked being with the boys, but by the second year, the girls' treatment had affected her enough to cause her to change her behavior. She had stopped hanging out with the boys "because of everything people used to say," and she had stopped playing basketball. "I don't really associate with them [the boys] very much this year," Marina said.

Marina also was treated badly by the girls outside school because of the way she behaves and, specifically, for the way she dresses. In our second interview, she explained what happens when she walks around her neighborhood:

Like, just in the summertime, right? It's hot, so I be wearing short pants, right? Or tight, or whatever. And then a girl's guy come up to me and talk to me, and this and this and that. And the girl comes up to me and asks me why I was out with her man, and this and this and that. And, you know, things like that. . . . Usually I get a lot of, I'm dressed like this, you know, it's like when I go to parties I look real nice. But I walk down the street and you see girls staring at me up and down, they're rolling their eyes because, I don't know why they do that. I don't know why. And those other guys, they be like whistling and be like, you know, Come over here; can I get your number? You know, this and this and that. And most of the girls dislike me, even if I don't look at them.

As noted earlier, Marina is considered a "bitch" by the girls on the street, who think she is trying to steal their guys just because she wears clothes that reveal her body and attract the boys' attention. Marina does not understand why the girls on the street, like the girls at school, react to her dress behavior by thinking she is trying to steal their guys. "God, that's so stupid," she says. "Why would a girl do that? Be fighting for a guy?"

Marina does not want to hide her body and she is not thinking about altering her dress habits to accommodate the girls on the street. She does acknowledge the style of the area by wearing jeans and T-shirts, which I saw her wear most of the time at school. But she is wishing that she could wear more things that are "erotic" and "weird," which is why she wants to go to France. She is wishing herself away from her neighborhood and her school, where her emerging sexuality and female identity are misunderstood and restrained.

Admiring Madonna as Strong, Sexual, and Successful

With my prompting, Marina says that what she likes about Madonna is "her style, the way she is. A lot of people criticizing her and she keep going on. 'Cause that's the way she is." Marina's unprompted remarks a year later confirm her earlier comments:

I really, really like Madonna 'cause the things she do on the videos, and she keeps going and going and going no matter what people say about her. It's like she has a very strong personality and she lives with herself, she loves herself, and she's very comfortable with the way she is. So, you know, she made some videos like that, even though people talk a lot of things about her, you know, she keep going.

Marina's references to Madonna's making videos, people talking about them, and "she keep going, no matter what people say about her" have to do with the general uproar Madonna stirs up every time she releases a new media product. Madonna has built her reputation, her immense popularity, and financial success on being provocative.

In the lyrics of her songs, in the dance and theatrical scenes of her videos, and in her business negotiations, Madonna challenges several establishments. She questions norms and standards of sexual morality by mock-masturbating during performances, wearing costumes that accentuate her breasts in a self-consciously absurd manner, acting out sex scenes with both men and women, and staging eccentric sensuous activity. She crosses class lines in the video for the song "Material Girl." After performing a song about using men to get money and jewels (in a scenario that deliberately references Marilyn Monroe's film performance of the song "Diamonds Are a Girl's Best Friend"), she rides off backstage and out of costume with a guy in jeans who drives a dusty, old pickup truck. In songs like "Express Yourself," and in her control over her own business enterprise, she tells women to take charge of their lives. What Madonna wears, says, and does as a performer and as a businesswoman push at the edges of propriety. Her "pushing" has generated popular and scholarly debates and controversy regarding the merits and power of her provocations.[4]

Madonna's performances express female sexuality, often commenting on the problems associated with doing so. As a result, she has become a huge celebrity and a powerful entrepreneur. What Madonna represents is spectacular success as a woman in the United States. She is rich, famous, sexy, and opinionated, and unlike many other celebrity women, she runs her own show.

Marina admires Madonna for all of these reasons. Marina watches music-video programming, during which she is able to view Madonna's videos, as well as watch discussions and presentations responding to her new releases and about her influence and wealth as a contemporary superstar. Marina is aware of Madonna's power and popularity, and, as she admitted in her writing cited earlier and in our first interview, "Yeah, I wanna be like her." Marina can see that Madonna has "made something of herself"; she has "that kind of life" that Marina wants.

Marina wants to be well liked rather than thought of as a "bitch" by the girls at school. Marina can see that Madonna is popular and well liked, even though she does things that provoke controversy—indeed, controversy has created much of Madonna's power and popularity. "I'm in charge" says Madonna, when commentators ask about scenes that suggest her own exploitation or sexual domination. Madonna is also in charge of a highly lucrative, multimillion-dollar media enterprise.

Marina is proud of her body and wants to dress it exotically. In the merengue she performs at school, she reveals that her homeland, the Dominican Republic, allows and even encourages her bold display of her body. Marina sees how Madonna has self-consciously constructed an image that is sexy, "exciting," and "weird." She admires Madonna because, even though she provokes controversy with her dress and sexual performances, "she keeps going and going and going no matter what people say about her." In saying that Madonna "has a very strong personality, and she lives with herself, she loves herself, and she's very comfortable with the way she is," Marina finds in the celebrity a vision of how to act and wear clothing that highlights her sexual features and an attitude for persevering in the face of the criticism this invokes from unfriendly peers and worried adults.[5]

Marina in some ways is already like Madonna, as illustrated by an anecdote I heard from a faculty member at AMS. Marina's second-year adviser approached her privately and asked her whether she was sexually active, just to make sure she knew how to protect herself from AIDS and pregnancy. Marina told the adviser that she was not sexually active, then went to the director of the school, Ms. Warner, and asked her whether she thought she was indeed sexually active. The director told Marina "no," as she assumed that Marina was more mature than most girls and would be thoughtful about that kind of decision. But Ms. Warner commented that people might think Marina was sexually active because of the way she sometimes wore makeup, did her hair, and wore clothes and because of how she carried herself. Ms. Warner told me that Marina smiled in response to this and said: "I'm a front." Marina told Ms. Warner that she intended to have others think she was sexually active and seemed proud that she had made this impression. But Marina reported that she was not sexually active. The boys at school were "too silly" and there was no boy outside school in whom she was interested (yet). Her success in presenting a "front" of sexual activity suggests she is a competent creator of self-image.

Reviewing Marina

Marina was an intelligent, bold, reflective, and strong Latina whose mother brought her to the United States in search of a better life. They had found a life that was better than that in the Dominican Republic in economic terms, but in the United States they had found new challenges. They lived in a tough, urban neighborhood where street life could be dangerous and where safety was found in small family quarters. Seeing her mother struggle to make a small income as a child-care worker, and seeing girls like herself get pregnant and stuck in domesticity or die from AIDS, Marina dreamed of going to college and having a successful career that would let her escape the limits of her local existence. She also challenged herself to learn about social realities, such as AIDS, teenage pregnancy, and drug abuse, to avoid them for herself.

Like most youth, including Christopher and Samantha (whose portraits follow), Marina used TV mostly when she could not be outside with her cousins and friends. But when she was on her own at home, she liked to watch TV because it is fast-paced and because it allowed her to express personal control. This functional meaning of TV differed from that of Christopher, who sometimes watched or listened to TV for company while doing chores, and from that of Samantha, who watched because she hated to read.

Like many young people and adults, Marina liked TV entertainment that portrayed characters, activities, and events that she recognized as part of her world, or as part of her desired world. Yet, also like many viewers, she called on a particular sense of aesthetics to judge the reality of the programs. Her tastes and judgments about programming were complicated and eclectic and associated variously with her identities.

Marina found meaning in programming about "real things" such as family life on *Roseanne*, even though some of *Roseanne*'s reality was not like her own. *Roseanne*'s family was working class and contained two adolescent daughters—similar to Marina's family situation. But Marina wished her own mother were more like the character Roseanne, who gained credibility as a "real" mother by being a highly popular TV figure. In this case, Marina lent "wishful believability" to a TV figure and TV activity, suggesting that she used television as one of her standard-bearers of living in the United States.

But Marina did not accept all TV depictions as realistic just because they were popular or because a familiar kind of family life was portrayed. When storytelling situations and aesthetic manners went against Marina's sophisticated sense of social norms, she deemed the program "dumb" and thus discredited. Like Samantha, who could not stand sitcoms that insulted people, and Christopher, who did not like "nasty" comedy, Marina preferred a certain style of realistic representation.

Yet she regarded television as a teacher about social issues. She watched programs to learn about some of the problems in her world, assuming that television has a responsibility to inform viewers about these contemporary realities. In this, she was similar to both Christopher and Samantha. And incidentally, Marina learned how to debate with herself about some of these problems. Indeed, she learned about different points of view that might exist within herself by watching a sitcom that depicted conversations between the different "sides" of a character. This program made Marina realize that her own different sides could have competing points of view about complex social issues. This was similar to Samantha, who will be seen to explore new perspectives and different ways to think about issues by watching TV. But as we will see, Samantha found alternative points of view not in fictional sitcoms but in talk shows that staged debates outside people's minds in a nonfiction format.

Marina may have relied more on television realities than did Christopher and Samantha to learn about social issues and to learn generally about life in the United States. Because she immigrated when she was four years old and had less experience of U.S. culture, and because of her low socioeconomic status, Marina looked to television for images of her better future life. She saw that the fictional Angela Bower had acquired the kind of good life she seeks, including a big house and expensive clothes. She also saw Angela's career, advertising, as an exciting and creative possibility for herself because it would let her figure out how to construct messages and images that "strike" people. Knowing advertising strategies would indeed help Marina project an image of herself that was confident, exciting, and sexual.

Consequently, Marina found particular meaning in Madonna's television image, because Madonna had constructed an image that was confident, exciting sexual, and, importantly, highly successful and popular. Further, Madonna had stamina and persevered in the face of negative treatment. Marina used this particular television image to cope with her own identity dilemmas, which arose from conflicts about her proud sexual image, her problematic peer relations, her forthright character, and her desire to be well liked and successful.

Marina was using a TV image that was partially "like" herself to address her identity dilemmas, in that Marina, like Madonna, was a consciously constructed, ironic sexual image. As will be seen, Christopher and Samantha also used TV-character images that had a particular configuration of similarity to themselves. But also like Christopher and Samantha, Marina was finding appeal in a television persona who represented qualities that she wanted to enhance, create, or bolster in herself. Marina's identity dilemmas were revealed in her use of television, and her identity dilemmas were "worked on" in her symbolic interaction with images on TV.

3

Christopher

*Settling into Images of Belonging
and Righteous Power*

hristopher's face is boyish and dark-skinned, and he wears his black hair closely cropped and smooth. His twelve-year-old frame is large and moderately bulky. He carries himself at a steady gait that contains an anxious concentration, and his brown eyes mirror the tensions suggested by this comment of his:

> "When I was younger, life was easier. . . . People focus more on you, like you at the time. You are the main focus. But now it's like, it's spread to like, they have hundreds of people to focus on, they can't just take the time to pay attention to one person."

An African-American, Christopher is the only boy I am portraying. Besides the typical difficulty of gaining access to student homes (see Methodological Notes), in the second year of my data gathering, the two other boys whose families I visited and interviewed year one of my study unexpectedly left the school.

Christopher became a focal participant when I noticed him performing like a TV show announcer or news broadcaster during a class visit to the TV studio at a children's museum to explore camera and control-room procedures. While waiting for his turn at the equipment, Christopher sat down at the fake talk-show desk, put his mouth up to the microphone (which was off), and started making up stories and giving fake introductions to special guests on his "show." His voice had all of the tone modulations and pitch variations that typical announcers have, and his comments were silly yet clever.

As I continued my research, I heard stories about Christopher's problems adjusting to AMS. Family rearrangements had caused him to transfer into the school in the middle of the year from the Midwest. Various faculty members were concerned about Christopher because he seemed unable to make friends, despite earnest efforts. While observing at the school, I noticed more of his performances of TV scenarios, but his peers did not attend.

Christopher went through many changes during my research. He moved into a new family situation, into a new neighborhood, into a new school, and into new peer groups. He also moved into adolescence and gained a new sense of his body, of his responsibilities, and of his possibilities. These changes were reflected in his uses and interpretations of television. At first, he watched a great deal of TV, mostly for company, and was enamored of a program that portrayed a man dealing with the problems of travel through time and space. Later, Christopher watched TV more intermittently and greatly admired a sitcom father who is widely known for creating a successful and positive image of African American family life. Over time, I learned that Christopher had found strength in his physique and a sense of "rightness" at home and school. He found strength and rightness in television, too.

Locating Christopher at Home, at School, and with Peers

Christopher lives with his father and stepmother in a modestly furnished five-room apartment in a handsome, old apartment building in Harlem. The neighborhood has a rich cultural heritage that is kept alive by the African American and Latin communities. But like many lower socioeconomic urban regions, the neighborhood suffers from crime, drug trafficking, and street violence. Christopher says that it is a hard place for him to live:

> Sometimes you can actually see [drug dealers] doin' the trade from my window. . . . You know how they are dressed, or they're always having cars that are, got all this snazzy gold, gold hubcaps, gold everything on them. Beepers, car telephones, bandannas. . . . [I see them go], 'Here it is.' They

take the money, get back into the car. People being robbed and stuff. I seen it.

While walking on the streets, Christopher has to watch out, because someone once tried to steal his hat and start a fight. "Like, 80 percent of the time," he reports, he has no safe place to go away from his house except school.

Christopher has had many homes. At age two, he left New York City with his mother and lived with her in several locations around Miami. There he spent time with his grandparents and other relatives after school while his mother worked as a hospital-lab technologist. At age eleven, he moved to a small Illinois town with his mother, and in the first year of the study, he had come to stay with his father and stepmother in New York. According to Christopher's stepmother and his adviser at AMS, he is with his father because he was neglected by his mother. Christopher himself indicates that he and his mother were not very close.

Christopher's father, Robert Stevenson, is a former Army man who now works as a security guard. He also heads a committee that is working to convert his building into affordable co-ops for the local community, and he conducts this business and holds meetings in the family's apartment. Christopher's stepmother, Alice Stevenson, was at home full-time recuperating from a serious car accident during the research. She was studying in an early-childhood-education program before the accident and intended to return. The Stevensons are active members of a local Christian church.

Robert Stevenson has six children from a marriage prior to that with Christopher's mother; all of these siblings are grown and living on their own, many with families. Christopher's new stepmother has three grown children, as well, one of whom lives in the same building as Christopher, two floors up. Yet although he has a large extended family, most of whom live in the New York City area, he is an only child in his home.

Alice Stevenson, who is lively, opinionated, and very congenial, talked candidly about the challenges she was experiencing with Christopher. She was just learning to "get along" with him, she said, having never lived with him before, and in a few months' time she had become aware of his struggles at school and with his social situation. She described him as a very smart person who "has academics together" but also as a "lonely child" who wanted very much to have friends and participate socially. On weekends and after school, she said, he "mopes around" and does not know what to do. When he reaches out, he is either "read wrong" or is "giving the wrong signals" in his attempts. In response to being rejected by his peers, he seems to look to adults "as a shield" or "security blanket." Alice said that she would like for Christopher to feel more comfortable with others and to have friends.

Christopher did not feel comfortable at home during the first year of the study. When I asked him about his home life in our first interview, he commented, "It's like a wall [between me and my parents], a real big wall." I asked him what the wall was made of. He said, "It's made out of fear, um, isolation, lots of stuff. Confusion." Then I asked him who had put up the wall. He replied, "I think I did, a few times."

Christopher had to learn how to fit himself into a new family order built around his father and a new stepmother in New York rather than around his mother and grandparents in Florida or Illinois. He also had to figure out how to live in an unfamiliar, challenging neighborhood. As time went by, Christopher's wall came down, and his fear, isolation, and confusion decreased. These changes were connected to, and reflected in, his school experience.

On his application for AMS, Christopher wrote about what he likes at school:

> I like to do science, social studies, and work with computers because all of these are interesting to me. I like science because you learn new things about the earth and planets. I like social studies because you learn about different people and their cultures. I like computers because I think that the way they operate is amazing.

Christopher described himself as a good student who occasionally did not do his homework. The AMS faculty members were impressed with him; his adviser noted that he had received the highest reading score on the standard achievement tests in the seventh grade. His science teacher considered him "a wonderful science student. His understanding and questioning have led to very provocative discussions in class." His social-studies teacher called him "a brilliant social studies thinker and writer. He works hard on things he is interested in, and he always knows the answer in class."

Further, Christopher showed "an impressive understanding of literature and an excellent command of language," according to teachers, and was a "talented fiction writer who has no problem generating ideas." According to a writing workshop teacher, "Christopher has worked hard and productively in Writers Workshop primarily writing adventure stories . . . where superheroes battle—and eventually win—against evil. His writing is fluent and full of active detail. . . . His mechanics are excellent." Christopher likes to read mystery adventures, detective adventures, and comic books about superheroes, such as "Wolverine," a character whose name he chose as an alias. (I will discuss this choice of alias later when I examine his television activity and issues of identity.)

Although faculty members considered Christopher smart and capable, they also noted that he had a tendency to "play along with" the others in his classes. Christopher's adviser said that he engaged in "immature behaviors which get in his way of social growth." His math teacher called his classroom activity "ridiculous . . . making noises, calling out, moving his desk"—actions that distracted others—and his social-studies teacher said that Christopher was "not always helpful. . . . Maturity consists of more than an occasional promise to stop talking."

Certainly, Christopher was not the only student about whom the faculty was concerned in terms of classroom behavior and attitude; some expressed similar dismay about Marina's and Samantha's classroom discipline. However, Christopher was proving to be one of the more perplexing students. In his second year, however, his behavior and attitudes changed so notably that, by the time he graduated from AMS, the faculty had given him a "Most Growth" award. His relationships with his peers had changed and grown, as well.

When he came to AMS, Christopher was assigned to an advisory that had lost a well-liked boy. In retrospect, some of the faculty commented that it was a mistake to have filled the spot without thinking through how some of the students might react to seeing their friend "replaced" by a stranger. So from the beginning, Christopher had entered an awkward social situation.

Instead of finding comfort in this group, Christopher found himself challenged. In addition, I watched him wander around the gym during break times and off times, hanging at the edges of groups, watching others, and trying to engage them in conversations and play. But the students did not talk to him; they did not make eye contact and seemed to edge him out.

I asked Colette about Christopher. Colette was a sixth-grade girl. As co-editor of the AMS newsletter, she knew much of the social lore that traveled around the school. She explained that Christopher "just doesn't fit in. He's annoying; he tries to play with you when you don't want to." She also mentioned that he wore jeans that were not baggy, and thus were not in style; they were also "high riders," or jeans that came up too far from the shoe. For Colette, Christopher's out-of-style clothing further symbolized how he "doesn't fit in."

I overheard other students make fun of Christopher's shoes, which were well-worn brown oxfords instead of high-price, popular-brand sneakers. For urban youth—boys, in particular—sneakers are a sought-after status symbol. Even those students who cannot afford the high-price brands promoted by celebrity basketball players make do with some kind of high-top.[1] Christopher's worn-out oxfords, which he wore during his first several months at AMS, definitely marked him as unlike the others.

In describing his perspective on his difficult social experience, Christopher referred to the size of the school and to other people's behavior. He said that finding friends was difficult because he was new and because "you have to choose your friends from only sixty students. You just have to get along." When school started in September, the students had almost all of the others to choose from, and friendship groups emerged gradually from the mass of sixty. But Christopher entered the school well after the students had determined their affiliations.

Indeed, many peers might have been rejecting him because of their established group solidarity and their perception of anyone outside the group as "them" instead of "us." Christopher described a dynamic that identifies the inside and the outside of a particular group of friends:

> *Christopher:* I been in lots of fights at AMS, . . . trying to play games. [The game is] they try to beat up on people, they are trying to just jump on you. There's a gang of brothers, and they go around, and they try to beat people who are not brothers.
>
> *JoEllen:* Who are the brothers?
>
> *Christopher:* You want names?
>
> *JoEllen:* Yeah, this is just for me to know. [Christopher gives me six names, all of African American and Latin American boys who are popular.]
>
> *JoEllen:* Are you a brother?
>
> *Christopher:* Nope. I don't beat up on people.
>
> *JoEllen:* They just beat up on anybody?
>
> *Christopher:* M-hmm. Then when you fight back, they really try to hurt you.
>
> *JoEllen:* So, who else has gotten beat up by the brothers?
>
> *Christopher:* Girls, boys.
>
> *JoEllen:* Is anybody safe from the brothers?
>
> *Christopher:* Teachers.

In this dialogue, Christopher describes a situation that ostensibly puts every student at risk of being beaten by the brothers. At the school, there were no reports of fights that led to a need for medical attention. But being beaten may not involve physical as much as social and emotional risk. Christopher may have ended up not with a bloody nose or black eye but with a loss in status and peer esteem.[2]

Notably, the "brothers" Christopher names all participate in basketball, the main sport at AMS. Basketball is one of the only viable sports at the school because of space and facilities. The gym is outfitted so that the central area is a full court, and there are two practice hoops on each side. Basketball games dominate gym times, breaks, and after-school hours, and boys dominate the basketball games.

Consequently, playing basketball with the boys is an important public context in which power and status among peers are negotiated. The "brothers" are some of the key players in these power games. They are either the biggest or the most adept players, which gives them status as game players, and subsequent power as peers, especially as males.

Christopher did not play basketball during his first year at AMS, because, he said, he was "not that physically fit." Also, his oxfords were not suitable for moving around on the court. Thus, Christopher's position as an outsider, a low-status "other," may have come not only from being "beaten" by the basketball-playing "brothers" but also from his status as a non-basketball playing boy.[3]

In his second year at AMS, things got smoother for Christopher. He made friends, many of whom were the "brothers" whom he had named earlier. He started playing basketball and wore inexpensive sneakers and baggy jeans. He was in the eighth grade, which gave him status not only as a senior but also as an established student compared with newly accepted students at AMS. He said that in his last year at AMS, as he prepared to go on to high school, "a lot of doors opened up. . . . Even the school's loosened up a little. . . . I got treated older. It's all in a year."

Reviewing his location in time and place, Christopher admitted that his new family and new neighborhood made him feel lonely, fearful, and confused. And at school, although he could shine academically, his behavior was considered immature and ridiculous, and his peers shut him out, seemingly because he was new, he annoyed people, he wore the wrong clothes, and he did not play basketball. Christopher felt that he could not garner attention; he was not safe; and he was an outsider in all of his new situations. Over time, however, he found comfort, encouragement, and safety at home; he made friends and joined them on the basketball court; and he earned praise for his social growth.

These changes were reflected, and his experience of these changes was revealed, in his interactions with and interpretations of television.

Christopher's Use and Evaluation of Television

Watching for "Company" and Entertainment

In his first several months in New York, Christopher spent a great deal of time in his apartment, because he had no friends with whom to hang out or exchange visits after school, and his neighborhood felt dangerous to him. His stepmother was recuperating from her accident for much of this time, which meant that she was often confined to her bed or gone for medical check-ups. This situation saddled Christopher with a good deal of chore duty around the house: He washed the dishes, swept the floor, cleaned the bathroom, and tidied things in general. TV was there for him while he worked:

> I like TV, because it's entertaining, especially when you're alone. I just like to, like, if I'm here alone, and I'm, like, washing dishes, I just like to hear the TV. It's like somebody's voice, like somebody's there. It's like somebody's talking to you. It's just that you can't talk back. But you can hear somebody's voice and that's, like, comforting when you're alone.

The TV was on quite a bit in the Stevensons' household, as Christopher's stepmother watched in the master bedroom and Christopher used the main TV in the living room.

Like most of his age-mates, Christopher watched many of the prime-time and early-evening sitcoms popular at the time. He watched these shows because they were popular and because, like many viewers in the United States, he mostly watched programs intended to entertain. He also watched afternoon cartoons, adventures, and mysteries, as those were available and entertaining to him.

In addition, Christopher sometimes watched late-night television with his father before he left for night shifts. At these times, television provided a context within which Christopher knew how to fit within a home full of new family rituals. As a familiar kind of activity, watching television provided a comfortable structure for Christopher to be in his father's company while they were still adjusting to living together.[4]

Watching Games and "Popping In"

After his second year at AMS, cartoons were out, and Christopher included watching basketball games in a shortened and intermittent viewing schedule. His shift to basketball viewing corresponded with his beginning to play the sport at school. He was watching to see how the games turned out and to discuss them with his friends and sportsmates. But he also watched different players to learn about the various positions and to pick up tips and strategies for playing. With this viewing, Christopher was purposefully educating himself so that he could interact with peers and play a better game. Both of these TV uses helped him build and maintain his social status and relationships.

Because of his basketball playing and because he had more social activities and after-school events to attend with his now friendly peers, Christopher was watching less TV in general, even though by this time he had his own television set in his bedroom. He explained:

> I don't watch as much TV now. . . . After school, I would either go play basketball, um, go home and maybe watch half an hour, sit down, then I would go outside for a little while, come back, and then I'll watch maybe some TV, but I wouldn't, like, I don't really watch, sit down and watch shows full, like beginning to end that much. I, like, pop in shows, and then I will go do something else, and then I come back and look at what's going on. . . . I'll be mopping, and then I will hear something interesting [in my parents' room], and then I'll just pop in and see what it is, then go back to work. Or I will turn on the TV and then see something, flip the channels around, turn it off, and go do something else. I don't leave it on. I just turn it off.

The only time Christopher "just watches" TV, viewing with more focus in his own room, is "at nighttime . . . let's say after nine o'clock. When all the work's done." At this time, he also reads mystery novels or adventure stories and often simultaneously plays basketball with a foam ball and net that is attached to his bureau.

Watching "Something That Could Really Happen"

Christopher's tastes and judgments about the content and styles of programs are not easily described and demonstrate the complicated and sometimes enigmatic nature of viewing. Christopher said that he liked funny shows but only if "they don't get too funny . . . they don't get ridiculous . . . they're something that could really happen. It could be real, it's not, like, impossible." Like most viewers, including Marina and most adults, Christopher wanted programming to be plausible or somehow believable to him.

Understandably, then, he found plausibility in sitcoms that depicted African American families and groups, such as *The Cosby Show, Fresh Prince of Bel Air,* and *A Different World.* But he also watched several sitcoms depicting White families and groups. The reality he is judging may be less familiar to him in terms of his identity as an African American. But frequently, the situations depicted on a show might seem familiar to him because of their urban locale (for example, *Cheers, Murphy Brown,* and *Night Court*) or their portrayal of family life as less than idyllic *(The Simpsons, Married . . . with Children, Roseanne)*—a reality he might find painfully familiar.

However, it may be that Christopher watched these popular sitcoms because they were popular and because they were lighthearted. He might also have been watching these sitcoms, along with *In Living Color,* so, like Marina, he could go to school and interact with his peers.

Looking for Scares and Clues but Not "Some Dead Monster"

What is believable in a situation comedy and what is plausible in other genres differed for Christopher. In adventures and mysteries, funny or not, situations and events were allowed to be "impossible" or in the realm of science fiction—that is, not based on reality as Christopher knew it. Fantastic things could happen in those genres, and that was part of their appeal. He liked *Tales from the Crypt,* a cable-based anthology series that presents absurd tales of suspenseful horror. The shows clearly are not real, but Christopher thought they were funny. "It's supposed to be scary, but it's not," he said. These shows are not depicting a reality with which Christopher was familiar, but he found them entertaining because they are funny and suspenseful. Humor and suspense were features he greatly appreciated in TV and in books, and if they were engaging he allowed for unbelievable situations.

Further, although he appreciated the suspense of mystery and adventure, the suspense had to provide him with "clues" and be somewhat predictable. He did not like the kind of suspense in which surprises occurred "out of the blue." Yet if something was too predictable, he found it boring and not worth watching. He implicitly understood the role of tension in story construction.

He also perceived the role of formulas in story structures and plot formats. During our second interview, he was not watching as many mysteries, because "now a lot of shows, they don't really have that many good mysteries on. It's always the ones that you can find out: Oh, she's the one who murders her husband, and she's always gonna get caught on trial." Christopher wanted clues but not formulas from his mystery adventures.

Christopher likewise did not appreciate any and all horror suspense, or any and all types of scare. For example, he did not like the kind of horror that involved killing people, people getting chopped up, bloody. Horror movies have a lot of mystery in them, like, you know, mind-boggling when they're walking through the house. And something jumps out the wall. But I want, like, a human to jump out the wall, not some dead monster with one eye hangin' out, blood runnin' all down, ax in his head.

Yet a "dead monster" portrays the "host" of *Tales from the Crypt*, which features unbelievable horror stories in a humorous vein—gore and terror presented with an absurd smirk. For Christopher, the saving feature of that horror is that it is all in fun; it is exaggerated, cartoonish horror, not serious terror by a real person with an "ax in his head." The "dead monster" who hosts *Tales from the Crypt* is a campy puppet figure residing in a coffin, not a truly horrific creature that is ready to "jump out the wall." Christopher enjoyed this program because it was obviously fictional; it was a construction of imagination and "not real."

Generally, Christopher's programming preferences were a complicated matter, a matter of balancing his own sense of reality with his own sense of aesthetics. He used his own sense of dramatic license to determine what was plausible on TV, what was funny or "ridiculous," what was acceptably scary, and what was sufficiently suspenseful. Christopher's sense of his own reality combined with his preferences for pleasure and enjoyment to evaluate plausible as well as engaging content.

Compared with his shift in TV habits, Christopher's tastes did not change greatly during the research period. He stopped watching cartoons in the afternoon but started watching *Tales from the Crypt*, which has cartoonlike qualities. Throughout the study, he enjoyed watching popular sitcoms and mystery adventures, including horror suspense that did not include gratuitous gory depictions. Primarily, he, like many viewers, looked for fun, lighthearted shows that seemed "real" to him. But he also liked fantasy programming that kept him suspended from reality, all in "horrible fun." Like many youths his age, Christopher seemed to be attracted to a kind of humor that is blatantly silly and fun to "play" with, perhaps to replace toys that he had outgrown.

Reflections of Christopher Through the Screen

Aspirations After a Superhero

As a pre-adolescent, Christopher chose the alias "Wolverine," which is telling. "Wolverine" was the name of a star character in the Saturday cartoon *X-Men*, an animated action–adventure series about a futuristic society. In the world of *X-Men*, mutants are a race of people who suffer discrimination by other humans. Mutants are recognizable because they have certain non-human features and outer-space-alien looks; they also have superpower capabilities of magical and mythical proportion. Some mutants have chosen to use their superpowers to "do good," while others use their superpowers in an evil manner. Because of their "differences" as a race, and because some mutants are "bad guys," many non-mutant humans want to eliminate all mutants. Quite often, good-guy mutants are framed to look like the bad guys.

The stars of the *X-Men* series are young, mutant do-gooders with superpowers; five are male, and four are female (despite the title), and they all work as a team. Under the guidance and leadership of a fatherly mutant figure, named "Professor," the *X-Men* characters live together in a mansion with high-tech, sci-fi communications. From this home base they learn about situations that require their assistance, and when they go on a mission, they transform their human resemblance by donning superhero costumes.

Wolverine is one of the more prominent and popular characters in *X-Men*. As his name suggests, he has wolflike features that make his handsome looks appear fierce and wary. According to the program credits, he has "heightened senses and accelerated healing ability" and an "implanted indestructible adamantine skeleton and claws." Dressed in his superhero costume, Wolverine is used as a "signature" image for the program, along with the characters Cyclops and Storm.

The cartoon character Wolverine maintains a high profile at AMS: He is popular with the boys and a few of the girls who are "into" adventure cartoons and comics. Students bring comic books and comic-based trading cards of Wolverine to school, and they sketch him in their journals, on the covers of their notebooks, and in their writing assignments. The TV figure of Wolverine is a heroic icon at school.[5]

Thus, in nicknaming himself "Wolverine," Christopher is allying himself with a good guy who is durable and invincible while fighting against the forces of evil in a world that is constantly unfamiliar and full of problems. Christopher liked stories in which "the good guy wins all the time," as in *X-Men*, and he preferred programs in general that showed "stuff about what's right," on which I will elaborate later. Because Christopher has lived through several transitions, he must find some comfort in imagining himself as a popular, strong, do-good character who can triumph over perilous and unpredictable situations.

Wanting to be "Cool," "Sensitive," and "Funny"

By choosing the name of a popular comic character at school, Christopher apparently shows that he wants to be well liked and popular. He further expresses this desire when he tells me explicitly who he wishes to be like: "I'd be a little bit like the *Fresh Prince of Bel Air*, and I'd be a little bit like Theo from *The Cosby Show*. . . . I'd be cool like Fresh Prince and sensitive like Theo." He also mentions Arsenio Hall, because "he's funny [and] he knows how to relax and talk to people."

Notably, these TV personalities are young African American men; they are a bit older than Christopher and are all popular figures on television. They are like him in some respects, which allows Christopher to identify with them,[6] but they also have characteristics he wants to acquire. If he were cool, he would have status; if he were sensitive, he would not "annoy" people; and if he were humorous, relaxed, and talkative, he would have fun and sociable interactions with his peers. All together, these qualities would bring him popularity and success in his social life at school.

Perhaps this helps to explain Christopher's acting out roles and scenes from television, taking on character voices and joking like a performer, as mentioned at the beginning of this portrait. Arsenio Hall, who does impersonations and tells jokes, is popular and well liked as a talk-show host. Maybe Christopher is acting out scenes from TV as a means of impressing his peers, so that they will come to think of him as funny and cool like popular characters.

Unfortunately, Christopher's acting like he is a popular figure on TV does not work at school during his first few months: His peer audience does not seem to appreciate his performances, and neither do his teachers. Over time, his performances transform, and his acting at school finds a more receptive audience.

Observing a Character Who "Leaps from Person to Person"

In our first interview, Christopher told me that an especially favorite show was *Quantum Leap*. He had almost memorized the opening narration explaining the dramatic series:

> *Christopher:* OK: "Sam Beckett theorized that one person can go back in time during his own lifetime. During the experiment he stepped into his project accelerator and vanished. He came back in other people's bodies, trying to save them from something bad, that it won't happen to them. If he

doesn't save them, he will die, lost in time forever. He leaps from person to person so one day he'll be able to leap home."

JoEllen: So he's trying to get to himself?

Christopher: Back to when he stepped into the accelerator. But when he gets back, it'll only be like five minutes since he stepped in, and he's going through this time-travel stuff for years.

JoEllen: And it's because the machine wasn't quite ready yet?

Christopher: Well, he expected to go back in time as himself, but he went back in time and jumped into other people's bodies.

JoEllen: And that guy who has the [small machine, a handheld computer the size of a calculator]?

Christopher: Al.

JoEllen: How did Al figure out that he needed to go find [Sam] and that there was something wrong?

Christopher: Cause [Al] is always with [Sam].

JoEllen: How come Al isn't lost?

Christopher: Al, he can go back to present time any time he wants. Like, right now, he can go back. . . . He presses this button, and there's this little light, and he steps in and—shoo! He disappears. [According to the program description, Al is actually a holograph communication. He is not travelling in time bodily like Sam; only Al's projected image appears to Sam.]

Quantum Leap is a science-fiction adventure, a suspenseful comedy–drama about a man lost in time. Even though the time-travel aspect is unrealistic, most of the lives that the main character Sam "leaps" into on the show represent familiar, everyday situations, "something that could really happen." In several shows, Sam deals with issues that arise from real historical circumstances, such as the riots that erupted after the assassination of Dr. Martin Luther King Jr. and the controversial investigation of John F. Kennedy's assassination.

The character Sam leaps into all kinds of lives, all kinds of bodies. Not only does Sam leap into the lives of people in periods of time and places in time that are very unlike his own, he leaps into bodies very unlike his own. Twice on the series, Sam, a White man, enters the bodies and lives of Black men, and once he leaps into the body of a pregnant woman.

This program appealed to Christopher on several dimensions. He said that it was funny without being "ridiculous" because the humor grows out of the "real" situations that the Sam character lives out. It also has suspense and mystery, elements found in Sam's figuring out which problem he needs to solve in the person's life so that he can leap out of that life. These dramatic features pleased Christopher and thus were aesthetically meaningful for Christopher. Relatedly, the Al character relies on a computer and on sophisticated communications technology such as holograph projection to act out his role as Sam's informant and fellow problem solver. As noted earlier, Christopher thinks that the way computers "operate is amazing," and on this show he got to see the computer perform amazing (albeit fictional) feats of data retrieval and synthesis through the magic of special effects. These special effects, representing computer capabilities, were also aesthetically meaningful for Christopher.

In addition, the program depicted people and situations that were new and somewhat unfamiliar to Christopher. One reason Christopher liked social studies was that "you learn about different people and their cultures." Although most of the characters on *Quantum Leap* live in U.S. culture, they exist in times and places in history that can seem like other cultures to someone as young as Christopher. Also, the unfamiliarity of the story settings, their different existence in time and place, represented something that Christopher missed about being younger, when "everything was new ... you had something to wake up to and I could learn ... and it was really interesting. ... I learned every day." The uniqueness of the story scenarios and predicaments appealed to his desire to learn something "new" and "interesting." The new adventures of the character Sam had storytelling meaning for Christopher.

Quantum Leap had important—and revealing—conceptual meaning for Christopher that reflected his personal experience. What he liked about this show was that Sam "goes through a lot of changing, with other people. And trying to save those people. And the close times he tries to save those people, the suspense." Christopher's identities as a confused son, displaced peer, and growing youth—his experiences as a person confronting many unknowns—are symbolized in his interpretations of *Quantum Leap*. Christopher is looking at what it is like for someone else who has been thrown into unfamiliar surroundings, what it is like for someone else who is going through "a lot of changing." Watching this program, he can see the character Sam figure out what to do and what to say when he is thrown into new places in time and space.

Christopher had real-life problems that needed to be solved, which created mysteries and suspense for him. When he watched Sam, perhaps he was comforted to see someone else addressing mysteries presented by life changes. Perhaps he was also comforted to see Sam succeed in solving problems week after week, always hoping to return home to his own body and his own time and place. Indeed, Christopher seemed to be attracted to a kind of superhero quality in Sam, a character who "tries to save" the people in the strange lives he enters. Christopher wanted Sam to save people and solve their problems, as he admired characters who acted heroically, such as the cartoon character Wolverine. Christopher wanted to see and hear about how to do things right—a sensibility that he expressed further in his admiration of Bill Cosby.

Looking Up to People Who "Handle" Things "Right"

In our second interview, Christopher put *The Cosby Show* at the top of his list of favorites. Christopher could identify with several features of this prime-time situation comedy. Christopher's family is urban African American; two parents are at home, and they are connected to a large and extended family. But unlike in the show, Christopher's parents were not in a high-level income or professional bracket, his neighborhood was not safe, and his house was not elegantly furnished. Yet despite these differences, Christopher found the show highly plausible, saying he knew people who were like the Huxtable family on *The Cosby Show*—not because they had jobs or a lifestyle like the Huxtables but because of "the way they would handle certain situations."

> [Bill Cosby] makes me laugh. I like a lot of the stories they do, things they do in the show . . . like how he can take a situation that, like, say, Theo [the son character] stole something from the store, and [Cosby] can make it into a situation where, you know, it'd be funny. Well, it wouldn't be funny that [Theo] stole it, but [Cosby would] make like a little joke out of something. But at the same time, he'd also be telling [Theo] that it was wrong to do what he did. [But on] *Married . . . with Children*, they would make a joke out of it; . . . they would, like, pat [the son] on the back and say, "Oh, I love you. And did you get me something?" *Married . . . with Children* is stupid. You know, it's, like, teaching kids that they can disobey their parents and laugh at their parents. And *Cosby Show* is teaching children that, you know, do something good for your parents, you know, it's about parents trying to raise their children right. And *Married . . . with Children* is, like, the parents don't even care about their children.

Christopher does not appreciate the disrespect that *Married . . . with Children* levels at its parent figures; he wants kids to behave, and he wants parents to show them how to behave. Parents are not supposed to not "even care" about their kids. Parents are supposed to "raise their children right."

The Cosby Show, which aired from 1984 to 1992, won critical acclaim and enormous popularity as a series that shed positive light on African

American family life. William H. Cosby Jr., who has a doctorate in education, intentionally created a series that emphasized the role of parents in fostering their children's healthy and successful development. Cosby wanted his program to counter the images of parents he saw on other programs, where, he has said, "the children were brighter than the parents. And the laughs were coming because the parents really weren't parenting."[7] Cosby worked in consultation with a Harvard University psychiatrist, Alvin Poussaint, to focus the show on what parents can do for their children and to generate messages about the benefits of education. Thus, *The Cosby Show* was specifically constructed to represent parents who "care about their children" and "raise their children right." Apparently, audiences found this aspect of the show appealing as well as believable, as millions of viewers regularly tuned into the program in part to get advice on good parenting.[8]

When discussing his changes over the year and a half of research, Christopher said that his father had been a significant influence in helping him settle into his new life, especially in the neighborhood:

> Now, remember, last year I was afraid to go outside, in the neighborhood? Now I'm bigger; I got more muscles. It's not like last year [when] I was all fat and bulky. But now, I started, you know, taking care of myself, lifting weights and stuff. So, you know, I don't have to worry about, like, the physical challenge, unless it's more than one or two people. Yeah, and my father's telling me, like, walk tall, and, um, you know, walk straight up, and don't look at people, don't be sayin' stupid stuff. And, uh, stuff like that. Don't be flashin' your money around . . . and think good thoughts. . . .
>
> My dad is always teaching me the right thing to do and giving me confidence in myself.

Thinking back over Christopher's life transition, these comments point to the identity dilemmas he faced when he moved and the identity work that he accomplished over time. Christopher moved in with a family who lived in an unfamiliar and often dangerous neighborhood. Just like at school, where the "brothers" challenged his entry and membership in their community, the neighborhood locals challenged Christopher's actions and presence on their streets. Christopher needed to learn how to establish a powerful identity in this neighborhood so that he would be recognized as someone who belonged there, as someone who knew the ways of the street.

Christopher's body grew on its own, but I suspect that Christopher's father encouraged his muscle development, as a small room in their apartment was devoted to weightlifting. But certainly, Christopher's father had shown him how to walk and behave, how to carry his body, and how to think about himself as he moved around the streets on his own. Robert Stevenson helped Christopher find a powerful street identity, which helped him feel less isolated in his apartment and more able to go out into the world. In addition, Christopher's muscle building helped him shape up for basketball and join his fellow players at school.

Christopher's preference for *The Cosby Show* mirrors his appreciation for his own father, a law-enforcement officer, a firm disciplinarian, and an understanding and caring parent, who taught Christopher how to walk around the new places in his life with his head held high. Christopher gained a new sense of himself through his father. Christopher found in Bill Cosby an image that bolstered and enhanced his belief in his father and, subsequently, his new belief in himself.

Over time, Christopher found a sense of correctness in his new home and transferred that sense of correctness to other TV interpretations. In the second interview, he also mentioned a new program, *Roc*, a situation comedy about an African American household. Christopher said he liked *Roc* because

> it's a comedy show, it's funny, like *The Cosby Show*. [And they're trying to teach] do the right thing. Don't cheat people, all kinds of messages. Like when Roc, he's a garbage man, right? And his wife is a nurse. And he always brings home stuff he found in the garbage, like, aw, this is a perfectly good washer, dryer, perfectly good VCR. And he got a used VCR that he found for their anniversary? But [his wife] started crying; she said, why couldn't you just buy me something new for once? And this is our anniversary—it's just like teaching people, be romantic and stuff. Stuff like that.

In this program, Christopher found another idea about how families should behave that he determined was "right." Roc should buy something new rather than salvage a gift for his wife, as that would show her that he loves her. Christopher said that the program has "all kinds of messages" like this.

It is relevant that Christopher was a churchgoing member of his neighborhood community, as he expressed a kind of moral righteousness about how kids and parents should behave, and even about how television programs should "behave." Not only should parents tell their kids what to do; TV should teach people about how to "do the right thing."

Christopher expressed his moral sensibility further when he compares the Cosby's style to other styles of comedy:

> I was shocked when I heard *The Cosby Show* was going off [the air]. Bill Cosby is my favorite comedian. 'Cause, you know, lots of comedians nowadays, they, like, their humor is, like, sick, nasty, you know, perverted, cursing kind of humor. Sometimes it's kind of funny, but, no—Bill Cosby, he can make you laugh without cursing and, you know, being nasty and perverted, stuff.

Christopher's righteous sense of comedy put him at odds with "a lot of comedians nowadays," but Christopher had settled into an upstanding life. He had become a confident member of his new family, respecting their teachings about doing the "right" things. His interpretations of TV's Cosby and Roc appear to affirm and fortify his growth in social and moral resolve, a resolve paralleling his newfound sense of belonging and confidence.

Reviewing Christopher

Over a two-year period, Christopher transformed from being a lonely, confused, frustrated, and fearful boy dealing with a series of unfamiliar situations to being a sociable, confident, and upstanding member of his new communities. He became comfortable and "paid attention to" in a new household, with new responsibilities and routines. A bigger, stronger body and his father's advice to "walk straight up" helped him feel less worried about danger in his neighborhood. By playing basketball with the boys and conforming to his peers' clothing standards of baggy jeans and sneakers, he eventually found the friends he sought.

Christopher's transformation from feeling confused and isolated to feeling confident, optimistic, and sociable was mirrored in his television habits. After finding friends and activities, he stopped using the TV for company at home and, instead, watched television mostly as a last-resort means of filling his leisure time. But he also came to use TV basketball as a means of developing and supporting his identity as a male peer.

Besides eliminating some cartoon viewing and adding basketball viewing, Christopher's TV tastes in general did not shift from year one to year two. Throughout this time period, he watched many of the same popular programs as his peers, locally and nationally, viewing prime-time situation comedies that were about "real" life. But as a unique individual, he preferred adventure mysteries that provided a blend of suspense and humor, as exemplified in his interest in *Tales from the Crypt*. These aesthetic and storytelling preferences contrast with the preferences of Marina and Samantha, both of whom generally enjoyed prime-time sitcoms about real life but preferred music programming and talk shows, respectively. These variations in tastes indicate the problematic nature of categorizing meanings for diverse youths—-or for any group of viewers.

Christopher's choice of an alias hints at his use of TV for identity work. Like many viewers, he appreciated the power of a cartoon character that could fight against evil and always prevail. Some respite from transitory stresses must be found in the predictability of this mythic world.[9] Yet Christopher's wishful identification with a superhero character was also strongly associated with the popularity of this character among his peers: He chose to name himself after a TV figure who was highly regarded by a group to which he wished to belong, and thus claimed a sense of peer identity.

Christopher's television interpretations give poignant expression to his identity dilemmas, as well as to his resolution of these dilemmas. In his first year at AMS, Christopher watched *Quantum Leap* to connect with a character who was lost in time and space; in this way, he gained reflective distance from his own "changing." By the second year, Christopher's newly settled identities as an admiring and respectful son of an urban African American law enforcer who was a churchgoer and community leader were symbolized in his interpretations of *The Cosby Show*, a program with a strong male figure who told parents and kids how to "do things right" and whose comedy did not rely on "nasty" humor. *Cosby* the program and Cosby the character affirmed Christopher's new sense of familial and social order and supported and enhanced his new sense of himself as a son who was well guided and cared for.

It is intriguing to note that Christopher moved from being attracted primarily to science-fiction and cartoon superheroes on TV (*Quantum Leap*'s Sam and *X-Men*'s Wolverine) to admiring real-life TV characters (*The Cosby Show*'s Cliff and Theo Huxtable and the cast of *Roc*). This suggests a kind of imaginative grounding, a settling down by moving from other-world fantasies to preferring earthly fictions—that is, from the imaginative world of mythic heroes, in which characters leap through time, fly in space, prevail over spectacular evils, and contend with extraordinary uncertainties, to the imaginative worlds of *Cosby* and *Roc*, in which family members prevail over everyday difficulties and contend with the familiar uncertainties of work, home, school, and city life. When Christopher's TV favorites shifted to *Cosby* and *Roc*, it was as if he was imaginatively landing within fictional ideals of his own life.

Stories—sung, read, or viewed—have long played a meaningful role in inspiring, challenging, teaching, and pleasing humans as they move through life (Bruner 1986). The television to which Christopher was attracted—the cartoons, mysteries, adventures, and family comedies—contained stories with features that particularly suited his aesthetics and elements that were identifiably familiar. They also had themes and ideologies that paralleled those in other areas of his life. Further, these stories seemed to resolve Christopher's changing sense of comfort while fortifying his sense of moral correctness. Thus, the TV stories Christopher preferred, and their characters, features, and themes, reflect his sensibilities about himself and his life. In turn, they contributed to his particular way of being at home, at school, and with his peers.

4

Samantha

*Pondering Images of Political
and Vocal Power*

A t thirteen, Samantha is discovering an attraction to speaking
out, in dramatic and public arenas. She explains that

> if you were to go up in front of the class and say something,
> where, you know, people are giving you the attention that's due,
> it's exciting, it's very exciting.... I like voicing my opinion in
> class.... I like people listening to me; I like people understand-
> ing what I have to say.

Samantha, like Marina, is tall for her age, but Samantha's
body is not full-figured. Instead, she is slim, yet strong and
athletic. Her hair is medium-long, wavy, and dark blonde,
and her bluish-gray eyes look pleasant and thoughtful. She
expresses herself in a quiet yet assured tone, and she walks
with smooth measure and stature. She generally conveys a
presence that is unassuming and congenial.

Samantha emerged as a focal participant because she was
one of the few students who approached me to ask questions
and continued to talk with me on her own. Samantha was curious about what I was doing at the school. When I explained
that I work like an anthropologist, a field she has considered
for herself, I gained her confidence and further interest. I was
surprised that she knew about the field of anthropology and was
impressed with how mature and collected she seemed.

We then had several chats at school, often during breaks
and gym class, where she usually sat on the sidelines with a

small group of friends or on her own. Samantha included me, alone and with her friends, and gave me "inside" information and insights. Thus, she became one of my key informants.

In my visits and talks with Samantha, I came to understand that observing and learning from the political and social worlds around her, which included television, is an important and valuable activity. I also learned that she was looking for knowledge and strategies that would allow her to participate in these worlds fully and expressively as a girl with a strong voice and a compassionate sensibility. She is a girl with a passion for speaking out, and concern for herself and others, who is struggling to figure out how to be a powerful female in male-dominated worlds.

Locating Samantha at Home, at School, and with Peers

Samantha, an Irish–Jewish American, lived in the Bronx, which, she said, gave her an edge at school. She noticed that her Black and Latin peers treated her differently when she told them where she lived—as if she had a tough life that was more like theirs. But she lived on the out-skirts of one of the safer and more middle-class sections of the borough, in an apartment complex that included a central yard with trees, green-ery, and walking paths. Samantha's surroundings were such that she could walk alone during the day and not worry too much. Yet shortly after our second interview, someone was mugged and killed in front of her building in the early morning.

Samantha's family lived in a roomy apartment (by New York stan-dards), where she had her own room. The place looked casual and unas-suming, with many books related to her parents' occupations. Both were in health-service professions; they also wrote. David Gardner was a clinical psychologist who worked with troubled youths; Beth Gard-ner worked at a center that educated and counseled adults who had mental retardation and gave physical-therapy treatment at home. Together, the Gardners were writing a book about stepfamilies, because they were a blended family: Beth had been married before and had a son, Samantha's twenty-two-year-old half-brother, who lived on his own in the area.

They were a blended family in other ways, too. Beth Gardner's fam-ily had lived in the Pacific Northwest, coming from an Irish–Scottish

Christian background, and David Gardner's family had lived in the Northeast, coming from a Hungarian Jewish background. They were not practicing a religion at the time of the study. Politically, the Gardners have similar backgrounds, as they were both active in the social movements of the 1960s and 1970s. Apparently, political activism goes back in time for the family: Samantha's grandparents were socialists who were active during the 1930s workers' movement.

Samantha's family was very important for her: She told me in our first interview, "I love all of my family." Several of her comments in the autobiography she wrote in the first year of the study suggested how comfortable she felt around them. In describing an annual picnic, for example, she wrote, "Those were the best times, being with family and friends that you trusted and cared about." On another occasion, she said that she was "extremely happy. My best friend and I are having a wonderful weekend together, and I am with my family. It doesn't get much better than this." Although some of her peers were distancing themselves from family to claim a sense of independence, Samantha proclaimed the value of being connected to family.

Samantha's teachers considered her bright and promising as student, even though she had what the school had labeled a "learning disability," and what she called "my problem." She had trouble reading and spelling, a situation that caused her to be assigned to "Resource Rooms" during her career as a student. Although she had difficulties reading and writing, she found ways to express her mature thoughtfulness, usually in discussions using spoken rather than written words. Her first-year adviser at AMS commented that Samantha's "deep concern for people seems to give her an understanding that penetrates to the core"; he also noted that she was "in many ways beyond her years." The teachers gave her many marks in the "good" and "very good" categories for her work and for her attitude. Her social-studies teacher found her to be a "good political thinker," and her reading and writing teacher said she was "interested in ideas, and can express herself orally very well. . . . She has a good ear for dialogue." Teachers found Samantha to be a compelling and very aware student into her second year, noting that her "strength lies in her communication skills."

Samantha's teachers also complained that she lacked concentration and focus at times but ascribed this partly to active "goofing off" on her part, which, she reasoned, was part of a natural process: "I had my year of goofing off. . . . I didn't care that much about my academic career."

Her status as an "almost" high-school student in eighth grade prompted her to be more serious. School was getting harder, and she realized that she also had to work harder, as she was thinking about law, anthropology, and acting as future areas of study.

Samantha told stories about being snubbed by some peers and being talked about in negative terms during her first year at AMS. Samantha's past friendships may have influenced the regard others had for her: In her first year at AMS, she was friendly with students who left the school early on negative terms. But it may be that her female peers regarded her disapprovingly because, like Marina, she liked to hang out with the boys. Most girls this age do not like girls' trying to befriend boys, as most girls assume that a girl who spends time with boys is trying to acquire them romantically (see Lees 1993). Samantha's emotional maturity and physical size made her seem older than her years, which could easily have threatened other girls who wanted to earn the boys' attention. However, Samantha claims that, in the seventh grade, she had no romantic intentions:

> I'm friends with most of the boys. And I don't have that many friends that are girls. But I don't mind. I've never really had. You know, I've enjoyed having friends that are boys, because I am athletic. And I do like doing things that a lot of girls don't. I just enjoy having friends that are boys. You know, boys go around, they might hit harder than girls, and they might shove a little more, but I'm used to that. I have an older brother. So, I imagine if you have an older brother, if a female grows up with a man who's not her father, then they will learn to get closer to males. And ever since I was young, I've always enjoyed being with males. 'Cause when I was younger, I'd, like, wear a skirt just so people would know that I was a girl. Then I'd pull it off and go out on the monkey bars, and go run around. So. . . I'm in between, I guess.

Yet Samantha's relationships with boys are perplexing. She has some romantic interest in boys, although not the boys at AMS. Like Marina, she is attracted to some neighborhood boys who are older and her brother's friends. And although she likes to hang around the boys at AMS, she feels that they discriminate against her for being a girl. At an all-school meeting at which students discussed discrimination, Samantha said that girls who wanted to play basketball, such as herself, were not able to participate fully because the boys did not think the girls should be playing. And even when girls did play, the boys avoided including them in game strategies and kept the ball out of their hands, which kept the girls from improving their skills. Thus, as Samantha put it, the girls were "doomed if you do and doomed if you don't" play. This exemplifies her keen insight into social interaction and, in this case, represents her awareness of the subtle yet frustrating effects of gender bias.[1]

Gender, race, and ethnic issues were complexly associated with Samantha's social experience at school. She did have a few girlfriends at school. Some she regarded as her equals "intellectually"; with others, she simply played double Dutch jump rope. She reported having a friendship with Marina and her Latina girlfriends, and I saw her talking with girls and boys of color regularly. Yet her designated "close friends" were White. Indeed, in Samantha's second year at AMS, she and her two closest friends were "the three White kids in the eighth grade."

Samantha acknowledged that she was sometimes swayed by her peers: That is what prompted her to spend a year "goofing off," and that is what subsequently influenced her to start being serious about school. She said that she was worried that she would get in with the wrong crowd in high school and might be influenced badly. She sensed that this was how she reacted to friends—she did what they did, and, "like, in high school, I could get caught up with the wrong people, and it would be just awful. Just be completely and totally awful."

I told her that, given her thoughtful nature, I doubted she would be unable to notice her friends' influence. Samantha explained:

> In a social situation it's a lot different. Last year, my friends were very important to me. I was going into a new school; I felt very insecure about myself, and I needed someone other than my family to kind of boost me up. And if it was my friends who would persuade me to do something rebellious or something I wouldn't want to do, but then in the end would kind of boost me up—that boost is what I needed, I would do something for that boost. That's basically what it was. . . . [But] I've changed. You know, I'm a different person, and I don't rely on people as much as I once did that are outside my family.

Samantha embodied contradictions, which indicated the transitory phase of development she was in; they also illustrated her complexity. As she was recognizing the power of peers in her life, she was also proclaiming her independence while hanging on to her family connection.

In sum, Samantha was a bright, reflective, emotionally mature girl who enjoyed relatively safe, urban, middle-class living circumstances. She had two parents who were sensitive to others' needs professionally and politically and seem to have influenced her to be socially sensitive and aware. Indeed, Samantha may have been overly responsive to others, yet she saw this changing to some extent. She was also sensitive to social interactions in which inequities and biases compromised her and her fellows' experiences—that did not allow her to learn to play basketball better or enjoy hanging out with the boys. Samantha wanted to learn to play like the boys and to enjoy being with them in games other than basketball.

Samantha's Use and Evaluation of Television

TV as "Play in Your Own House"

Samantha said that she liked television the most of any of her family, but it was only something to do when she was alone and bored, when there was no possibility of being with friends or talking on the phone. Her attitude was similar to the attitudes of her classmates, who also said they preferred being with others and engaging in physical activities (sports, dancing, playing outside) to watching TV.

But she could get hooked into TV, seeing it as a way to mark time that was easier than other lone pursuits, such as reading and writing. Because of her difficulties with texts, she "hates to read." Literate activities are not relaxing or entertaining for her on her own. But television— "It's just, you watch it 'cause it's just like an excuse to do anything. It's just entertainment, that what it is. It's not used for like any psychological purposes or anything like that; it's just entertainment, and people enjoy it. . . . It's like play in your own house."

Samantha liked this "play" only within her own house; she did not like to go to friends' homes for TV "play" and did not like friends who spent too much time with the TV on.

> *Samantha:* My friend who lives in [my old neighborhood], the television is on twenty-four hours a day, even if nobody's watching it. She has two in her house: She has one for watching television, and one for playing Nintendo and video games. And every day either the radio's on or the television set, twenty-four hours. . . . Maybe once a month, if I'm sick or something, I can sit in front of the television, all day. But she could do that the whole year. Sitting there, watching television, never going outside. She has a beautiful yard; she has two brothers and sisters that she could go outside and play with. Her friends are all where she lives. . . . And I go over to her house sometimes, I get mad, I didn't go over to her house to watch television. I could be at my house to watch television. . . .[And she watches] whatever, whatever. She has all the cable stations, whatever's on . . . [and] after a while—say, a couple hours after that—I say, You wanna go outside?

> Or you want to go to my house? Or something like that. . . . Sometimes she will, and sometimes she won't. If she doesn't, then I'll go home, and I'll help my grandfather or something.
>
> *JoEllen:* When you guys watch together, do you talk?
>
> *Samantha:* No. Not at all.

Because the friend does not talk while she watches TV, Samantha cannot abide this activity when they are together. Interaction is very important to Samantha; it is essentially what friends are for. In her first-year autobiography assignment, Samantha wrote:

> In order for you to be a good friend you must care about this person, and know their faults and if they do something wrong just let it roll off your shoulder. Let your friends create other relationships and sometime if they wish give them time to be alone by themselves. But mainly the most important suggestion I have is to listen and talk. If you just do one you might drive your friend crazy. Listen to what they have to say and if it is a problem try to your best ability to give a solution.

Samantha titled this section, "The Rules of Friendship." In this writing, she demonstrates aspects of her social sensitivity and maturity by suggesting that friendships involve caring, acceptance of individuality, and flexibility. But, especially, she notes that "the most important suggestion I have is to listen and talk."

TV as a Family Ritual of Coziness and Commentary

I was able to watch television with Samantha and her family, participating in one of their typical weekday evening routines, during our first set of interviews. While I was there, they nestled into their couch and easy chairs, taking opportunities to sit close and "cuddle" (Samantha's term).[2] This gathering around the television happens fairly regularly, but the family does not watch "whatever." The Gardners reported that they tended to watch educational programs on the public stations, including news, documentaries, nature shows, and selections from Masterpiece Theater (PBS). But they also watched shows that were more like "play in your own house," such as reruns of *Barney Miller* and *M*A*S*H*, which they considered "classics," and the sitcoms *The Simpsons*, *Roseanne*, and *Murphy Brown*, which were popular at the time.

The Gardners told me that they identified with characters on TV. David Gardner said that he was like Homer Simpson, and Beth Gardner said she was like Roseanne Connor. They took delight in comparing themselves to these characters, because they realized how very different they seemed from these characters on the surface. David said that he was sometimes unaware of himself, like Homer, the father character in *The Simpsons*, and Beth described herself as a wisecracking, easygoing woman who ran the household, like the mother and lead character in *Roseanne*.

This kind of reflection and commentary typifies TV viewing in the Gardner household. The family told me that they were "loud complainers" while watching TV; that they had a hard time not talking back to the tube because it was, to them, "a vast wasteland." While viewing together, they voiced opposition about portrayals or themes in certain shows and commented on aspects of programming, like the critical viewers in R. Lembo's *Thinking Through Television* (2000). The Gardners noticed gender, race, and class stereotypes and biases in news perspectives; they were also cognizant of the commercial ploys that are so prevalent in episodic series. David Gardner characterized most television as "three guys on a couch with a laugh track." Like the viewers in Lembo's study, David Gardner seemed to recognize the "formula" that much programming has to adopt to produce volumes of time-filling shows. Because Samantha is "modeled after my parents, 'cause they are the people who I spend my life with," she was also critical and reflective of television.

In our second interview, the Gardners had adjusted some of their perspectives on television in ways that were almost paradoxical. On the one hand, they had purchased a new TV set that had a larger screen and could be hooked to stereo speakers. They seemed to need to justify this to me, explaining that they usually did not like to buy new things—especially items about which they complain or that they feel represent materialism, an aspect of American life about which they are generally critical. But, they said, they had seen these big, fancy TV machines at friends' houses and realized that they could enjoy some of their public programming better if the picture and sound were improved. They wanted to treat themselves because TV is something they share as a family, so they said the purchase was a "sociological and psychological" decision to benefit their family gatherings.

At the same time that they were purchasing a new and bigger TV set, Beth said, she had become upset the amount of time kids spend watching television without thinking about it. She was upset with herself for not noticing sooner that the kids just watch TV when they are bored instead of thinking of other options. Beth then wondered aloud about what she might have done differently and what she might do now.[3] Yet she also noted that a pattern had been established over "twenty-some years," and that it had been useful for her to rely on TV when she was making dinner or when the kids came home from school and she was working. If they were watching TV, she felt, "They're home; they're safe." Still, after all these years, she assumed that watching "stupid and awful" programs (which she said were the norm) "has to have an effect."

Choosing Programs That Have "Some Class" and Pro-Socially Entertain

At night, Samantha watched many of the prime-time situation comedies that her cohorts selected, which effectively positioned her as a member of her school's peer mainstream. But her particular list of favorites included shows that she often watched with her parents: *The Cosby Show*, *The Golden Girls*, *Murphy Brown*, *Roseanne*, *The Simpsons*, and *The Wonder Years*. Generally, she was attracted to these shows because "they hold my attention, and they kind of make me give a silent smirk or something. . . . They make me feel good . . . because when the canned laughter is on you're laughing along with it. You're not just sitting there bored." She also said that these shows "have some class to them"— unlike *Married . . . with Children*, a show she hated because

> they're insulting to everyone, even to that stupid dog. It's just awful! Everybody's making fun of each other. And I don't like the sitcoms where everyone is making fun of each other and calling each other stupid and things like that. You know, if there's nothing else on, I guess I'll watch that. Except I'll never watch *Married . . . with Children*. It's just too much.

The Simpsons and *Married . . . with Children* are both known as programs that poke fun at family life and American stereotypes, so I asked Samantha to explain the difference between the two (besides the fact that one is a cartoon and the other uses real actors). Samantha claimed, "I guess people can relate to *The Simpsons*. There are, like, stress points that you wouldn't normally stress, and then when you see it done with other than human figures, it's kind of cute to see it."

Although both programs make fun of "typical" family life and other aspects of American society, episodes of *The Simpsons* generally end with an implicit, and sometimes explicit, pro-social message or moral. Very often, this message or moral has been presented by one of the female characters—either the mother or the daughter. *Married . . . with Chil-*

dren, by contrast, is generally amoral and aggressively boorish in its presentation of messages or morals. The motto of this program appears to be "everyone for herself or himself" as each character looks only to please individual wants. The mother and daughter in *Married . . . with Children* are the smartest and cleverest in the cast, who are all selfish, petty, and conniving characters, contrasting with the female characters on *The Simpsons*, who are mostly sensitive, wise, and altruistic.

Samantha's sensibilities, and her mother's, more closely matched those of the female characters on *The Simpsons*, explaining why Samantha could not tolerate the amoral themes and "insulting" aesthetics of *Married . . . with Children*. In addition, Samantha's family had a declared interest in educational fare and public-broadcast programming. Generally, these kinds of programs are thought to have some socially redeeming value. The more popular mainstream programs that Samantha chose—*The Golden Girls, Murphy Brown, Roseanne, The Simpsons, The Wonder Years*, and certainly *The Cosby Show*—have been acknowledged as shows that explore social issues in the limited manner allowed by situation comedies and that present provocative yet mostly pro-social messages. For example, various episodes of *Roseanne* addressed topical issues, such as domestic violence and tolerance for gays and lesbians, and *Murphy Brown* was known for its feminist stance. Samantha found these programs meaningful because their stories, values, and ideas were in line with the political and social sensibilities of her family. Samantha said that her parents were "very political . . . they talk [and] read political books." Likewise, Samantha had attended several summer camps that were oriented toward social activism and community involvement. Samantha's preferences and judgments about prime-time programming were thus associated with her identity as a daughter, her identity as a citizen, and her compassionate and pro-social sensibilities.

Learning About "So Many Things That Are Happening"

Samantha's favorite afternoon programs were *21 Jump Street* and talk shows. She watched *Tiny Toons* (an animated series) intermittently and glanced at other shows while flipping through channels during commercials. She also said that she would watch "whatever is on," but only if her preferred programming was not available while she was trying to fill her time alone.

She watched *21 Jump Street* mostly to see Johnny Depp, an adolescent heart throb at the time. But the show's stories and concepts also aligned clearly with Samantha's sense of social responsibility. The main characters on *21 Jump Street* are young people who have become under-cover narcotics agents who work in high schools to capture drug deal-ers and keep students from using drugs. The values and ideas of this program are socially redeeming, which put it in the same league as Samantha's nightly viewing fare (with the exception that *21 Jump Street* is a serious drama).

Samantha's favorite afternoon fare, however, is talk shows.

> *Samantha:* Basically, there's nothing else on at 4:00, and I enjoy talk shows a lot. I'm a talk-show-aholic *(little laugh)*. And when I stay home . . . on days that I'm sick, I lay there and watch talk shows and talk shows and talk shows.
>
> *JoEllen:* Why do you think you're a "talk-show-aholic" ?
>
> *Samantha:* I don't know. It's interesting to see those people and see the pub-lic's reaction toward them.
>
> *JoEllen:* Do you mean the hosts or the . . .
>
> *Samantha:* The visitors who are up on the panel. That's why I like it. They have some issues where I go, Oh god, I can't believe this is really true. And sometimes they have issues, like, political people up there that really get into it.
>
> *JoEllen:* Give me an example of people [about whom you think], "Oh, god, is this really true?"
>
> *Samantha:* Like neo-Nazis and stuff like that. Like, we all know people like that really exist, but we don't want to know, you know, and that's why they put 'em on these shows. 'Cause it does get ratings, you know? It gets the number one. "Let's kill all the Jews. Let's kill all the Blacks!" All of a sud-den you've switched to that station and you kind of gulp.

Samantha declares an interest in talk programs because of their pres-entation of "issues" and "political people." Again, she is attracted to pro-gramming that has some kind of educational value or somehow addresses topical social issues. In addition, she proclaims her need for social interaction, which is particularly evident in her remark, "It's inter-esting to see those people and see the public's reaction toward them."

Samantha fits the profile of female viewers that S. Livingstone dis-cusses in "Watching Talk: Gender and Engagement in the Viewing of Audience Discussion Programmes" (1994). Livingstone finds that non-viewers in Britain regard talk shows as "uninformative" and "senseless" because of the manner in which they explore topics. But regular view-ers, male and female, consider the shows "interesting" because they allow "ordinary people to have a say in public, including the opportunity to argue with experts," which characterizes the genre as a democratic forum

(Livingstone 1994: 434–35). Livingstone argues that women who watch talk shows find program topics to be morally, socially, and politically meaningful, using C. Gilligan's (1993) theories about gendered differences in moral development in tandem with S. Benhabib's (1992) discussion relating the private and public spheres. Livingstone suggests that women find talk shows compelling because the topics are personally relevant, and because everyday people—usually women—are providing contexts for topics. Talk-show viewers also complicate topics rather than resolve them. Talk-show panels discuss topics such as domestic violence, divorce, sexism, racism, and poverty using personal narratives and commentary as illustrations, which relegates them to the personal or private realm in a male-dominated framework. Male viewers find the specifics of narratives and commentary in and of themselves unsatisfying and are more concerned with how topics are argued and resolved—that is, they want the discussions to move into the realm of logic and principle. But for women, the details of personal stories contribute to a more comprehensive understanding of real human dilemmas in the social world, which, according to a feminist framework, are part of the public sphere and inherently moral and political.

Like Livingstone's viewers, Samantha is curious about the people who appear "on the panel" and is interested in the studio audience. She is like an anthropologist-viewer observing people who seem to be in a culture different from her own ("Oh, god, is this really true?"), yet wondering how to co-exist with people who are so different from her ("like neo-Nazis and stuff like that"). Watching the studio audience, who ostensibly are ordinary people ("the public"), interact with people on the panel who are outrageous by comparison ("Let's kill all the Jews. Let's kill all the Blacks!"), Samantha finds social, political, and moral value in the discussions. While watching, she challenges herself to consider how she should think and feel about these strange others. T. Liebes and E. Katz (1990: 100–14) would characterize this as a "referential" reading: Samantha relates the real people on the show to her own real world.

Samantha's viewing of talk shows and the social issues they explore could have been contributing to, as well as helping to abate, some nervousness she had about the future. When I asked her what she imagined about her future, she said she figured on getting married and having kids, but she was not exactly sure what she would be doing professionally or where she would live. "There's so many options out there for me," she said. However, she did worry sometimes about what might happen:

> It can get pretty scary ... just to think about what the future will bring. 'Cause you never know, because there are so many people out there, you know.... You see all the homeless, and all the stuff that's going around, teenagers and prostitution, all the drug problems going around, and there's more stuff that no one's knowledgeable of.... So many things are happening, you just say, you know, that could be me one day. You could try not to think about it at all. That's what I try to do. It doesn't work, though.

The social world presented on talk shows can look bizarre and scary, because panels present topics and situations that lie sensationally outside mundane everyday existence. Samantha's view of the future as scary might have been influenced by her everyday viewing of TV's "ordinary" people talking about scary and unusual social experiences; this, in turn, might mean she was a victim of the Cultivation Process as proposed by Gerbner et al. (1986). However, Samantha's real world included encounters with real homeless people, who heavily populate the area around her school and the subways she rides, and hearing about the problems of teenagers through her father, who works with troubled adolescents. The actual world surrounding Samantha would not let her forget "all the stuff going around," even though she tried.

However, Samantha's gathering information from talk shows about bizarre aspects of the world may also have helped her to prepare better for an unknown future. Perhaps she was educating herself to face the uncertain "realities" of her own life by exploring the "scary" realities presented by people on talk shows. Because of her difficulty reading, talk shows became a more palatable way for her to learn about some real social worlds outside her own.

Watching the Talk Moderators

Samantha watched both Oprah Winfrey and Phil Donahue regularly, flipping back and forth between their talk shows, although she was usually drawn to one topic more than another and so stayed longer with one program. She also preferred Donahue as a moderator:

> Oprah is a little bit, like, she gets on my nerves. 'Cause when she has, like, a victim up there, it's very disturbing. And she's just kind of, like, the person is up there crying, instead of, like, going for a break or something, she'll go: "Tell me more, tell me more. Come on, come on, tell me more." And it's just, like, you know, enough is enough. Let the person breathe. It's kind of dis-

turbing to see someone, like, so insensitive and so uncaring. In such a position where that person needs someone to care, and for her to just to be like:
"Come on, go on; it's OK if you cry and break down. Actually, that's what I
want. It will get me ratings. Come on." You know? It's just, I don't like her.

[But Phil Donahue] kind of reminds me of a lawyer ... how he tries to
get straight to the point, he doesn't let them dilly-dally.... [And] he always
cracks little jokes, you know? That make, like, the audience and everyone else
really enjoy it, when it gets really intense he does that.

Drawing again on Livingstone's study (1994) and Gilligan's framework of gendered differences (1993), Samantha sounds "typically"
female as well as male in making these comments on talk-show dynamics. Livingstone finds that viewers, male and female, tend to notice and
comment on different interactional styles of hosts and studio audiences,
which she claims is a "critical questioning of the communicative mode
of address of discussions" (Livingstone 1994: 436). Samantha questions
the manner in which the moderators handle the topic and the participants. Samantha is "disturbed" that Oprah can be so "insensitive and
uncaring" that she would coax a "victim" to "cry and break down" rather
than "let the person breathe." Samantha wants Oprah to be like Gilligan's (debatably) typical female, who is concerned with caring and relationships rather than rights and responsibilities. Samantha critiques
Oprah's behavior because it is geared to "get [her] ratings"—Oprah is
a responsible business person rather than a caring host. At the same
time, Samantha suggests that when Donahue "cracks little jokes" so
that the audience can get relief from the intensity of the program, he
is helping the audience "enjoy it"—and thus implicitly caring for them.

In Livingstone's study, men tend to be critical of the style and intentions of the host and the program, while women question how the audience is selected, wondering how specific "ordinary" people come to be
in the audience. Ironically, when Samantha claims to like Donahue better because he is like a "lawyer [getting] straight to the point" and not
letting participants "dilly-dally," she is talking more like male viewers
who want the discussions to be resolved rather than elaborated with personal or emotional details. Yet Samantha sees Donahue's jokes as a caring act—something a typical male would not do. Oprah is the typical
male here, pushing people to cry for ratings. Samantha's commentary
on talk shows and their hosts' behavior illustrates the problematic nature
of specifying gendered differences, because Samantha responds at times
categorically like a female and at others like a male, and characterizes
male hosts according to feminine standards and vice versa.

Samantha's empathy for "victims" on the talk-show panel is linked to her compassionate and sensitive qualities—qualities that are complemented and perhaps fostered by both of her parents, who are necessarily empathic as "helping" professionals. In addition, her critiques of talk-show hosts who probe panel members just to improve their ratings make evident her keen observation skills and her critical awareness of programming, which have been nurtured by her family's "loud complaining" about TV.

The Meaning of Talk Shows

Overall, the meaning Samantha finds in talk shows is related to her appreciation for informative programming about social issues, which is associated with her, and her family's, political and social sensibility. Samantha believed that the media have a responsibility to inform people and that ultimately everyone should know more:

> I think there's a lot of things that people should know about that they don't. Like the news should tell a little bit more of the truth. And a little bit more what's really going on. And not try to hide the public, [but] let the public kind of pick out what the public chooses they want to hear, and choose what they want to watch. Not just like for [the media] to guess.

Relatedly, Samantha liked talk shows because of her explicit valuing of everyday talk—her optimal means of gathering and conveying information, given her problems with written language. Samantha explicitly mentioned the value of talking to maintain friendships. In her family as well as at school, talking was encouraged and supported, even when the talk engendered conflicting points of view. Samantha came from "a very open-minded, strong family where your opinion should be voiced— even if the society or even your family doesn't agree—it should be voiced." Yet Samantha herself was actively struggling with this notion.

Reflections of Samantha Through the Screen

"I Don't Really Have Role Models"

When Samantha compared herself to people on TV whom she liked, she could identify partly with certain characters:

> On *Roseanne*, you know, the two daughters? I kind of feel in between the two of them. . . . Like one of them [the older daughter] is, like, this girl who is real smart and who is always thinking about boys, and the other one [the

younger daughter] is always playing sports, you know, playing with the boys. And I feel in between them, like. But before, I was more like the younger one.... [But] I don't see myself [being smart-alecky like them]. Maybe to my friends when I'm kidding around or something, but I don't talk to my brother like that, and I don't talk to my parents like that.

Samantha related to characters who engaged in activities that are often opposed to each other: being "real smart" versus being athletic; dating boys versus befriending boys. Samantha was admittedly "in between" in both of these areas. She still wanted to play sports and jump rope and generally "goof off" with her friends. But she knew she had to get more serious and be "smart" at school, because high school was going to be more challenging academically. And Samantha wanted to hang out with the boys but also to date them. She associated being younger with a time when it was OK just to play with boys, without "always thinking about" them and without the problems that go along with dating, such as tensions among peers and the risks associated with sexual activity. The two TV daughters helped Samantha recognize that she was no longer a child but was not yet a teen.

But Samantha rejected any direct relationship between herself and TV personae. She said, "I don't do that to myself; I don't say, I'd like to be like her. I just, you know, I like different people for different reasons. I wouldn't like to be anyone other than myself." Samantha's emerging independence and self-creativity shine through here and were bolstered when I asked her whether she had role models:

Not at all.... Not on television.... I don't really have role models. I want to model myself on Samantha. You know? I want to be Samantha. I don't want to—you know, of course I'm gonna be modeled from my parents, 'cause they are the people who I spend my life with. But I don't want to be Beth; I don't want to be David. I want to be Samantha. I don't want to be, whoever, Roseanne Barr, Murphy Brown, or anyone, for that matter, other than myself. And who that is yet, I'm still not sure. But every day it's maybe a little better.

Samantha is like her family, yet she also is not; her self is still unknown but emerging "every day." She fervently wants to establish identities that are distinguishable only as Samantha "myself," not as "anyone" or "whoever."

Yet Samantha may have been looking at others on TV and in reality for certain qualities, and even for particular techniques, that might assist her desire to "model myself on Samantha, [even though] who that is yet, I'm still not sure."

The Value and the Risks of Speaking Out and Being "Spicy"

In our first interview, Samantha reported:

> I like the lady who plays Murphy Brown. She puts a little spice into her. . . .
> And my father likes her, so I watch it with my father. . . . My father got me
> into it. He likes her, too; she kind of gives it a little something. . . . She's kind
> of aggressive.

Once again, Samantha declares her strong connection to her family and shows how influential they can be. Yet these remarks also provide more clues to Samantha's identity issues. Her most salient concerns are oriented around her sense of herself as a political citizen and her sense of herself as female. How can she be a woman who strongly expresses her opinions if she is nervous and soft-spoken? How can she be aggressive and feminine at the same time?

Not only did Samantha appreciate talk; she also wanted to wrangle over issues. "I love debating," she said. She was hoping in high school to get into a special law-studies program, an honors project at the school she would attend.

This partly explains the appeal of the Murphy Brown character, a sitcom persona who wrangles on-screen with almost everyone she encounters. In *Murphy Brown*, Candice Bergen played the part of a television journalist with a reputation for being outspoken and for confronting interviewees on camera using provocative and direct approaches. Putting fictional guests in the hot seat and zinging them with pointed questions had won awards for the Murphy Brown character and the sitcom-created news program for which she works. The Murphy character was known for being equally provocative in her personal life—so much so that, in 1992, she incurred the wrath of Vice President Dan Quayle, who publicly denounced Murphy for having a baby out of wedlock. The *New York Times* considered the uproar and aftermath of this event front-page news (see Wines 1992).

The creators of *Murphy Brown* wrote a special episode in response to Quayle's denunciation and to the subsequent media attention paid to the program and the issue of single motherhood. The program episode incorporated Quayle's videotaped remarks as if Murphy were seeing them on her own TV in "real time"; then she and the show's other characters lambasted the vice president. Although Murphy found herself pondering her decision again (similar to some of the show's episodes about the character's pregnancy), the ending of the episode showed her strongly defending her position as an independent woman choosing to have a child without marrying.

It is likely that Samantha greatly appreciated the "debate" atmosphere that *Murphy Brown* actively espoused. Indeed, Samantha admitted that the TV characters she preferred

> have a quality about them that is tough, that doesn't take crap from anyone, which also attracts me to them, which I consider myself as, as well. That I don't take crap from anyone. . . . I was brought up not to take crap from anyone. . . . It's not necessary for me to take it. I mean, I know when to keep my mouth shut, and I know when I'm able to speak my mind.

Although Samantha liked characters, like herself, who had a "tough" quality and did not "take crap," she did not behave aggressively like the Murphy Brown character. Samantha did speak up for herself, as well as for others, as shown in her critique of the boys at school who would not let the girls play basketball. But when she spoke out, her warmth of spirit and her compassionate tone drove her voice and her presentation.

Relatedly, Samantha confessed that she felt nervous when she spoke in front of others. By her description, she trembled when she spoke:

> You know, in social studies, we had to write speeches, and I was up there, and I was trembling. . . . It's bad enough that the words slide off of the page. I kind of memorized it [the speech], and I still did good, but I was so frightened. And I sat down, and I was still shaking.

Samantha's jitters were certainly a reasonable and common response to performing in front of people. However, they also point to conflicts associated with her developing identities. Samantha "loves" debating and she wanted to express her opinions. Speaking out—to "complain loudly" about things—is part of her heritage. She was even considering law as a profession. But if she was "so frightened" presenting herself in formal speaking contexts, how could she take up law? How would she be politically powerful? How could she "speak [her] mind"—without trembling—to a public crowd?

Although Samantha did not want to *be* like Murphy Brown, she did want to know how to *act* like her. If Samantha could act like Murphy Brown, she could speak her mind aggressively; she could "put some spice" into it. As a keen and thoughtful observer of social dynamics, she sensed the power that lay behind Murphy Brown's forcefulness. Samantha's father liked Murphy Brown's aggression; it was the "something" that attracted him to the character and "got [Samantha] into it," too. Samantha knew that her father, a powerful influence in her life, was drawn to this quality. She also saw that a television character could become the focus of Washington politicians and the national media because of her aggressiveness and independence—qualities that are traditionally considered more male than female, and qualities that are generally required for success in Western patriarchal systems.

Samantha indeed noticed that the Murphy Brown character was a constructed entity. As she said in our first interview, she liked "the lady *who plays* Murphy Brown" (emphasis added). In our second interview, I asked Samantha whether she still liked Murphy Brown, and she confirmed that she did:

> I like her character. Her character is really great. And, you know, like, she does those Sprint commercials? And sometimes you can see a little bit of her Murphy Brown in her. You know? So, it's kind of, like, she made the character, the actual actress.

Samantha is not only attracted to the qualities in the character of Murphy Brown; she is also attracted to the person who created the character whom she likes. She has observed the actor Candice Bergen playing two different parts in two different contexts and noted their similarities. Doubtless, the Sprint commercial Samantha mentioned was meant to capitalize on the success and visibility of the sitcom *Murphy Brown* (a common strategy in advertising), so the similarities that Samantha sees probably are intentional. Nevertheless, Samantha attributes the similarities to Bergen's acting abilities, perhaps because figuring out exactly how the actor created the image might make it possible for Samantha to act out these qualities herself. If Samantha can see how "some spice" is crafted, she will be able to construct herself as a persona who speaks to the public without being frightened. Indeed, part of the appeal that acting has for Samantha is that "you could play different characters, and no one could find out what you're really like. I mean, if you're good enough, you could play anybody." Samantha wants to take on roles that will let her "go up in front of [people] and say something, where you know people are giving you the attention that's due. . . . It's exciting, it's very exciting."

In her second year at AMS, Samantha became involved in some drama projects and performed in front of her peers. Some of her nervousness about speaking in a formal setting diminished, and she found herself helping to organize a demonstration against the Rodney King verdict and the unrest in Los Angeles that followed.[4] When I asked how these things came about, despite her fears, she explained, "If you do it more than once, you get used to it. And it's not so much of a fear as it is a requirement for you, even a challenge." Determined to give voice to herself, she pushed herself to learn how to craft politically and vocally powerful versions of her self.

The Problem of Beauty and Romance

Samantha's observing how to act like powerful TV images subsumed a desire to look like powerful images. In our first interview, she admitted: "Like, if I see a beautiful lady on TV, I might say, I wish I could look like that." Like many females, Samantha recognizes the cachet of good looks. But unlike acting in an aggressive and outspoken way, looking beautiful is not something Samantha can learn to "do," especially given TV's standards for female beauty.

Females on television represent a narrow set of appearance standards: TV requires that they be young-looking, thin, well dressed, and glamorously Aryan (that is, White).[5] These beauty standards misrepresent females' actual physical differences and diversity in appearance related to age, race and ethnicity, class, and cultural style. Television, as the "most mass" medium, promotes privileged, patriarchal ideals for feminine appearance, which effectively gives the TV image of beauty a popular, although limiting, power.

Samantha was aware that people on television "are all too good-looking." She saw that television was presenting images that are not "normal" but are nevertheless popular and attention-getting. Thus, her wish to look like "a beautiful lady" on TV acknowledges the power of feminine beauty.

Samantha acknowledged the power of feminine stories as well as beauty. When I asked whether she wanted to be on television, she said she wanted to be in a soap opera. The soap opera she chose was actually a fellow student's version of the popular Spanish-language telenovella program *Pasionara*. As mentioned earlier, a group of Latinas at AMS wrote and circulated extensive scripts, filled with melodramatic romances and domestic situations, soaps' standard fare. Samantha's ideas for herself were appropriate for the genre:

> I'd be the main character . . . sailing on a boat to Italy . . . and then when I
> get there, I'd take a big nap and eat some chocolate and get a backrub. . . .
> I'd make so much money I wouldn't have to do anything. I'd just lay around

and watch television all the time I want! I'd watch myself on every soap opera!
... [And] Tom Cruise [would be with me].... It's my fantasy!

Even though Samantha's tone is sarcastic, she imagines herself in a situation in which she is pampered in a romantic idyll, and even though
she makes money, she just "lays around." She is a "lady-in-waiting" for
chocolate and backrubs. Her companion is Tom Cruise, a popular, handsome actor who is frequently cast as a romantic hero. Samantha's TV
fantasy, though not entirely serious, is characteristically feminine.

Can Samantha fantasize about being a beautiful lady, find pleasure
and romance, and also construct herself as an independent, aggressive
person who speaks her mind? The problem Samantha may have being
a "spicy" and vocal woman is a problem for feminists in general. If she
tries to acquire power in a male-dominated system by adopting male-
identified characteristics, she can be criticized for not being feminine
enough. Indeed, the character Murphy Brown is criticized on her own
program, as her "extreme" autonomy and mode of professionalism form
the basis for much of the program's humor. A. L. Press (1991: 41) notes
that "Murphy is almost too cool, too calm, too competent, and the
show continually reminds one that these characteristics are quite
humorous in a woman, or at least are striking enough to make those in
her company uncomfortable."

If she wants to be taken seriously, Samantha cannot act aggressively
and independently without looking like a beautiful lady and having
romantic dreams. But the images of beauty that Samantha uses as a
standard discriminate against most women's bodies and styles, including her own. And her soap-opera fantasies of doing nothing, getting
backrubs, and cruising with a romantic film idol counter her intentions
to act like an assertive speaker. Like many females, Samantha must
negotiate conflicting imaginations about how to present her self to the
world, and TV both helps and hinders her emerging sensibilities.

Reviewing Samantha

Samantha was strong, thoughtful, determined, and sensitive. Her family routines and beliefs had shown her the importance of critical discussion and expressing opinions, being socially and politically aware, and
having compassion. They had also shown her the value of family fun
and closeness while "playing in your own house." In addition, Samantha attended a school whose philosophy was well aligned with her fam-

ily's, further supporting her development as an outspoken, insightful, informed, and concerned member of society.

Samantha enjoyed more comforts, in terms of finances, space, safety, and class prestige, than did Marina and Christopher. Samantha did not experience the racism that Christopher knew as a boy of color or that Marina knew as an immigrant with a Spanish accent. But despite her circumstantial advantages, Samantha, like her peers, knew about the difficulties of living in the city. And as an emerging adult, she, like them, also contended with contemporary stresses associated with drug use, sexual activity, and economic instability that could lead to joblessness and homelessness. The problems she saw around her made her feel unsure of her future.

At home, Samantha was safe, and because she found reading difficult, she watched television rather than read for entertainment. But her entertainment had to have some positive or educational value to her. She did not want to be "insulted" by programs that only made fun of people; she insisted that stories and themes have some moral or pro-social messages. Her tastes were similar to Christopher's, as he did not want to see "nasty" humor and liked programs that taught people the "right" things.

Samantha's educational, pro-social requirements influenced her preference for talk shows. Because she valued talk in general, she used TV talk shows when actual talk was not available: They provided her with "virtual" talking interactions while alone. They also reinforced her belief that ordinary people's opinions needed to be voiced.

Talk shows' treatment of topical issues contributed to Samantha's learning about the social and political world, and might have influenced as well as abated some of Samantha's nervousness about the world and her future. She said that a lot of scary things were going on "out there" and that this prompts her to feel uncertain about how her life would advance. She believed, in fact, that media should be doing a better job of informing people about what was going on. In that way, Samantha was like Marina, who wanted the media to tell people like herself "what's going on" and not just be "in a fantasy world." Samantha watched shows that had some social and educational value in her eyes to forge further her politically aware identity.

Samantha's identities were works in progress, and sometimes in conflict. She saw that acting aggressive and outspoken like a boy got attention, but Samantha's manner of talking and behaving was quiet and unassuming. So she challenged herself to learn to act "spicy" like Murphy Brown, a TV character who appeared to be independent, opinionated, competent, and successful (though perhaps unwittingly) at drawing public attention to social and political issues.

If Samantha learned to say what she thought without fear, she might gain the admiration of her father, schoolteachers, and feminists. But she might make some people uncomfortable, because females are supposed to be timid and sensitive. She could not take on male qualities exclusively at the risk of appearing insensitive, unfeminine, and unromantic— just like Murphy Brown was on her own show.

So Samantha would learn to act like "anybody," to give herself all of the options. This is both different from and similar to how Marina and Christopher used TV images to address their identity dilemmas. Marina looked to images to figure out how to craft herself, but as a sexy, successful woman. She was not looking for strategies to act like someone else; she already acted like Madonna and she wants to keep acting that way. Instead, Marina was looking at Madonna as an economic success and for an attitude that would let her "live with herself."

As for Christopher, he was looking at TV images for ways to craft himself as a basketball player. But when he watched both *Quantum Leap* and *The Cosby Show*, he used TV images to think about the changes in his life and to affirm his belief in the strength of families and doing things right. TV helped him create a physical and peer identity, cope with confusing identities, and value a new family identity.

Because Samantha is unique, her particular dilemmas were unique. She observed television images as they displayed acting processes, so she could craft qualities she needed to speak her mind and make a difference in the public sphere without compromising her private sense of "Samantha."

5

The Dynamics of
Everyday Learning

The following conversation is from an interview with Annie,
Jamaican American, age 11:

> *JoEllen:* Do you think television gives you new ideas?
> *Annie:* Talking back to my family, talking back to my mother. But
>   I don't wanna talk back to my mother; it's not right. . . . The
>   only way I talk back to my mother is I say it in my head. I say
>   stuff in my head. If my mother gets me mad, I talk to myself.
> *JoEllen:* Did you used to get mad at your mom, or is this a new
>   thing?
> *Annie:* This is new to me, this is new to me.
> *JoEllen:* Do you think it has to do with the TV?
> *Annie:* I think it has to do with the TV. The TV puts stuff in
>   your head that you don't usually get in my country. 'Cause
>   you hardly watch TV in Jamaica. They have a music program,
>   and it is on up to nine o'clock. And then it just stays off until
>   four o'clock in the afternoon, and then comes cartoons, and
>   then the TV signs off at ten o'clock at night. So then you
>   could do work.

As the daughter of immigrants who still visited their
homeland, Annie had the opportunity to compare her experiences in "my country" to those in the United States. In
Jamaica, programming was more limited than the nonstop,
multichannel barrage that characterizes American TV. Some
might wish that Jamaica's limited TV schedule could be
duplicated here in the United States, and some also might
think that Annie had been corrupted by American TV
because it had made her want to talk back to her mother.

Annie's comments point to what Annie had derived from her experiences in different cultures, but not just different national cultures. Annie suggested that she had acquired ideas from the culture of television—"talking back"—that had been moderated by ideas from the culture of her home: "it's not right." So she talked back silently, "to [her]self," indicating a triumph of the values of her home over those of TV. But TV culture had triumphed in a different manner, because Annie had "stuff in [her] head" that had not been there before. She had imaginary material that allowed her to express her feelings of anger yet not suffer the consequences were she to give voice to those feelings out loud.

Such interactions between home culture and TV culture played out for Annie in other aspects of her life and in other dimensions of her imagination. For example, Annie's comments about programming in Jamaica suggest her implicit awareness of how TV is associated with everyday life patterns. She noted that the scheduling of shows left a gap at the time when most people were working at jobs or in school. Also, TV went off the air early enough for people to "do work." Her words hint that she watched more TV in the United States than she did in Jamaica because TV was more available here. She indicated that there was a logic to TV scheduling and said that a "they" was responsible for this logic. So she might have been attributing the new ideas she had gotten from American TV to some real people—albeit strangers—who worked in the industry, much as she might attribute the values she got from her home to her very familiar family.

Like Annie, the portrait participants Marina, Christopher, and Samantha had feelings, knowledge, and other "stuff" in their heads, some of which was detailed in the previous chapters. I looked closely at these young adolescents because I assume that all people are unique and that all lives are diverse, complex, and dynamic. But it is also crucial to investigate how different people's experiences dovetail, because I assume that lives are shaped by common structures and systems. In this chapter, I look comparatively at the portrait participants' experiences, discussing how these three different individuals learned in some similar ways from their experiences of local life, life on the screen, and the systems that surround both.

Acquiring Social Drives and Making Symbolic Links

For these youth, motivations for the future in some kind of occupation arose from family and neighborhood cultures. Marina, Christopher, and Samantha had acquired specific values and ideas from their home and community that drove their quests to move into better economic or political sets of circumstances. These quests for improvement were particular to their personal natures and to their life situations, yet they generally reflected American sensibilities about upward mobility and social freedom. Although Marina and Christopher honored their families' particular integrity, their homes had inspired them to get away from their working-class situations. They wanted to advance toward careers that are respected and well paid, and thus gather prestige and material comforts that are more than just getting by. Samantha assumed, though perhaps tentatively, that she would maintain her middle-class status. But she also hoped to be a person who engaged in activities that would build a more fair and just world, furthering the progressive values she had acquired from her family.

H. Markus and P. Nurius (1987) term the convergence of past experience and future visions of identity "possible selves." In this study, the "possible selves" of Marina, Christopher, and Samantha were motivated largely by their home cultures. This confirms other studies and builds on common sensibilities. Because homes are the initial and ever-present places that youths encounter every day, home cultures are largely responsible for their fundamental values and thinking. It follows that home cultures then filter learning from other cultures that youngsters encounter later in life, or perhaps less often (depending on their circumstances), such as school and peers (Heath 1983; Leichter 1979; Ogbu 1985; Willis 1977).

In this study, families and communities influenced young people's patterns of interaction with TV, as has been found in other studies. Also, home cultures set parameters for what these young people acquired or wanted to learn within television culture. In TV symbolism they found specific strategies that could help them flesh out their "possible selves" and accomplish their quests. Marina found TV images that indicated some ways to "[make] something of herself," building on her mother's model for economic improvement and on Marina's own determined, bold nature. Christopher found images that helped him reflect on his life changes, imagine profitable business plans, and defy racist strictures on socioeconomic mobility, responding to the urgings of men in his life and to the constraints of his African American heritage. Samantha found images that showed her how she might construct herself as an informed, incisive, and assertive public speaker, continuing the activist spirit of her family as well as widening her options to "play anybody."

Basically, these young adolescents acquired strategies within television culture that helped them configure their individual yet also home-motivated versions of the American dream. The television industry intends to provide images and messages about "the good life" in U.S. culture (Kellner 1990; Lipsitz 1990), as TV functions as a promoter of consumer capitalism as well as as an electronic showcase of democratic politics. What this study shows is how, in this kind of TV culture, young people find their own specific "symbolic links" that connect their current situations, their possible selves, and the "good lives" into which they want to move. A similar dynamic occurs when examining their everyday learning in peer and TV cultures, although there the "good life" involves their engagement with friends and acquaintances.

Marina, Christopher, and Samantha all had problems with their peer cultures, although in different ways. Like most youths, they were motivated to belong to a group of peers, and they desired to have satisfying social relationships, romantic and just friendly. But Marina's hanging out with boys and her sexual "front" made her the target of snide remarks and peer rejection. Christopher's status as a newcomer, his lack of experience playing basketball, and his out-of-style clothing led peers to regard him as an annoying outsider for several months. Samantha's interest in befriending boys prompted many female peers to ignore her, and her wish to play basketball met resistance from the boys.

Each of the students responded to these peer dilemmas by acquiring strategies from TV-culture symbols. Marina took comfort in Madonna's reaction to criticism and rejection, which was to persevere and "keep going." Christopher watched Sam Beckett on *Quantum Leap* at first to learn how to cope with being out of place and time, and he later looked to Bill Cosby to fortify his father's encouragement to deal with things in a positive, "right" manner. He also watched basketball to talk and play better with peers. Samantha observed talk shows and Candice Bergen's acting so that she could learn, vicariously, to stand up and be heard by her peers without being frightened, an experience she found "very exciting."

Whether consciously or not, Marina, Christopher, and Samantha acquired strategies within television culture to deal with being snubbed by peers with whom they desired relationships. In this respect, peer cultures, like home cultures, guided these young people's social dreams, while television symbolism provided them with ways to negotiate—imaginatively—personal dilemmas associated with their social dreams.

Different Kinds of Everyday Learning:
Acquiring "Ends" and "Means"

Young people such as these acquire what I term "guiding motivations" within local cultures. Through their face-to-face interactions at home and with peers, they learn what they want for themselves in their future lives and what they want now socially. They look to television culture to acquire "imaginative strategies" for acting on their dreams and hopes for the future and for coping with dilemmas of social relationships (Fisherkeller 1997). TV material gives them symbolic ways mentally to work on what they learn through real people and real situations of their lives. The difference between these types of everyday learning processes is a matter of ends and means; guiding motivations help define the substance of the adolescents' goals and aspirations (ends), while imaginative strategies help the adolescents work out, in their minds, how they might accomplish their hopes and dreams (means).

One might perceive guiding motivations as more durable kinds of everyday learning, because they set up a framework of ends or goals. R. G. D'Andrade (1992), Strauss (1992), and others interested in culture and the mind might consider guiding motivations to be similar to "master motives," as they are associated with overall human interests in achievement and affiliation. Master motives are connected to basic human physiological needs and ecological functioning, but these are given particular emotional and social character through the workings of culture. For example, motivations to marry in the United States, where individual choice is the norm, would take shape and have meanings that would be very different from motivations to marry in those cultures where families dictate who may wed and when.

I have coined the term "guiding motivations" to suggest the particular role that day-to-day local cultures play in refining the master motives of a culture at large. I argue that these young people's motivations to succeed and relate socially have been guided by the specific people and situations of their home and peer cultures. Thus, Marina, Christopher, and Samantha have acquired specific goals and longings from their daily interactions with their families, neighborhoods, friends, and acquaintances.

Compared with guiding motivations, imaginative strategies are more replaceable, transitional, or alterable processes of cultural learning, because they function as a means toward already established ends or goals. As D'Andrade (1992) might interpret this, imaginative strategies are subordinate to the guiding motivations. I am assuming that those learning processes that fashion people's goals are more durable than those learning processes that function as means, but this is only the case if goals are given enhanced value compared with means. The saying "The end justifies the means" indicates such an enhanced value. I am assuming that imaginative strategies would be replaceable, transitional, or alterable as means because they are functional only as long as they can be applied, imaginatively or actually, toward specified ends or goals. That is, a strategy might be learned and then unlearned, or perhaps revised, if it did not function appropriately or effectively as a means toward a durable goal, or it might be discarded or set aside once the goal was accomplished.

Take, for example, the case of Christopher, whose guiding motivations remained generally the same from year one to year two of the study, but whose imaginative strategies shifted because some specific goals were met. Christopher hoped to become a successful entrepreneur and desired to have a base of friends to hang out with at school or in his leisure time—motivations shared by many, and not just youth. Christopher's particular professional aspirations were guided by significant men in his home culture, and his longings for friendships were guided by the urban male culture at his school and in his neighborhood. But in year two of the study, Christopher's use of television symbolism (weaving together his goals, particular situation, and sense of self—his imaginative strategies) adjusted. He had settled into his new home and found a small group of friends at his new school—that is, those specific goals had been met. Thus, after looking to the lost-in-time character in *Quantum Leap* to wrestle imaginatively with his own "lost" experiences at home and with peers, he turned to *The Cosby Show*. There he found a humorous version of his own dad, who had been encouraging him to walk tall. And he turned to televised basketball to sustain his new relationships with boys at school. In his mind, and through TV, he had new means toward the same ends.

In some cases, guiding motivations might be acquired from television culture, and imaginative strategies might be acquired from home, peer, and school cultures. It is important to investigate this in further research. Likewise, home and peer cultures themselves may develop guiding motivations that are inspired by TV culture, then filtered through to young people such as those in this study. I will discuss this later.

But age is important to consider in terms of the dynamics I describe here. As these young adolescents are just beginning a move away from childhood and into adulthood, their families of origin are still vital aspects of their everyday life. Parents and caregivers still have ultimate authority over them. As young people grow older and move away from their families' daily presence by going to college, joining the work world, and living on their own, young people's guiding motivations might then be acquired from other cultural sources, as specific goals change with age and experience. In the Epilogue, I explore how Marina, Christopher, and Samantha had changed, and how they had remained the same, when I interviewed them three and eight years after the completion of this study.

Also, these young adolescents came from families that presented themselves as supportive and secure emotionally, and Marina, Christopher, and Samantha regarded their families as valuable sources of guidance and nurturing. Young people growing up in home cultures that are seriously disordered or neglectful may be acquiring guiding motivations elsewhere, or they may be learning in a negative manner about life's goals.

Peer cultures, which are often regarded as threats to the guidance of home cultures, can guide learning about life goals in a negative, as well as a positive, manner. These young adolescents experienced the pain of rejection, name-calling, and stigmatization in some of their peer interactions, although they remained motivated to belong to a group of friends. The drive to feel membership in a group of peers is strong (Brown 1990; Savin-Williams and Berndt 1990). Indeed, it is so strong that youths sometimes will engage in dangerous behavior just to join or stay members of a peer or friendship group. I mention this hesitantly, as I do not want to contribute to the pathologization of adolescents in general, or of peer relations in particular. According to N. Way (1998), a great deal of attention is paid to statistical minorities of youth who engage in negative activities and behaviors such as violence, substance abuse, dangerous sexual activity, and failure at school. These are certainly serious issues, and complex peer relations can contribute to these problems. But, as Way (1998) notes, the majority of youth appear to get along in life without becoming part of the statistics in these areas, and her teen participants find much satisfaction and value in their relationships—even if problematic. Scholars, the popular press, educators, and policymakers frequently ignore young people who are doing "alright."

Although their peer relations were difficult, Marina, Christopher, and Samantha were not engaged in any of the negative behaviors typically associated with youth. Notably, the peer cultures at their school, no matter how socially and emotionally trying, were not the type to guide these youths toward engaging in extremely dangerous or unhealthy behaviors. The problems the faculty dealt with regularly were related to discipline and to cases of harassment linked to gender and race. It is a credit to this particular school culture that such problems were, to the most part, kept from escalating beyond verbal antagonization. Yet for the portrait participants, television culture was also there to provide positive strategies for imaginatively coping with or changing their peer-related problems.

Assuming the positive role that real people and real situations play in ideal environments, and given the learning dynamics I describe (the durability of ends; the replaceability of means), many people are likely to prefer that young people acquire their guiding motivations from local cultures than from media sources. Indeed, most critiques of the influence of TV and other media say that they teach the wrong things and in the wrong way. Many people would not want youth to be acquiring imaginative strategies from TV culture, especially if these "means" to an end are replaceable, transitional, and alterable processes of learning. In light of existing worries that television is encouraging us to be fragmented and ever-changing, it would be difficult to claim that young people's use of TV to strategize toward the future or to resolve personal dilemmas is positive. And some might ask: Although strategies from TV culture can help young people imagine moving toward their futures and help them solve dilemmas, will TV actually help them accomplish their dreams or "fix" social problems? And should it?

Before I address these issues, I must complicate them by discussing how young people's learning from their local cultures and from TV culture are interrelated in terms of substance, but distinct, qualitatively, in form and style. Everyday learning in contemporary cultural situations is messier than the previous analysis might suggest.

Complementary Learning: Parallel Contradictions of Power

Although Marina, Christopher, and Samantha learned in different ways from their local and television cultures, they learned complementary lessons about social power *across* cultures. The lessons are complementary in that prevailing power dynamics informed all of the structures and activity of their experience. At home, at school, with peers, and through television, each student learned about the interrelated power and problems of gender, race and ethnicity, class, and other identities. Likewise, they learned about standards for success and for group belonging in the United States (Fisherkeller 1999).

Marina's peers and the adults at school taught her about the problems involved in displaying her mature body and behaving in ways that suggested she was sexually partnering with boys. Because of gender norms that are historically patriarchal, females face many double binds with respect to their body image and interest in sexuality, and this situation is exacerbated when females are minors, like Marina. Yet Marina wanted to present herself as a sexual subject, even though she was not participating in sexual relations at the time. She admired Madonna, a TV symbol who knew about the problems females face in displaying their bodies and behaving as sexual subjects but, at the same time, was persevering and had achieved power and economic success. Indeed, Madonna is successful—spectacularly so—not only despite, but certainly because, she is sexually provocative. And like Madonna, Marina wanted to move up from a working-class background by "making something" of herself—not unlike what her own mother did by moving to the United States.

Yet moving up is not as easily accomplished as the American dream suggests. Many social, cultural, and political forces operate to keep people in their place (see Sennet and Cobb 1973). It is especially difficult for immigrants, who are often discriminated against. And unfortunately, although Marina is smart enough to figure out how to move up in life, her Dominican accent and her use of non-Standard English (during the research) could be obstacles (Suarez-Orozco 1989; Weis and Fine 1993).

Marina's admiration of Madonna's particular "style" of success, and of Madonna's "keeping going" in the face of derision, indicated that Marina had acquired her own sense of the conflicting cultural standards and norms associated with female sexuality and status mobility. That is, she knew she could not be "like" Angela Bower, a proper Anglo lady, even though Marina wanted the good life that Angela possessed on TV. Through her local experiences and interpretations of TV culture, I saw Marina learning about a complex and tension-filled set of power relations linked to her age, gender, race and ethnicity, and class.

Christopher's male peers taught him about the power of participating in basketball, and men at home taught him about the power of being an entrepreneur. Christopher overcame being physically unfit for basketball by working out, watching games on TV, and learning from the informal coaching of his school teammates. Thus, he resolved a male-identified problem of appearing weak and non-sports-oriented. It was more difficult for him, however, to resolve the "problem" of his racial identity, which could easily stand in the way of his becoming successful in business circles dominated by White men. Further, his working-class identity, like Marina's, could get in the way of his being accepted in the professional world, which prescribes codes of conduct constructed by the middle and upper classes. But his father's urgings taught him that African Americans should walk tall. And in admiring Bill Cosby, Christopher acquired a positive cultural representation to support his dream of being a Black male professional. His TV interpretations, seen in relation to his actual experiences, suggest that Christopher was learning about a complex and tension-filled set of power relations linked to gender, race and ethnicity, and class.

Samantha learned the power of speaking out from family and from educational experiences that emphasized the value of citizenship and working for social change; she also learned this from her feelings of excitement and importance when talking in front of schoolmates. She could see the power of speaking out on television through the character of Murphy Brown, who at the time was gaining the attention of millions of viewers and listeners. However, Samantha felt a fear of speaking in public that, although common to both sexes, is more often found in females because they historically have been silenced by society.

When she spoke up about the boys at school and their biases in basketball, and when she admired Murphy Brown's acts of aggression, Samantha indicated her awareness of the norms for playing games and getting attention—that is, being competitive, independent, and assertive, or behavior that typically is established and encouraged by males. Yet Samantha also sensed that when females used these tactics, they might be excluded, ridiculed, or "doomed." Also, she sensed that females might struggle with sensitive and romantic sensibilities they possess and value—behavior that is established and encouraged typically by females. Through her actual experiences and her TV interpretations, Samantha was learning about a complex and tension-filled set of power relations connected to gender.

My analyses suggest that these young adolescents learned about salient social power relations from actual life and TV in a parallel, inter-related manner. These young people were drawn to TV figures whose fictional experiences of power relations linked to age, gender, class, and race resonated thematically with their experiences of non-TV life. J. T. Klapper (1960) would argue that the young adolescents' predispositions are prompting them to choose media fare based on their existing tastes and opinions, and so their television interpretations are merely rein-forcing. But I am working within a cultural and interpretive framework rather than a "communication effects" framework. The lessons these young people learn from their TV choices do not necessarily reinforce the lessons of their actual experiences of social power relations. And it is not clear that these viewers were accepting, resisting, or opposing dominant ideologies of programming in a categorical manner, as cul-tural studies of audience often argue (see Fiske 1987; Hall 1980; Willis 1990). Marina, Christopher, and Samantha found meaning in and learned from TV figures who struggled with some of the same issues as themselves, but these issues of identity and social power are highly problematic and dialectical in nature. These young people's under-standings about identity and social power were variously negotiated—that is, their understandings may have been challenged, elaborated, diminished, and perhaps invoked by TV. For example, Marina looked to Madonna's persevering attitude and thus learned a way to "live with herself" while she also learned conflicting values associated with her body. Christopher appreciated Bill Cosby's teachings about the "right way" to do things, as he did his father's teaching, at the same time find-ing an image that helped him dream about escaping the kind of life his father leads. Samantha admired Murphy Brown's aggressiveness and learned ways to speak out, as her family did, but she also learned that for females, this behavior carries a high measure of risk in public life and in personal relationships.

All three were learning, across their experiences, about contempo-rary conflicts and dilemmas of a changing society. Paths to identity for-mation and social power are not clear and straightforward, as they may have seemed in the past. In the past several decades, different cultural groups, such as feminists, civil-rights advocates, progressive activists, and others, have worked to balance the social-power scales. These groups have brought about changes in society, but at the same time, dominant societal forces also have worked to maintain the status quo and created backlashes against any sense of progress (Faludi 1991). Thus, young adolescents such as those in this study are coming to terms with new identities and power relations on grounds that are shifting and contested, whether those grounds are televised or "live" (Lembo 1997).

The Power of "Making It"

While local and TV cultures provide complementary lessons about identity and power, television as a system provides distinctive lessons. The portrait chapters describe how Marina, Christopher, and Samantha regarded certain TV figures as personally and socially meaningful within the fictional worlds of programming. Yet Marina, Christopher, and Samantha also saw these TV figures as publicly powerful within the nonfictional realm of corporate media institutions. Marina acknowledged that Madonna was an extremely popular performer who produced her own shows and videos; Christopher was aware that Bill Cosby was a very wealthy actor, ad pitchman, and television businessperson who had produced several programs featuring African Americans; and Samantha took note that Candice Bergen, the actor who played Murphy Brown, made phone-company commercials and attracted real-world politicians' and journalists' attention. These youths knew about the constructed and commercial nature of television: "It does get ratings, you know," Samantha said. They knew about the roles people play in the making of television: "They're running out of ideas, so they added new characters," Christopher noted. And they knew about the kind of riches and recognition TV people get when they know how to participate in the image- and story-making world of TV: "TV is for them to make money, for actors to have a job. To advertise things," according to Marina.

These young people saw their favorite TV figures as actually (that is, nonfictionally) successful in a system that rewards image and story creation economically and publicly. Thus, these young people were learning about social power relations not only in the local social worlds of their lives and through the stories and characters they are drawn to on TV, but also through the profitable institutions that provide these meaningful fictions to them and to millions of others.

Previous research on young people and their understandings about the commercial aspects of media focuses primarily on their awareness of advertising or is concerned with how young people are socialized as consumers (Alexander and Morrison 1995). My analysis broadens this realm of research and suggests that, through TV, young people are learning, at least tacitly, about the value of working in corporate media industries and about the terms of participation in a corporate capitalist (rather than democratic) public sphere. In today's world, media conglomerates generate billions of dollars of revenue in communication services and media commodities,[1] and publicity and advertising play an increasingly significant role in the U.S. marketplace and politics. Through their meaningful interactions with TV symbolism and systems, these young adolescents are learning accurately (though not completely) about social power and success in the real-world institutions that structure their experiences.

The Dialectics of Multiple Cultures and Learning

The idea that these young adolescents understand TV people as being part of "real" worlds of power and success in the United States points to complex social dynamics that pertain to everyday learning. I claim that these young adolescents learn within their local cultures in a manner that is qualitatively different from the way they learn within TV culture. Yet in the United States, all local cultures exist within the same larger culture that encompasses TV culture. The people in these young adolescents' homes and in their peer cultures also observe, and perhaps talk with others about, the power and success of TV people in the United States, whether those people's accomplishments come as characters in constructed TV stories or as the constructors of the TV stories themselves.

Although the family members in this study seldom talked explicitly about these aspects of TV culture, it is highly unlikely that they were oblivious to the presence and status of celebrities and of the power-mongers of media production. The cachet that goes with being "in the media" is ubiquitous, and many parents, like Samantha's, are aware that the people who make media are not only economically successful but also politically powerful. The families and young adolescent peers in this study witnessed the growth of cable television, VCRs, computers, video games, and the Internet—expansions that increased the presence of media in society and, at the same time, the implicit value of media production and consumption in the economy. Also, these young adolescents' parents and caregivers came of age in the 1960s and 1970s, when civil-rights activists, feminists, antiwar protestors, and other critical groups in the United States gathered momentum, due partly to the reach of television (Meyrowitz 1985). Thus, the understandings these young adolescents had about the success and power of TV people may have been shared—or, perhaps, sometimes primed—by their home and peer cultures.

At the same time, home and peer cultures may themselves have been guided by the ideologies of accomplishment that are promoted through television fictions, as well as through stories of fame and power associated with the making of television and related media. Like many other immigrants, Marina's mother figured that she could make a better life for herself and her children by coming to the United States. It is likely that some of her information about the promises of the American dream came from her experiences with television culture—whether firsthand (such as viewing TV exported from the United States to the Dominican Republic) or secondhand (from talking with relatives and friends who lived with TV culture in the United States). Although Marina acquired her specific motivations for success from her home culture, her general aspirations were rooted in TV culture. Television might then be seen as a promoter of certain "master motives" (D'Andrade 1992) in the United States, which were appropriated and given particular shape by Marina's mother, then reappropriated by Marina in her own manner.

TV culture is produced by people living in U.S. culture; thus, the values and ideologies found on television are themselves negotiated versions of the nation's general values and ideologies. What can be seen in the participant portraits is how different kinds of home cultures have given particular shape to the "TV-cultured" American dream, and how young adolescents have acquired their home-culture versions of the "TV-cultured" American dream.

This acquisition process is similar for the focal participants' peers. Yet, peer cultures engage with television values and ideologies *as peers* as well as as children of particular home cultures. Young adolescents' experiences as an age group in a particular place and time, and as schoolmates, friends, and neighborhood chums, bear on how they use TV and on how they learn through TV culture. For instance, unlike peer cultures in other times in history and in some other cultures, the peers in this study were (and are) surrounded by myriad media and communications technology and a boggling array of consumer artifacts. These are realities of the material and social world these youths took for granted, even if they did not have access to the actual technology or items of consumption and encountered them only via media messages and images. Thus, the youth in this study, as a group of peers, understood that television is but one of many options people have for leisure, getting information, and interacting with others. And for them, TV was often the only option. Many of these adolescents regarded television as a necessary given, as shown in their disbelief when I informed them that I lived without cable TV (for a time). The idea that anyone did not have full access to television choices made some of their jaws drop.

In addition to regarding TV as useful and necessary because of their time in history and social location, these youths knew about TV as an industry because of their geographic location. Marina, Christopher, Samantha, and their peers lived in a city that is one of the headquarters of media production in the United States. They were aware of this aspect of their hometown in many ways. They knew about people who worked in media industries and the buildings that housed those industries, such as Bill Cosby's complex of studios in the Borough of Queens. They noted the locations of production listed in film, TV, music, and video-game credits, which sometimes became a source of conversation. They also saw media scenes and products being produced in their own neighborhoods and on the TV programs that provide viewers with behind-the-scenes coverage of media construction.[2]

Thus, acquiring guiding motivations from local cultures and acquiring imaginative strategies from TV culture are not entirely distinct processes. On the one hand, local experiences are situated in material and social realities that are considered actual or more immediate and tangible than media realities. Learning from actual experiences is grounded, and so guiding motivations can be seen as primary. On the other hand, TV experiences are regarded as removed from the local and the actual because of what appears on the screen. Images and messages are seen as intangible and non-immediate because they are representations, not the lived presentation of actual everydayness. Indeed, TV representations are often elaborated and idealized reconstructions of everyday experiences. For this reason, learning from TV experiences is secondary.

However, our local experiences are mediated by aspects of TV culture that imbue the actuality of home and peers. At the same time, our TV experiences are not only interactions with screen representations; they are also interactions with presentations of the actual systems of corporate capitalism. Consequently, young people's learning about themselves, others, and worlds of power and success is a dialectical weaving together of the meaning of experiences in local life, through the TV screen, and with corporate media systems. This complex of cultural learning is similar to the "dialogics" of language acquisition and discourse circulation, as examined by M. Bakhtin (see Emerson and Holquist 1981).

Given the dialectical and "messy" nature of cultural learning, and given the situations and circumstances of the contemporary world, what are the implications for young people's identity formation? What are the consequences for cultures and society? And what should we do if we want young people to learn to be powerful and successful, yet also help us change those aspects of the world that are inequitable and inhumane and that otherwise compromise our cultural and civic ideals? I explore these questions in Chapter 6.

6

The Dilemmas of Growing Up with Multiple Media and Cultures

The following conversation is from an interview with TeniyaSerita, Puerto Rican American, age 12:

JoEllen: Would you want to be on TV?

TeniyaSerita: I would like to first start a commercial, and then start doing TV. Commercials, like, so I can get the feeling of talking and stuff on television instead of acting out first. Well, on commercials you sort of act, though, but it's more speaking than anything. 'Cause when I see cameras and stuff I get nervous speaking. Like when they tape me and stuff. So I would like to get the feeling of it first. Commercials, and then acting later.

JoEllen: What would you like about it?

TeniyaSerita: I would like the fact that my friends are watching me *(laughs).* I don't know. The fact that, really that, well, I'm getting paid. The fact that I get a chance to be on television 'cause there are not that many people who can be on, get on, get accepted to be on television, something.

TeniyaSerita's comments about appearing in commercials before being on "regular" TV suggest she has a sense of her own abilities as a potential TV figure. She feels that she will need some experience at speaking to commercial audiences before she can take on acting in front of people on "regular" TV. I know that TeniyaSerita is familiar with being in front of audiences, as she has studied ballet and modern dance for many years and has performed with prominent New York

City troupes of young dancers. She has even danced solo in citywide venues, not just in recitals for parents and friends. Why is she tentative about being on TV, and why does she want to practice with commercials first? She says that she is "nervous" about the camera; it is something about "when they tape her."

TeniyaSerita's limited experiences in front of videocameras have not felt comfortable, not unlike many people's first encounters with this technology or with public-performance contexts in general. Yet TeniyaSerita assumes that there are steps she can take to get rid of her nervousness in front of the camera. Presumably, her dance experiences have taught her the value of learning a performance in pieces, practicing, and rehearsals. So she seems to understand that she can evolve toward being on TV by learning its pieces—in this case, ads, which these days are only seconds-long "pieces"—and by practicing speaking for the camera. Taking these steps will help develop her acting abilities for "regular" TV. She imagines she would like placing herself at the center of her friends' attentions if appearing on TV. She also imagines she would like being on TV because she could get paid for doing so and because not very many people get such an opportunity.

TeniyaSerita was not alone in picturing herself as being viewed by others, or in envisioning herself as an image on TV or other venues. Marina, Christopher, and Samantha had similar visions about themselves appearing before others, and they also had ideas about actually creating these possibilities. It is likely that many young people develop ideas about themselves as images, drawing on cultural forms that have been provided by commercial media such as TV. Yet young people's visions of themselves as images might be regarded as detrimental rather than legitimate aspects of their self-formation. At the same time, these young people's self-as-image visions might not surpass the level of private imagination or of fleeting local displays. These issues are problematic if worlds of image construction (such as TV) constitute the contemporary public sphere (commercial or civic), and if the public sphere is so conceptualized in the minds of young people themselves. If we want young people to participate powerfully in this "image-conscious" public sphere, their self–as-image visions need to be regarded as legitimate and given recognition—not just in their minds, but in actual public forums.

In this chapter I discuss how these young people sometimes constructed themselves as images and the implications this holds for their development, as well as for the culture at large. I also examine their awareness of television culture as an image-construction system that draws on multiple forms of communication. Finally, I explore the role formal education plays, or should play, in young people's learning to participate in the public realm, both as workers and as citizens. How should we help young people grow up if image worlds contribute to their self-formation and if image-construction systems increasingly characterize the contemporary environment as a whole?

Selves Forming in Mediated Cultures

Marina, Christopher, and Samantha regarded TV figures as personally meaningful in the fictional worlds of programming. These young people were attracted to TV-story characters who wrestled with identity dilemmas and issues of social power issues that complemented their experiences in their local lives. They each used their favorite programs and characters to address issues relevant to their daily lives and identity development. This use of television resulted in their learning tacitly about themselves, but their learning was primed by what they had acquired from their homes, school, and peer experiences.

These findings bolster conventional understandings about the use and power of TV. Under particular circumstances and in specific situations, people take up the meanings of media such as television at a narrative level (Lembo 2000). In this way, cultural ideologies embedded in television storytelling (such as sexism, racism, and classism) are accepted, while others are rejected or negotiated (Fiske 1987; Hall 1980).

Many adults worry that young viewers merely accept the ideologies of TV stories and thus maintain the inequities and biases of the culture that these stories reflect. And even if viewers reject or negotiate TV ideologies, the systems of cultural inequity and bias are not necessarily changed. Adolescents such as those in this study, whose sense of self and future possibilities were limited by the inequities of their local lives, were also constrained by the biased sets of media imagery they selected as means of constructing and presenting their selves. Marina, Christopher, and Samantha might have found a means of understanding themselves and their situations through TV. But they were unlikely to find a viable means of changing the outside world for the better.

This is a political and social problem if principles of democracy and humanity underpin our ideals for young people's development and learning but do not inform the workings of everyday life and media narratives. In principle, all young people should be given equal opportunity and access to circles of power and authority. As V. G. Paley, author of many books on young children learning the ways of the world through social interaction, says in her book: "You can't say you can't play" (1992). But in actuality, many young people are kept from "playing" successfully in society because of racism, sexism, classism, and other discriminatory processes. Most media narratives do not offer young people any means of challenging these processes of discrimination. Media often skirt politically sensitive issues or offer simple resolutions that placate the audience rather than encourage change.

But concerns about media use and power go beyond these conventional understandings and problems. The biases of TV culture exist at structural levels as well as at the levels of content and narrative, where media power is typically located and critiqued. Postmodern media theories claim that the commercial ideology of media production combined with people's constant consumption of changing media imagery (particularly television) has encouraged the development of selves that do not cohere around a traditional set of social norms and that it has created a culture that is shifting—for better or worse (Jameson 1991; Kellner 1992). These theories assume that the continuous flow and superficial nature of commercial media represent a culture that has been destabilized. These theories also assume that people constantly take on and throw off the variable identities and roles conveyed by media narratives.

In the previous chapter, I argued that television provides young people with imaginative strategies for building on the motivations provided primarily by home and peer cultures. This argument partly supports postmodern claims about selves and culture. For as means to an end, the imaginative strategies that television and other commercial media provide are ephemeral and useful only as long as young people need them. As a case in point, Christopher identified with the lead character in *Quantum Leap* only while he was feeling "lost" in terms of his material and social locations. In his mind, he took on and threw off the identity of Sam Beckett the TV character (who was lost not only in time but also in social location) because he eventually found his sense of place in own his life. Thus, young people can appropriate, adjust, and discard—in their minds, at least—the identities or social roles associated with TV characters and stories, much as people do with visible style trends in fashion, music, and decor. And as will be seen in the Epilogue, as these young people's lives changed, their interests and tastes in TV and other media cultures changed, as well, even though the motivations of their local lives continued to guide their uses of TV and other material.

Television culture is more than a conveyer of message content, more than a storytelling medium, and more than an ephemeral "clothes rack" or "tool kit" (Brown et al. 1994) from which people can appropriate symbolic identities and roles. Television culture is a system of image construction that is a persistent feature of the contemporary world. This system involves real people and real institutions as image makers, people who are regarded as powerful members of society and of the world because of their ability to produce and distribute media imagery— whether we like it or not. And if young people acknowledge that image-making is a systematic and powerful activity, then they might find a kind of stability in regarding media imagery as a means of constructing self and society, even while they might not find coherence in the narratives of media imagery. Young people who appropriate, adjust, discard, and create images of themselves by drawing on commercial forms—for example, TV symbolism—are engaging in processes that are consistent with the practices of cultural structures (such as corporate media). Given a constantly changing system, people who hold on to the idea of image construction and, in turn, people who see themselves as image constructors create new kinds of stability. These new kinds of stability are based not on individuals' sense of coherence but on their sense of the persistence of image-construction systems and in the consistency of image-creation processes.

Recall that Marina held on to the idea of image construction when she talked about people being able to project a sense of confidence about their bodies, regardless of their shape and of their clothes. Marina felt that it was important to think about "how you want people to see you as." Using these words, Marina placed herself—or, perhaps, others ("you")—in some kind of public arena in which people pay attention to clothes and bodies. Marina claimed that how clothes and body are perceived is a matter of attitude. If a person projects a sense of self like that of a model, others will regard that person as a model. Thus, like TeniyaSerita, Marina had given thought to how she was and could be an image creator. Marina perceived of herself as an image creator via the medium of clothes, and TeniyaSerita imagined herself to be an image creator speaking and acting for the TV camera.

I observed Christopher acting as if he were on camera at a local museum (see Chapter 3). The studio set was outfitted like a late-night talk show or news program. While waiting for a demonstration of the equipment, Christopher sat down at the talk-show desk and began to speak into the microphone (which was off) as if he were the host of a talk show introducing his "guests." He actually played a talk-show host for his own camera when he interviewed his grandmother for a home-made video. He wore a suit and tie, in the tradition of male talk-show hosts, and referred to notes on a desk. Christopher's understandings about himself as a creator of images are implicit here.

Samantha pictured herself (ironically) as a pampered "lady" in a soap opera, getting backrubs and eating chocolate. This was her "fantasy," her "playing with" appearing before an audience in her mind's eye. On a less fantastic level, she indicated that she wanted to learn to "play anybody" so she could perform more competently within public contexts, such as assemblies and demonstrations. Her desire to speak and act competently in front of others led her to live theater productions, where she gained in the craft of acting onstage. Thus, Samantha saw herself as an image creator while playfully fantasizing about a televised fiction, while learning to perform in plays, and while speaking out in front of a public.

Erving Goffman might dispute my claim that these instances demonstrate how TeniyaSerita, Marina, Christopher, and Samantha held on to the idea of image construction and saw themselves as image creators. Goffman (1959) and others might explain that these youths were engaged in the presentation of self in everyday life. They did present themselves in the everyday "dramas" of their lives. These dramas were bound by existing cultural norms for social interaction and group membership—norms that prescribe how selves are presented (Geertz 1973). Marina presented herself as a girl who was proud of showing her mature figure while peers told her that she had crossed gendered and sexual lines of propriety. Christopher joked around and dressed like popular male comedians, but he was not able to get anyone but his grandmother to listen. Samantha pretended that she could be a royal lady in a romantic melodrama, a traditionally feminine dream; at the same time, she actually behaved like a crowd leader who was passionate about social issues, embodying the idealism of youth and the politics of her family. In these ways, these young people presented themselves in roles and as identities constructed according to established sociocultural rules they had learned, informally, through daily interactions with others.

But sometimes, the selves these youth presented involved their taking on something *in addition to* the social roles and identities that were co-constructed within the dramas of everyday life, whether those dramas were actual or mediated. Sometimes, the selves these young people presented involved constructing images for others to view as audience members, not necessarily as fellow characters in lived dramas. In some situations, these individuals were—in their minds, at least, and sometimes in actuality—placing themselves in front of others as *forms* of communication, forms that could be recognized as images largely due to TV culture, similar to the manner in which fans appropriate and represent popular imagery (Jenkins 1992; Lewis 1990). These forms of self-presentation are almost exclusive to television culture, or if they are not exclusive, they can be recognized as having been standardized by and promoted through television culture or made generic by commercial media. TeniyaSerita imagined practicing to be a commercial spokesperson and TV actor in general—not for a specific product or show—and enjoying her friends' attention to her appearance as a TV image. Marina saw herself as a clothing model who consciously projects a fashionable image, no matter what clothes she wears and even if the clothes she wears are not themselves fashionable. Christopher played a talk-show interviewer for the camera, re-creating an image of any of the late-night talk-show hosts on TV. Samantha pictured herself as a star in a standard-format TV soap opera.

The instances described here reference what Lembo (2000) explains as a kind of viewer "play" with television images. According to his conceptualization and documentation of TV viewing culture in the United States, these young viewers have constructed "celebrity moments" for themselves, as they have drawn on images that they know were produced systematically by corporate media. Their engaging in "image play" of this nature is a type of image-based viewing, according to Lembo, because unlike in narrative-based viewing, they acknowledge the idea that television in general is a commercial enterprise and that, in addition to representing "real" relations, it presents viewers with images that are manipulated and exchangeable (Lembo 2000: 209–12). Viewers engaged in image play know that the stories and characters on the screen have been fabricated strictly for the purposes of viewer consumption, not just for purposes of narrative development, and so can be manipulated for commercial interests.

For example, recall that Samantha knew that the people appearing on daytime talk shows, regardless of their identity or role, were supposed to be outrageous ("like neo-Nazis and stuff") so the shows could increase their ratings ("they get the number one"). Also recall that Samantha did not like the way in which Oprah Winfrey seemed to manipulate her talk-show guests, no matter who they were, so that they would display upsetting emotions; she pointed to Winfrey's prompting guests to cry or get angry, at which point the camera could swoop in for close-ups. In these ways, Samantha acknowledged how talk shows in general, and Winfrey's strategies in particular, result in the fabrication of imagery solely for ratings, for the TV camera, and thus for the commercial-image production system itself.

In the commercial television enterprise, fabricated images are commodities, often of generic, formulaic types. In this system, celebrities are the ultimate commodities, because they are images produced solely to promote themselves and the practices of image construction per se. In this system, Madonna, Bill Cosby, and Murphy Brown are celebrity personas as well as characters. Living in a culture that traffics heavily in the production and consumption of celebrity personae, the creation of "celebrity moments" for themselves by TeniyaSerita, Marina, Christopher, and Samantha—that is, constructing themselves as personas before an audience—could be seen as a contemporary norm.

The construction of selves as images as a process of self-formation is not unique to television culture: People presented themselves as visual forms (via dress and mannerisms) long before television, film, and photography became pervasive aspects of society. Cultural migrations since the dawn of civilization as we know it brought people's attention to differences in clothing and non-verbal behaviors that were unique to regional and ethnic identities. Stage, street, and village performers have long been mindful of the adornments and manners suitable to appearing before audiences. The upper classes and the royalty of most cultures throughout history have engaged in rituals of ceremony and of the everyday that involve visual displays (Geertz 1983). Such displays have been mimicked at times by those seeking to be seen by others as members of the elite groups, such as those with new money who attended supper clubs in New York City in the late 1800s and early 1900s to observe, and to be observed, as if they belonged to the aristocracy (Erenberg 1981).

But now, photography, film, television, and other image-based media (including computers and online software) allow people's visual forms of self-presentation to be captured and distributed via technological mechanisms. These "captured" forms of self-presentation can then be viewed by audiences that do not have to be present in the space or at the time of image creation. Thus, people's presentation of their selves can be circulated and recirculated among many people, some of whom may never know the selves being presented in mass-media forms in any face-to-face contexts. In this way, some selves—such as celebrities—are known only as media images.

Youths today know many selves that are only image creations on TV and in other media and thus are not aspects of their actual, face-to-face interactions. Indeed, this situation prompts many adults to worry that as forms of media grow in the world, and as youth are absorbed in media cultures, they increasingly will be out of touch with actual reality. But the young adolescents in this study understand—at least, in a tacit manner—-that television is an image making system *in actual reality*. These young people know that, in the real world, TV images are prolific, continuously available, and often formulaic. Their everyday experiences with the images and messages the TV system produces provide them with pleasures and meanings that are very real to them, whether we think of them as substantive or superficial. And they have learned that many of the people who appear as images on the screen (such as Madonna, Bill Cosby, and Murphy Brown) can gain fame, money, and status in actuality. They also know that some of the people who produce TV images (such as Madonna, Bill Cosby, and Candice Bergen) are "really" successful and powerful as public figures—both commercial and civic.

In a culture that values images and image creation so thoroughly and systematically, both on-screen and off, we should expect young people to imagine and create themselves as images in their minds or before audiences of some kind. Yet constructing themselves as images does not replace young people's presenting themselves as identities or social roles, and their selves are not merely a collection of images, arguments that are posited by postmodern critics (Kellner 1992). No matter what, young people construct themselves as members of "real-life" social groups that are grounded by the conditions of their actual (as opposed to virtual or mediated) lives. Marina, Christopher, Samantha, and their peers all drew from their relationships with people and physical environments to construct their sense of themselves as identities, social actors, and images. The self in this process is an agent or creator, whether it draws on local face-to-face experiences, encounters with commercial images, or interactions with other cultural forms. As Goffman suggests, the self at some level is an ongoing mindful process, not the product of situations and circumstances (see Lembo 2000).

In sum, I argue that postmodern selves are consistent when weaving together fragments of the constantly changing commercial imagery system, but also organized, though sometimes in a contradictory manner, around the located norms and values of home, school, and peers. Conceptualizing self-formation as consistent and organized does not necessarily mean that individuals feel their selves to be coherent; although the processes are consistent and organized, people's self-experience might be disjointed. Indeed Marina, Christopher, and Samantha were living with many ambiguities and contradictions.

But perhaps selves have never been coherent in the lived dimension. Notions about selves as coherent in times prior to the postmodern may be conceptually idealistic or simply nostalgic. We do not have grounded accounts of how "ordinary" (that is, non-elite) pre-postmodern selves experienced their own presentation in the everyday or of the roles that forms of communication of the time, such as books, music, oral storytelling, and dance, played in people's actual self-formation. In light of this, and given what I argue about people constructing a consistent and organized self-sensibility in television culture, concerns about a lack of coherence may need to be rethought.

Participating in Multiple Cultures

The young people in this study understood, implicitly and explicitly, that constructing images of themselves was expected in the postmodern world. And they were aware of the processes involved in creating themselves as images on the screen, as demonstrated by TeniyaSerita's citing the need to practice for the camera by starting with commercials, and by Samantha's wanting to learn to act, to "play anybody."

I think we should expect young people actually to present themselves as images and provide them with the means to do so. Then, when girls like Marina walk around as if they are fashion models, or boys like Christopher act like TV talk-show hosts, they can be part of actual worlds of success and power. I make these arguments and claims because, like these young people, I conceive of image construction—like language construction—to be a valued activity in the contemporary environment.

Let me say this another way: If youth are not given access to and education about image-making tools and techniques, then they are bound to feel relatively powerless in the official domains of image making. After all, as TeniyaSerita recognized, not many people get to be on TV. Young people like her might picture themselves as images, but these private imaginations rarely lead to their actual appearances in the media. This is particularly the case for people of color and for those in economically disadvantaged circumstances in the United States. TeniyaSerita's opportunities to be viewed publicly by audiences of mass media are rare to nonexistent, or they are confined to stereotypical or negative kinds of depictions (Gerbner et al. 1994; Gray 1995; Means Coleman 2000).

Yet it is not only people like TeniyaSerita who experience being left out of the image-making systems, even though they may dream of being seen by peers or others. Indeed, youth in general get to look at image-making only as consumers. What youth learn informally as image consumers prompts consideration of what they learn, or do not learn, about images and image making in formal educational contexts.

Note that TeniyaSerita perceived a difference between commercials and television, even though she encountered ads via TV. For her, commercials involved speaking to the audience more than acting in front of an audience. Presumably, she recognized two standard formats for advertising in the United States. Both depict spokespeople either talking to the audience or narrating over images to promote, in an explicit manner, a product, brand, or service. These formats and purposes clearly mark commercials as constructed and as "sales pitches." By comparison, most TV programs depict people and action as if they are "real" events, though staged for entertainment. The construction of most TV programming is intended to be less noticeable than that of ads, so that viewers (like theater-goers and readers) can suspend their disbelief and engage with what Lembo (2000: 182–85) calls the level of real social action. Also, most television programs are not selling specific products in an explicit manner, although the boundaries between ads and programming are blurred constantly and increasingly—as seen in the infomercial and edu-tainment genres and as exemplified by cross-media promotions and product-placement strategies.

But in her distinguishing between commercial advertisements and dramatic programming, TeniyaSerita noticed a difference between two different modes of communication within the same medium, TV. She was not unusually perceptive in her distinguishing and evaluating modes of communication on TV: Her peers Marina, Christopher, and Samantha were similarly perceptive. These young people evaluated TV programs on the basis of how their constructed elements allowed viewers to engage with characters, stories, events, and topics that they considered relevant, pleasing, and plausible. In this respect, they were not unlike viewers who are younger (Davies 1996) and older (Lembo 2000).

These and many other viewers' perceptions of the different modes and constructed elements of television have developed through viewers' everyday experiences with TV, not through formal instruction. By watching TV, by discussing TV with others casually, and by "playing" with TV elements when, for example, joking, singing, and dancing with peers (see Dyson 1997), young people learn about television as a complex cultural form. But their informal learning about television and its constructed modes and elements is not valued by formal education systems. Learning in TV culture does not align with learning fostered by schooling systems, where print literacy—not media literacy—prevails. I think this is a problem for young people and for society, as well.

Consider what it means to be well educated and therefore a powerful member of society. Traditionally, being well educated involves being literate, or knowing how to read and write. Generally speaking, knowing how to read and write leads people to better-paying and higher-status jobs; it also gives citizens access to the facts and the discourse of political and economic activity. So ideally, reading and writing support people's participation in the workforce and in democratic processes.

Institutions of schooling intend to foster the development of reading and writing by teaching young people how to deal with printed symbols and by evaluating how well young people understand and use printed symbols. In turn, literate students learn to be competent decoders as well as skilled encoders of printed symbolism. To be competent and skilled, students must accept the role and the value of printed symbol systems in culture. Put another way, when people are literate, they know what to make of, and do with, print symbols, because they understand the role print symbols play in society and the value these symbols have for culture (Heath 1983; Tyner 1998).

Yet being powerful in the contemporary world involves being able to understand and use a vast array of corporate media, such as TV, film, music, magazines, computer software, and online technology. Business markets and political campaigns know this and invest immense resources and energy to construct advertising and public-relations programs that sell their products and promote their agendas, activity that supports and maintains corporate media systems. Media industries themselves engage in elaborate promotions and campaigns to sell their own symbolic products, such as programming, video rentals, CD recordings, concerts, fashion journals, video games, and Websites—to name but a few. Indeed, this is where celebrities as commodities most often play a key role.

Corporate media produce their symbolic products and advertising using printed text, but they also rely heavily on a variety of visual images and sounds to convey meaning. But no matter what form these media take, their goal is to create an image, using multiple media symbols in ways that audiences and consumers will find appealing, meaningful, persuasive, instrumental, and moving. Producers (such as TV and movie creators, actors, musical performers, supermodels, and computerware designers) who succeed in creating and constructing symbolic products that bring about these audience engagements are considered powerful members of our culture—and of other cultures, too, as global markets expand. Media makers' power is indicated first by their increasingly lavish incomes, and second by the nature of the attention they are given by the press, government heads, and the public. In short, their symbolic contributions to culture are valued economically, politically, and socially.

The actual people who create the messages and images of corporate media systems, and who are valued for this, complicate notions about being literate, or well educated, in the contemporary world. The producers, directors, PR spinners, advertisers, actors, musicians, animators, and many other makers within corporate media know how to work with many symbol systems besides print; they know how to decode and encode symbol systems associated with audiovisual and digital communications as well as print. Thus, corporate media makers know how to read and write, but they also know how to comprehend, analyze, evaluate, and produce multiple media forms (Bazelgette 1997; Tyner 1998).

Ironically, formal education systems in the United States rarely acknowledge popular media forms as legitimate, and they do not encourage competency with audiovisual and digital communication. Indeed, most educators argue that popular media should stay out of the classroom, and they discourage, overtly and covertly, students' associations with these forms of communication outside the classroom, as well. Typically, school officials regard the media, especially television media, as corruptive forces or as distractions (Seiter 1999; see also Murdock and

Phelps 1973). Such notions about media prevail even as teachers and parents respond to pressures to install computers and online systems in every classroom and to provide all students with access to the messages and images of global networking systems. In part, this has to do with the hype surrounding computer-based communications as the keys to success and as educational tools that can replace pencils, paper, worksheets, and reference books, rather than as commercially created and distributed media. Thus, being well educated in the information age is still strongly associated with being able to understand and use print forms—not with understanding and using multiple media as *different* forms of communication.

Yet as consumers, young people today are aware—though perhaps not consciously—that commercial media rely on multiple forms of communication beyond print symbolism (especially advertising; see Nava and Nava 1990). Their sense of the multiple forms and means of communication develops in a manner similar to the sensibilities we all develop about the function, use, and value of language as a form and means of communication (Dyson 1997; Heath 1983). That is, through their everyday engagements with popular media, young people understand that print symbolism, audiovisual forms, and digital communications work together in a complex manner and that they can be used and understood in different ways and in a variety of contexts—much like language. In addition, young adolescents know that many of the people who work in commercial media industries make a good deal of money, and gain the attention of journalists and politicians, by using multiple forms of communication. In other words, they have learned, at least tacitly, that engaging in the making of multiple media forms is a credible and powerful means of economic survival and of participating in public life.

TeniyaSerita said that she would like "getting paid" if she could appear on TV and that she would like to be on TV because not many people can do this. But people like TeniyaSerita usually do not learn in school about how to "get paid" to be on TV, or how to make TV at all. Schools are still places for reading and writing, even if those activities are sometimes computer-based. However, I am not suggesting that we merely train young people to be media makers who reproduce corporate media systems, and thus maintain the status quo. Far from it. I engage in research and teaching activities driven by a desire to reform media systems and practices. In that way, I am not unlike many scholars and educators in media and cultural studies who strive for changes for the common good.

Media education is a long-term means of producing social and political change for the common good. Broadly speaking, media education helps young people learn about the roles media play in society and in everyday life by prompting critical examinations of systems of media production, the products of these systems, and how people construct meanings about media. In theory and in practice, the word "critical" is crucial to media education. To accomplish necessary changes, young people need to understand that there are problems with the existing media systems and products and that these problems have serious consequences for themselves, others, and the world at large. Thus, media education, if integrated into school curricula, should not just provide a new kind of job training in the information age. Media education should help young people become pro-active citizens in local and global contexts.

However, teaching youth to be critical of the media, and only that, can be counterproductive if they understand that making media is a powerful means of becoming economically and politically successful in the world. Young people who have hopes for themselves are likely to feel confused, cynical, or powerless about change if they are merely told that these huge systems of corporate media need to be rejected or altered entirely. I have witnessed this phenomenon among college students in media and communications programs through the years. Others have discussed similar dilemmas working with adolescents in school and community-based educational contexts (Buckingham and Sefton-Green 1994; Tyner 1998).

Ultimately, we need to help youth succeed—as consumers and as producers—within ideological systems that value many forms of media making. In addition, we need to help youth participate in democratic spheres that value critique, reflection, and action. This is no easy task when corporate capitalism and democracy are often at odds with each other, as demonstrated by historical battles over access to and regulation and production of the media. These battles are now taking place at global as well as local levels, and with new media as well as old.

How can we help young people understand and use multiple media in ways that build on their dreams and hopes for the future, our ideals for just and fair societies, and existing knowledge of the workings of the postmodern world? Those who work with constructivist perspectives will want to learn the particulars of different young people's dreams, hopes, and knowledge to connect these, in a grounded manner, to cultural ideals (Fisherkeller 2000). As the portraits of these young adolescents demonstrate, home, school, and peers play influential roles in youths' sense of themselves and their possibilities. Likewise, television culture figures powerfully in their self-formation, their learning about power and success, and their multiply literate development.

Scholars and educators must continue to ask how young people weave meanings for themselves across the complex dimensions of their everyday lives. We must continue to ask how youths' evolving sensibilities, which incorporate their "real life" and TV experiences, suggest research and teaching directives. Given these imperatives, I turn again to the voices and experiences of Marina, Christopher, and Samantha. The next and final chapter reports on what these young people told me about their lives at high school and college and presents their interpretations of television and other media cultures from those periods in their lives. Thus, I close this book with these youths' own words providing suggestions for further research, teaching, and creating change.

Epilogue

Marina, Christopher, and Samantha, Continued

everal months ago, I thought I had lost Marina when I called her mother's apartment and reached a pizzeria instead. I panicked, thinking I would never find her. Scouring my notes from our follow-up conversations, I found the name of a college to which she was going to apply, and called. It turned out that she was there. I felt very relieved, and lucky, when I heard her voice.

It is difficult to keep track of participants in longitudinal studies because of situations such as this. But despite such difficulties, I encourage others to engage in long-term, in-depth studies, especially with young people. Gathering detailed "on the ground" accounts of how individuals weave their lives from multiple threads of existence over time will help us in many ways. On a scholarly level, such work will help identify dynamic patterns of human development that are both common and distinct for different kinds of people in a variety of situations. On a personal level, it is rewarding to watch youths grow up and see how they meet new challenges.

The accounts that follow rely exclusively on audiotaped interviews. Unlike in the initial study, I did not visit the schools, places of work, or homes of these youths regularly for several months. Thus, I cannot check their words against observations of behavior and circumstance, although I can draw on my knowledge of contexts similar to those they

133

experienced and of the TV (and other media) they mentioned. However, I am able to make connections among the words they spoke later and the words they spoke when younger and, thus, identify themes of self and growing up particular to each individual.

I quote these three participants extensively, with little or no analysis. This is purposeful: I want to let Marina, Christopher, and Samantha speak for themselves as much as possible here. I also want to invite readers to add their own insights and analysis for further discussion. Thus, I close not with extensive final statements but with questions and speculations to explore.

Samantha, Later: Looking to Go Deeper

At age eighteen, Samantha was living in a dormitory at a state college just outside New York City. Having "survived" high school, as she put it, she had decided to stay close to home for her higher education. High school had been difficult because she had started out at a large, traditionally structured public school, where she "got involved with the wrong crowd." After she went "crazy for a month or two," her parents pulled her out of that school and put her into an alternative high school whose scale and philosophy were similar to that of AMS. At the new high school, she said, she had gotten her "act together," especially when she realized that she might become a "super senior" (a fifth-year student) if she did not stop "messing around."

In the summertime during her high-school years, Samantha had moved into a leadership role at the camp she had been attending since childhood—a camp that in principle and practice nurtured socialist views akin to those of her family. Working with children in the camp, Samantha began to think about becoming a teacher, a profession she thought aligned well with her and her parents' general interest in helping people via social service. Also during high school, Samantha met the man to whom she had become engaged to marry just a few weeks before our college meeting. When Samantha told me about her engagement, they had not yet set a date, as she intended to finish college, and her fiancé was still sorting out his own career focus. In her first year in college, Samantha said, things were "still early on, and nothing is written in stone in my life yet."

I asked eighteen-year-old Samantha about her earlier interest in public speaking. This is how she explained that drive to speak:

> I think I'm realizing when I was in junior high school, I knew very little. The more I know, the more I realize I don't know anything. And, um, it was very easy for me to speak up at AMS. It was a very comfortable environment, and, um, I was very passionate about everything, and I didn't know what to do with everything I was passionate about. I just had so much passion inside me. And there was no particular reason why.

Then she explained that she had developed a more reasonable approach to speaking her mind. Her age, and her increased awareness of needing to support her passionate claims with "evidence," had led her to temper, but not silence, her speaking.

> I didn't know anything about the world in junior high school. I thought I did, which most adolescents feel, I guess. And the older I get, the more I realize that I just can't yell and scream about everything. I really have to learn about it. I really have to know about it before I can do something about it. 'Cause the older you are, the more people want evidence and the more people want to know really why. You just can't say: "Because I think so; because this is the way it is." So I still definitely stand up, if something is wrong, but I don't scream and yell about everything anymore. And it just has to do with age. And learning things.

In these words, I see Samantha's thoughtful nature shining through. Also, I see keen insights into the nature of being outspoken. Whereas as a young adolescent she wanted to learn how to act outspoken, as a late adolescent she appears to want her speaking-out acts to be fueled by a "really why" and to be informed with learning about the subject at hand. Perhaps she gained her insights through an internship she held in high school, working as an assistant at the local public advocate's office. Her task was to assist someone working with a "real politician" who had to keep "up with current events." She termed this politician "real" because he "smiled and shook my hand, and his teeth were all capped and they were all white and all beautiful. And he just shook your hand like he meant it." Working with his office, Samantha might have come to understand that, to act like a "real" public speaker, she needed to be knowledgeable as well as motivated.

By the time she had reached age 22, many things had changed. Samantha had graduated from college, ended her relationship with her fiancé, moved into an apartment not far from her grandparents, and found a job in New York City. In college, she had majored in literature and written her senior thesis on dyslexia, which included her own experiences as illustrations. Indeed, she left her final pages unedited, "deliberately, to show, like, me and my difficulties." Her engagement had ended during junior year in college, because she and her fiancé had been "fighting and fighting and fighting. And I was going in one path and he was going in another path. And it just, you know, it was a lot of fun, and I loved him very, very much, but, you know, I wanted so much more." She said she was sad they had not stayed friends but also proclaimed: "I don't need someone there to feel secure; that's not where I'm at. And that's where I was. And it's good to not be there anymore, let me tell you!"

Most recently, Samantha was living happily with a female friend she has known since they were both quite young and who shares many of her political sensibilities. Samantha had moved into this apartment (which her mother and her friend secured while she was gone) after returning from a summer spent traveling overseas. She had immediately begun to look for a job and found a position as a caseworker in an organization that provides social services to people who have HIV/AIDS. Her job entailed

> a lot of rules and regulations. But that's not the hard part; the hard part is that the agency is pretty crappy itself.... My supervisor ... has no people skills. And doesn't really know how to relate to people, doesn't know how to make eye contact, doesn't know how to talk to people. You don't really need someone who has to know all the rules; you want someone who can actually communicate with you, and she can't. And it's unfortunate. And I actually am supervising someone, who's the opposite of her in some ways. And he's crappy in his own way, but just the opposite. He's outgoing, he's in your face, but he just doesn't do his work. But he always looks busy.

Samantha was proud to be in a position of some power and responsibility but able to employ her own ample "people skills." She also felt the value and importance of her work through her everyday contact with the people who were her cases. She had been compelled to look into unionizing her co-workers because of their working conditions and dissatisfactions. Given this, her future was a bit uncertain in terms of security but steady in terms of aim:

> I know that I could lose my job 'cause I'm on a six-month probation period. And they could easily, like, you know, you wanted to unionize and now you've lost your job. I gotta find out what union I could get involved with. I have to figure out which union deals with nonprofit social services. And I'm gonna talk with them and figure out, you know, what's the process. I pretty much know 'cause my grandfather was telling me what the process is. And then, in the same time, [I'm going to] send out resumes, because I'm not staying there forever.... I'm just not gonna sit there and take shit, you know? I mean I

don't feel like that's what I'm about, you know? I don't think I deserve that, or anyone else there at work deserves that.... And if I unionize, honestly, I feel like there's no more noble way to leave a job. Like that.

Looking beyond her immediate situation, Samantha mentioned several kinds of future goals. She wanted to travel more, to go "someplace far and unique." And she wanted to learn to make pottery, or do photography, to "have some creative energy" in her life. She was considering going to graduate school to get a doctorate in applied psychology, but it was a "seven-year commitment" about which she had to think seriously. And notably, she was

> starting to think about what do I really want to be involved in. Like, I'm thinking about this political organization that deals with the [local colleges]. They are really involved right now in anti-Nike stuff. So we have Nike literature around, and we're going to go to their store and hand out Nike literature. And give something to the corporation, and stuff like that. And, like, that's all well and good, but I'm kind of ready to get in deeper. I'm just really worried about this new presidency coming up. All this talk about what they're trying to take away from the population, things like this. And I just want to be involved at another level.

Samantha looks to be following in her family's politically active footsteps. Despite the changes in her life, her interest in "get[ting] in deeper" seems to draw on her drive as a young adolescent to know more about acting like a strong, independent, and outspoken person. Her interactions with television are in line with many of her consistently developing sensibilities.

Television Through the Years: "You Could Just Flip It Over"

As an eighteen-year-old college student, Samantha spent much of her time going to school and studying. She also spent most of her free time with her fiancé, working on drawing and painting projects for a class, or "run[ning] around a little bit to keep me sane.... I do everything I can to stay busy." She reported watching very little television, which was a switch from high school. During that time, TV had been a "home in the evening, don't really know what else to do, get something to eat, sit in front of the TV until dinner time" activity, which is how she described watching "all the time" then. At twenty-two, she sometimes watched television in the evenings after work, but only when her roommate was not available to talk with, or if she was not on the phone or meeting with friends, parents, or grandparents, which were her first priorities.

When she did watch TV, she viewed whatever happened to be on ("flip flip flip"), as she had no allegiances to particular programs and was using TV as "passive entertainment." Besides watching TV, Samantha read novels regularly. Most were recommended by friends or family, particularly her mother, who had become a full-time writer. Samantha also listened to music and went to clubs with friends to dance, although she did not do so often because of the expense. She used "fast" music at home as background to get her going in the mornings and to do housework and chores, but she said she had eclectic tastes overall. At eighteen, Samantha used school computers for homework and e-mail, and at twenty-two she did not have a computer of her own, although she was thinking about getting a laptop to access e-mail.

Samantha did not specify any favorite TV programs during high school, except talk shows, which she watched occasionally at eighteen as well as at twenty-two. She said talk shows were "compelling" when she was eighteen because

> I still don't believe that people will go on national television and tell their fiancé or their husbands or their wives that they've been cheating on them for the past five years. That's just uncomprehensible [*sic*] to me that people actually do that. And they're just getting really outrageous. Maybe it's that I'm getting older and I've changed, but they just seem really outrageous at this time.

During college, she said, she watched the soap opera *All My Children* every day.

> *Samantha:* Just 'cause I enjoy it. Just 'cause it's funny and entertaining and ridiculous as well.
> *JoEllen:* What's funny about it?
> *Samantha:* Just like, it's like talk shows, but not in a "let's sit and talk about it" [way]. It's a "let's do it" type of way.

Samantha was attracted to programs about whose content and format she was actually quite critical. Indeed, Samantha's critical sensibilities about talk shows have a history, for even when she was a "talk-show-aholic" as a young adolescent, she knew about the tactics the shows used to appear "outrageous."

Indeed, Samantha's sense of the difference between talk shows and soap operas referenced critical approaches to the workings of different programming genres. According to her, talk shows and soap operas were both "funny" and "ridiculous" because, although the situations handled by both formats are everyday domestic matters (that is, marriage, divorce, adultery, and so on), they are presented in a melodramatic and outlandish manner, emphasizing the extremes. But talk shows and soap operas are different, she said, because the former genre only talks about such matters, while the latter genre depicts these matters in action.

Samantha's evaluations of most programming, and of the media in general, suggest a critical knowledge of the overall workings of television. A program she liked when she was both eighteen and twenty-two was *ER*, which she watched because "it's cute . . . it's not fulfilling anything." Yet she was "very excited" when *ER* came on because, compared with other shows she watched that took "up time and space and like mind energy," *ER*

> seems pretty realistic. And everyone's not beautiful, and everyone's not these wonderful people sleeping with everyone else. They all seem to have pretty original personalities. It's interesting to see how a hospital works and runs. Not that it's exactly realistic. . . . Sometimes it's just too nice and too good. And people's personalities aren't conflicting as much as they should be in that kind of situation.

Perhaps Samantha's college experiences had informed some of her interpretations of this and other programs. Comparative analyses of texts and genres are a central aspect of literature studies, her major. A film studies course she took along with a college roommate—who, like her father, was drawn to non-mainstream, independently produced, and sometimes foreign movies—made her into what she calls a "movie snob" because she could not tolerate Hollywood-style blockbuster movies that were "disgusting and boring." They prompted her to consider making films of her own.

> It's just so interesting, you know, you can take something and do something with it. You know, not do what everyone else is doing with it. It's just amazing how you could just flip it over. It's the same media, it's the same thing; you just make it feel like it's saying what it should be saying. So the things that I watched, that influenced me, you know, it made me look at the world differently. Like, I remember after watching certain films, when I walked into a room, I was like . . . looking at it in like a frame. And it was kind of like, if I had a camera right now . . .

These experiences, and her parents' continued practice of "loud complaining," seem to have influenced her critical analyses of media more generally. At eighteen, Samantha was skeptical about news media, which she thought were

> very subjective about who gets on TV and who doesn't get on TV. [It's] made very black and white, and there's not much leeway for people's opinions. All media, especially news, gets things very black and white. . . . Like, how much of it is kind of bending the rules a little bit to make it look a little better? Or slightly twisting it just a little bit?

Not only was she wary of what was being said on the news; she was also wary of who was doing the saying, and how they were saying it:

> Knowing that they're not reliable is enough for me to realize that everything they say I shouldn't always be like, " Oh, okay," and I shouldn't always naturally just believe because some white man on TV tells me so. I shouldn't just naturally go with it because this man that I've never seen before tells me it's true. And they're probably not as interesting in real life as the media make them out to be. I don't believe that, like, Dan Rather is more believable than Tom Brokaw or anything like that. I just believe that they're all kind of reading off of cue cards and not really getting too much into what they're saying, and their bosses are telling them how they say it. Not necessarily what they say but how they say it. . . . Different tones of voices and different orders of saying things can really turn something good into bad, or vice versa.

Samantha claimed that the "bosses" of newscasters were not truly responding to the public's need to know. Instead, they were responding to corporate interests:

> What's best for you—the individual getting the media—is [decided by] the corporation that's actually letting the media be heard. . . . It's really not for the public. It's really for the beneficiaries, and what their opinion or what their role is, rather than to inform the public about what really happened. Which is a shame, because the public needs to know.

At twenty-two, Samantha remained critical of the news in a similar manner, and included printed news in her assessments:

> Why is the mass media such a guru when they are so obviously opinionated? They just use larger vocabulary, are geared toward a higher-class population. So this is why it takes me a whole week to read the [*New York Times*]. I read it section by section. What are they really trying to tell me? Are they calling me to action? Or are they calling me to just kind of accept? Do they want acceptance, or do they want action? It's never really clear. . . . It is all smeared and buttered with this fancy vocabulary. All these people that I work with could never read it and understand it. Why is that?. . . Why does that seem OK to do that?

Ever the social critic, Samantha continues to wonder about the workings of media and whether they contribute actively, or appropriately, to public participation. Likewise, she continues to speak up about and take action on social and political issues, drawing on her family's socialist heritage. I can only wonder how the news, and perhaps politics, might benefit if she were to create an alternative news forum or run for public office.

Christopher, Later: Finding His Place, Again

Christopher described some of the stresses he had faced at seventeen when I asked him how things had changed.

> *Christopher:* Well, things aren't as fun as they used to be. Things have gotten harder. You have a lot to think about, the future and everything, what you're going to do with your life. You've realized things, just about life in general, about people. You know, even at AMS, you know, things were easier, you know; you really didn't have to deal with all the problems that are going on. But now as you get older, you see things that really didn't matter back in junior high school, but . . . that really do matter now.
>
> *JoEllen:* Things like what?
>
> *Christopher:* Everything. Really everything. College is more important now. Really finding your place, like, you know, finding your place in life really is starting to become more important than junior high school. Decisions that you have to make, because I've found that, like, during these past years there have been more decisions that you have to make, either good or bad.

After middle school, Christopher started at a high school that, he reported, was "falling apart" because of "intruders" who prompted fights, pushed drugs, and robbed students. This made going to school generally unsafe for Christopher and affected his studies. At the same time, he was dealing with a medical situation that called for surgery and visits to doctors and hospitals. Thus, Christopher said, "I had to miss so much school; I had to fall so far behind."

Because of an injury sustained in a fight, he managed to transfer to a "good school" in the middle of his sophomore year and in the school's diverse and safe atmosphere, Christopher got himself onto the honor roll. Economics became a new favorite subject, accompanying social studies, as before. He had friendships that were satisfying, and even some romances.

But life at home turned tense at seventeen, when his relationship with his father changed. "Communication is bad, . . . and, it's like he expects me to be, like—aw, man—like perfect. You know, do nothing wrong." Describing his father as "harsh," Christopher reported that he wished he could stay with an older sister who lived nearby and had kids of her own who were about the same age as Christopher. "I'm almost jealous, because her kids can, like, come and talk to her about anything," he said. "She'll help them. Just being able to talk to your parent eliminates so many problems."

After high school, Christopher moved out of his father's apartment to get away from him. Through fortuitous connections, he later found a job within a large financial institution and attended a local community college. After a year, he dropped the college courses, in part because of the demands of his job, which he needed to pay his apartment rent and to support himself. In addition, he was excited about being involved in the world of high finance and trading.

After many months dedicated almost exclusively to working long hours, days on end, Christopher began to investigate college programs in business and finance, because he knew he would need a degree. He also wanted to meet people his age and have a social life. His job supervisors agreed to provide him with some college funding and summer employment and encouraged him to apply to one of the Ivy League schools in the Northeast. My most recent meeting with Christopher when he was twenty-one years old took place at the end of his first year of studies at one of the most prestigious universities in the United States. Because a professor there had become a close mentor, Christopher was considering majoring in the study of government as well as business. "I've never loved learning as much as I do now," he reported. "It's totally shifted from like, um, I just need a degree to, like, wow! I really like doing this; I love this, you know?" He was even considering becoming a teacher in the schools or a professor.

Christopher's relationship with his father was repaired over the years. Due to Christopher's accomplishments, "people in [his] family were just amazed," and his father "gave [him] a lot of respect." As Christopher said: "You know, getting a job, an apartment, a car, going to [an Ivy League university], he just kept saying, 'Wow!' Like, I guess now he sees me as an adult, as a man now." Also, Christopher described a kind of silent agreement between them that fostered acceptance. He told me that when he was not spending school breaks and summer weekends with various extended family members—because he is "family-oriented"—he was talking, on the phone or in person, with the woman to whom he was engaged to marry after they finished college. At twenty-one, according to Christopher, "things [had] changed dramatically, like total 180, for the better."

Television Through the Years: "I'm Actually Seeing How I've Changed"

At seventeen, Christopher was watching less TV than before because of his social life outside the home, increased homework loads, and care for a new dog. When he was at home, TV was part of his activities, even though he was not

> like, *in* the show.... I'm not even watching it.... It's like someone being there. [After school, I] watch television, listen to music, mostly. I don't even use the computer much, really. I really use it for school, not really for entertainment.

As he had before, Christopher used TV as background and engaged in simultaneous activities (see Lembo 2000). At the same time, he used computers for what are considered formal educational activities, while he used television and music as "purely entertainment."

At seventeen, Christopher deemed the hit sitcom *Seinfeld* his favorite show. He and his closest friends all watched the program, then talked about it in school the next day. Christopher showed insight in pointing out the similarities between his friends and the feature characters on *Seinfeld:*

> *Christopher:* [My friend], that's like George [on the show]: He, he's like, like a pessimist. He really doesn't think about the positive sides of things. You know, he's really on the negative side of things. Like, he'll think the worst of something, and I could say especially when it comes to things like girls. Like he doesn't, if a girl would say "yes" to go out with him, he would start worrying about "Will it last? When will it be over? Will she dump me because I'm short?" or something. Stuff like that. He just worries, worries, worries about things. And he's always like, not really lying, but always, you know, trying to weasel his way out of doing things. Like, you know, we say, "Let's play basketball" or "Let's just go outside," and he'll be like, "Oh, oh, oh. You know, the funniest things happened: I'm not able to go outside, my clothes got stuck in the laundry machine." Just this big, he would make up this, just this, instead of just saying, you know, "No. Don't feel like it," he'll make up an excuse and everything. Even though we all know it's an excuse, and he does, too. It becomes like a joke all of a sudden, you know. And one of my other friends is like Kramer [on the show] because, you know, he's like really outspoken, like, you know, um, like a daredevil. You'll dare him to drive, ride down this hill on his bike with his eyes closed, and he'll probably do it. He's, like, funny like Kramer.
>
> *JoEllen:* And you said you're like Jerry Seinfeld?
>
> *Christopher:* Mainly because I'm trying to talk both of them out of doing things. That's how Seinfeld [the character] is with Kramer and George. Or either I'm trying to talk them into doing something that's good—like,

say, he wants to, um, like with my friend that's like George, it seems like it's always about girls. I say, you know, "Why don't you just go say hello?" He's like, "No I can't say hello! She hardly even knows me." "I'm not asking you to go ask her for her hand in marriage; just go say hello. And then he's—or I'm trying to talk him out of not doing something, like. Just really trying to, you know, talk him out of not doing something or talk him into doing something, like Jerry does with Kramer and George. But there's no Elaine [the only female feature character]. I think now, the girl I used to go out with is like Elaine now.

Notably, Christopher's adolescent friends were Black and Latino (labels he and they used), unlike the feature characters on *Seinfeld*, who are all White adults. Nevertheless, he noticed similarities in how his friends respond to everyday social situations and circumstances and in how the characters on *Seinfeld* act in response to everyday phenomena, though staged for comic purposes. Thus, the specific surface features of the characters and situations that Christopher liked changed over the years: *Quantum Leap* and *The Cosby Show*, earlier favorites of Christopher's, differed from each other and differed from *Seinfeld*. What remained consistent was Christopher's interest in the underlying social and emotional activity of TV fictions.

Christopher's television and other media interactions and interpretations at twenty-one suggested that his fundamental viewing interpretations were consistent. Christopher said that, because of his work, university schedule, and social life, when it came to watching TV, "it's just, I don't have the time. That was one of my past times." And as at seventeen, at twenty-one he was using computers, as well as online and "new" technology, exclusively for formal educational purposes.

Christopher commented early when we met that he was eager to talk about media. I asked him why he was so excited to talk about that, and he reflected on his own changes in circumstance as they related to his TV viewing habits and to the significance of certain programs:

My mother, I lived with her up until I was about eleven years [old], up until I came to New York.... It was hard for her as a single mother and having a career that demanded a lot of time, and so a lot of times I found myself at home alone, and my only friend was the television. You know, my mother didn't want me, while she wasn't there, like, going outside, where I could get hurt. So she really, like, created the perfect environment for me, like toys and games, use the phone whenever. I grew up on TV, and the most influential show was *The Cosby Show* for me. Like, I still, while I was up at [the university], I had a lot of slack time during the afternoon because of my class schedule. I was tempted for a while just to get extra money, but I realized that while I was there, I should just focus on school. But in the afternoon, like about two o'clock, I watched *The Cosby Show* [reruns]. And, you know, it brought back a lot of memories. 'Cause I remember what I was doing when I first saw this episode in prime time. Like, it didn't make me feel old, but, like, times have changed so much since then, 'cause they would always show the year that it was on, and I was like, Wow, that was 1987! You know?

Christopher went on to evaluate how *The Cosby Show* had played a role in his own and in his friends' developmental experiences:

I remember seeing the last episode, when Theo [the son character] graduated from [New York University]. You know, that TV show impacted not just me, 'cause I speak to a lot of my friends about TV, and it's always like "*The Cosby Show, The Cosby Show, The Cosby Show.*" ... [But] there's no more programming that really emphasizes maturity, responsibility, growth. Like, um, like with *The Cosby Show*, you really saw everyone in that house, even the parents, evolve. Move into different stages of life. Going from being offered drugs at school, to, you know, what they're going to do after they graduate. To just the day-to-day things that happen. Like, I could relate so much, 'cause, yeah, they picked on me, too, for dressing like this or talking like that.

Discussing the importance of the 1980s *Cosby* program in his and his friends' lives prompted Christopher to ponder current media and their influence on other youth:

That programming, I can't think of anything on television now that's like that. ... TV is not so much about entertainment now as that I'm actually seeing how I've changed. How society is changing. ... What used to be acceptable isn't acceptable now, and the impact that television is having on youth. And right now I think that a lot of television programming is just being very reckless with their responsibility. That goes for all media; that goes for television, and especially music. Like, I personally love hip-hop, and I like some rap, but some of it is just a little too much, you know, like with all the gangsta rap, and I can't relate to that. 'Cause to me there's no relation. I can't relate to gangsta rap at all. I'm old enough to understand that, um, like, you're not going to do everything that you hear in the music, you're not going to do everything like you hear on TV, you're not going to emulate everything you see on television. But what these producers and everyone who's writing television programs are not realizing is that they have adolescents, you have children, that are watching TV, even more now, [and] they actually—it's showing a notion of "this is how life is." And this is how we should be acting, this is what we should be saying, this is what we should be. The producers are not taking any responsibility for what they're producing on the screen. I'm not saying that dramatic events, like, shouldn't be talked about—not at all. But their context is not necessarily to educate; it's more to shock.

Christopher's values and sense of self did maintain a kind of consistency through the years, as shown most by his renewed regard for *The Cosby Show* and what it had given him and his friends as they grew. *The Cosby Show* was, and still is, a representation of reality familiar to, and preferred by, Christopher (and presumably by his friends), because it showed families dealing with everyday contemporary life in a positive manner (that is, helping kids resist drugs, figure out what to do after graduation, and so on).

Beyond this consistency, however, Christopher demonstrated an increasing confidence in himself that certainly was informed by his accomplishments over the years. At the same time, Christopher's evaluations of television, and of other popular media, had grown more critical. His critical sensibilities appeared to be informed by his real life and media experiences, building on his beliefs in good triumphing over evil and in ideas about the common good.

> And I know, um, a lot of adolescents who are going through such terrible times, trying to conform to what they see in music videos, to what they see in ads, to what the media says is cool. The media have become so bold; like, they will literally say this is cool, this is not. Go with this, don't go with that. And it's a marketing ploy. I won't necessarily knock that, because you also have to understand it's a profit motive. That's why I can't do investment banking for a living anymore, because you know they'll crush anyone. If there was a choice between a school and a mall, they'll build a mall. And if it's a choice between saving a monument or putting up some new high rise, the monument goes. I mean, it is clearly ... I mean, if there's anything that is "evil," it is investment banking. That's a powerful statement, but I see they're just ruthless. It's no place for someone with a heart. There's no place for them. 'Cause that's what I had to do; I had to conform to this, like, rough and gruff kind of thing. You know, cursing people out over the phone 'cause they haven't delivered bonds. And it just wasn't me; I just couldn't do it anymore. So, but, um, that's what television has done. And I think it's, um, I don't know what to say. There needs to be a new wave of television programming.

I could not agree more. Maybe Christopher should start that cable company he imagined running when he was a young adolescent—and invite Bill Cosby to his board meetings.

Marina, Later: "It's Like I'm Neither–Or"

At seventeen, Marina was a junior in an alternative public high school that she liked, even though it was "a lot of work." She said she had "changed a lot" since we had last spoken, and I asked her to describe and explain these changes:

> Um, I guess I'm more dedicated toward school. I still have fresh in my memory most of the things we talked about in the last interviews and, um, some of them were about how I used to dress to impress other people. And that used to be important for me to get other people's attention, but now I am more comfortable with who I am as a person, and not what I look like or how I come off to, for other people. So I've learned that, and I feel more comfortable with who I am now. And before, I was still a child, which I still am, still an adolescent, but I've grown, I was like in the sixth and seventh grade when you interviewed me. I used to be a little tomboy, and I used to play and make jokes and make people feel bad to impress other kids. I don't do that anymore. So, I've changed a lot. You could say internally—the way I see things and how I feel about myself.

When I asked her what or who was responsible for these changes, Marina named the director of AMS, as well as advisers at high school. She said that her two sisters had taught her, via "the good things" and their "mistakes," as well. Both of her sisters went to college and were the first in their family to do so, which made Marina "proud." But both of her sisters also got pregnant and had children

> at a very young age, and I've learned from that, too. I remember at the last interview you asked me what I wanted to be, and I said I wanted to be a mother, and then I was reading through that, and I was like, "Oh, my God. How could I have been so stupid?" That's not what I want to be now. I mean, of course I want to be that, but once I follow myself and realize myself. Once I have my career, once I have my good job, my house, my car, I wanna have everything, everything for my kids. So that takes a lot, and I've learned that through watching all my cousins get pregnant at a young age. Almost all—a lot of my girlfriends that I used to go to school with and my sisters—and just watching how hard it is to have a child. And especially at a young age. Trying to go to school, trying to have a job, trying to grow up, too.

As an immigrant and as a female, Marina had to confront many conflicting expectations, as was seen in Chapter 2. But she had grown, and she gave credit to her home and school experiences for the role they played in helping her grow and learn. She also gave credit to herself for "questioning" norms in general:

> I guess I've always defied the feminine role, because ever since I was little I used to love to play with boys' things. I used to be a tomboy. I guess it always happened like that. And I like to question things. Always. If my mother used to say, "No you can't do that" I used to always want to know why. Why I

couldn't do this? "You can't go to the store." "Well, why?" I used to ask her everything. I mean, I never used to stay shut. I always wanted to know why.

These "questioning" traits seemed to align well with those fostered by Marina's small, progressively minded high school.

> All my grades this semester have been distinguished. It comes from the atmosphere that is in the school and how much effort they put into a child's learning, and, I guess, from me, too, because I love to learn. So even though the school runs like that, this doesn't happen to every child over there, because a lot of people are failing, probably because they have problems or they just don't like school. But for me it's different. So I'm doing great, and I love the school and how they teach and what they teach. It's going great.

Things continued to go well for Marina, as she graduated and received a scholarship to attend a small liberal-arts college a few hours outside of New York City. At twenty-one, she was a senior getting ready to graduate and writing a thesis on Latin American culture and international politics, an interest that had grown out of her own and her family's experiences as immigrants. When we last met, she was waiting to hear about admission to graduate schools. She intended to study anthropology and become a professor, because "I've always been interested in human nature and culture. And, um, just really getting to the core of what makes us human beings and what makes us have things in common. What do we all have?"

Although her academic experiences had been stimulating and rewarding, college had been difficult socially and personally.

> I guess it's been hard being away from my family. That's the hardest thing. Also, being in a school where there's only 1 percent of us that are actually poor. And it's actually a really good university. It's a small liberal-arts campus; it's a diverse university. But still, it's actually a very hard clash. The hardest shock was to be around a lot of wealthy people, especially from very, very different [backgrounds]—not only social backgrounds, but different . . . Living in Spanish Harlem is what I'm used to, the African American community as well as the Latino community, but not necessarily the White community, and also Asians and a lot of international students.

In addition to this culture "clash" on campus, there had been tension at home. Marina's mother had become very ill over the years, and sometimes Marina had to go home to tend to her. At these times, Marina felt "borderline," as she put it:

> It's coming home and dealing differently with my family, like things that I was unaware of, that, like, the tree cannot see from the forest. Like, when I'm at school, I see the female subjugation within Latino culture—within the

Dominican family, specifically—the way that women are raised, the way that we are kind of stuck in the cycle of poverty, and the way we re-create it and re-create it. Like, there are my fifteen- and sixteen-year-old cousins that are pregnant. And it's like, I want to be really sympathetic, and I am, but at the same time I'm like, Get your ass up! You know, why don't you do this; why don't you do that? I'm just very conscious that it didn't happen to me like [it] did [to them]. I mean, I could have, I don't know. . . Maybe their parents didn't raise them like my mother raised me. And it's very hard, like, being the same person when you are outside of the family and coming back, and kind of, they're like, you're trying to be White, or that I sound very differently, the way I dress is very differently now. And just the way I am in general. It's just really hard. I've become an outsider, where it's borderline, where they respect me but at the same time they think that I've become too white-washed. . . . [At school], I'm really rambunctious and loud and obnoxious, and then when I come home, it's like, What's wrong with you? You're quiet; you're not acting the same! That's what it's like, you know. It's like I'm neither–or. . . . It's a hard meaning to deal with.

Marina's struggle is familiar to the many generations of immigrants in the United States who have had to negotiate the borders of identity and culture. Perhaps some, however, have not confronted this struggle quite so consciously. Marina's comments reminded me of her earlier struggles with being "borderline" as a girl in a culture that was, and continues to be, conflicted about women being strong, assertive, sensitive, sexual, smart, successful, and feminine at the same time. Marina's struggles with cultural borders have continued through the years, and are often reflected in her television interactions.

Television Through the Years: "They Don't Really Want to Be Ethnic; They Just Want to Be for Show"

Marina was at home often at seventeen, because, she said, she did not "like to be in the street so much" anymore. At home, she spent time with her boyfriend of four years and with her sister, helping her take care of her toddler son. Also, she had a great deal of schoolwork. Marina listened to music at various times, and her tastes were eclectic, although she was drawn to what she called "oldies" from the 1950s to the 1970s and to "Spanish music" from her mother's youth, because the "lyrics are beautiful." She had pulled away from listening to rap because, she said, the lyrics were "nasty and violent." She also liked to dance. When Marina watched TV, she viewed

mostly rented videos or, like, Spanish soap operas. I don't know why. Spanish soap operas. . . . It's like recently I just started like watching one of them, and it's because my cousin just came from Puerto Rico. I know we're Dominican, but she used to live there, and she came and she likes them, so I just started watching them. They've become so silly, and you just become used to them, so I just. . . . That's what I've been watching. And they give them during prime time, so I no longer watch the shows that I used to watch. I used to watch, like, *Martin, Living Single, Roseanne.* Now I don't be watching those shows anymore.

I asked Marina about the movies she rented. She said she "especially like[d] funny movies, like Jim Carrey movies, Eddie Murphy. I also like to see movies that like, they're acclaimed with, like, Emmy nominations and things like that." Marina's media tastes seem to have been influenced strongly by her home culture and pop culture, as demonstrated by her interest in Spanish fare as well as mainstream, award-winning movies. But at the same time, she said she "hate[d]" the sitcom *Seinfeld*, the TV program that had the highest ratings at the time. Instead, she preferred *Murphy Brown, Cheers*, and *Coach*, which were on late at night before she went to bed. She mentioned really liking the character Christine on *Coach*.

> I love her. [From her, I learned] about relationships and, like, all the things that they go through. It's like, things similar to me and my boyfriend, as to how men can be so childish. And she's just so great. Like, he's kind of sexist and, like, a coach or whatever, but Christine, she's sensitive, but yet at the same time she's a very strong woman. And I like her character.

I wondered about her prior preferences for strong female TV characters. In reflecting on these earlier preferences, she reported a "self-conscious" yet also instilled interest in feminism.

> I remember that last time we were talking about Angela Bower, [the character] from *Who's the Boss?* That I liked her, and Roseanne [Barr] and Madonna were my favorite women. Even though I don't watch TV as much anymore, they are still kind of like my role models. And now [the character] Murphy Brown, too. And I guess it's because they have a trait of what I like and that is, you know, feminism. So I guess even though I don't show it as much, it's always been instilled in me self-consciously, and I guess that's why I like them so much. And I still do. So I guess that that comes from everywhere, and it also comes from the oppression, just thinking that just because I have male cousins, and my aunts let them go out at night, and the girls, they could be older and they don't let them do the same things just because they're females. And they have to cook for them and they have to clean for them, and I question that. Why do we have to do that? It has to be equal or nothing, you know? So I guess it comes from that. From everywhere. But mostly from me, because I want to make that change. Especially from the culture that I came from.

Marina's later TV and media habits and interpretations continued to illustrate her thoughtful yet conflicted negotiations of herself as a female, Latina, and upwardly mobile immigrant. She talked about getting into the "culture of college," which, she admitted, involved "youth-culture-type" activities:

> I got into *Friends, Party of Five, Beverly Hills 90210.* I used to never watch that, but it's just that my friends would get together, like on Wednesday night, and order pizza, and it just makes it really cool for everybody to take a break, to not go to the library or whatever. When I was a freshman I used to live in a house with thirty people, and it was fun to get together to watch a show, so I started getting into those shows, and *X-Files,* too. I had never watched it. And then I'm into these, like, youth-culture-type things at college, and I started to like them.

But at twenty-one, Marina was watching TV on her own, and very seldom, because of her schedule and household situation. By that time, she had only one favorite TV show, the sitcom *3rd Rock from the Sun:*

> *Marina:* That's an amazing show. That's the only show I watch now. Like, after freshman, sophomore year I forgot *Party of Five,* but the only show that I'll make time to watch if I have the time is *3rd Rock.* But I don't have much time to watch television, unfortunately, or I watch videos when I have the time, just to keep up with the music and the "fads" *[said sarcastically].* But I love *3rd Rock*
> *JoEllen:* Why?
> *Marina:* They just make a parody out of everything. They just make fun of us, you know, since they are supposed to be alien, and they are trying to be like normal—like , who's supposed to be American—and they are, like, trying to fit in. And it has to do with just being foreign and just how ridiculous like some of our cultural values are.

I asked her whether she had a favorite character on the show, and she replied: "Sally. 'Cause she's so unconventional. Look at her boyfriend: He's this fat, ugly cop who she just loves to have sex with. It's just, like, whatever, you know. I love her. And then, um, Harry, 'cause he's crazy. It's a great show." This led to a discussion of how the show was a bit like anthropology, or the study of people trying to figure out how a culture works and how to be part of that culture. As Marina put it:

> And it's, like, for any immigrant, you know? That, like, things that aren't normal for them are normal for other people, and [vice versa], and how they have to fit in. And it's funny how people take like the most natural things for granted. So that show is questioning every single thing that you can imagine and really mak[ing] fun of it. Just like the family structure: this man that has a kid . . . lives

with his brother and sister, but where is the wife? And the kid looks Asian, kind of Asian, but the father is White, and it's a very very weird setting.

Marina found the show to be very relevant and meaningful, given her own experiences of coming to the United States and fitting into a predominately White and middle- to upper-class college. Indeed, several times during her interview at age twenty-one, Marina described how she battled constantly with her desire to stay true to her home culture versus her wish—and need—to adapt to the culture of school. Also, she struggled with being easily swayed by commercial styles and images. She saw that others, even those not like her, battled with multiple desires, even though others' battles might take place on different grounds. In the following comments about *Bamboozled*, a movie by Spike Lee that she considered "lovely," Marina shows some understanding that young people are "foreigners" in different cultures, even when these cultures are not national or college-based:

> I have friends—well, not friends really, just kids—and they are, like, ghetto boys glorified, like the baggy jeans, the hip-hop look, Ebonics[1], the lingo. Like, "Let's 'blade; what's up." Ghetto talk. And at the same time it's like: You go home to New York or wherever, to a mansion, and you have no idea what it is like to be Black or to be poor. You know? And it's just, like, romanticizing all this stuff. It's, like, what part the Black entertainer has as, like, being funny, a great musician. It's, like, the only venue you have to actually make it. If so, are you doing it for your community or just to be the entertainer of White people? So it's like you keep propagating the same system, even though you may think it's not. But really, you know, that's, like, the whole message of the movie: Who are you doing what for?

These words, along with those in the next excerpt, show that Marina has an explicit awareness of the role that media play in structuring some young people's competing sensibilities in multiple cultures and of the roles that multiple cultures play in how the media operate, as well. She also argues that she is not immune to media appeals:

> Recently I've noticed that it's cool to be Black or Latina—a certain physique, the way that you look. Like, I've been asked about commercials and about comedians and actors, if I would like to go into it because I look like me, like the TV wants to be very ethnically diverse. But I have to say, they don't really want to be ethnic; they just want to be for show. Like the Gap commercials. They want to make us into little cutouts of the same thing, just in different colors. Like, all you guys wear khakis: You are Black, you're Asian, you are brown-skinned, you are White, but all of you guys wear khakis. You know, it's like they are just trying to fit you into one tin mold, but different colors. They superficially show diversity. What I see in the media [is that] we are

just being molded to the same styles, the same thing that the culture right now is craving. And, like, because it has been created for us, we don't create it, and we don't question it. You see an image, you see a blush, and that's what's in. For example: I am not. . .I never say "never" anymore because I hated the '80s in terms of style, [but] I loved the music, but it was so tacky. And it's coming in. And watch how in a year or two I'm gonna be wearing all the things that I hate—the little rhinestones, the big hair, you know? It's gonna be so ingrained in us through the media. So we are not gonna question it, and I include myself in it, and I consider myself a very knowledgeable person. But these are images that, whether you like it or not, you are gonna follow them. You know? And that's what I see. And I see it and I do it, 'cause it means something to fit in. Especially youth culture, you know? It's not like anyone putting a gun to your head to do it, but it's just, like, if you see something that many times, that's what you are going to start liking, without questioning.

Yet Marina indeed questions the media. When I asked her to talk about the media "in general" at age twenty-one, her self-professed feminism came through loud and clear. Indeed, her feminist perspective had advanced to a point at which she was concerned not only about issues of female development and possibilities but about male development and possibilities, as well.

My nephew, since he was very little, we let him play with dolls, but we never let him play with guns. We figure he's going to be a father, so it's like, let him play with dolls. So it's like, now, it's becoming so great and wonderful to be a girl that I think the backlash is coming, especially in the media. Because it's not cool to be a boy anymore. It's cool to be a girl, 'cause we can wear the baggy jeans, the hair, we can wear anything we want, we can drive a truck, we can be self-assertive. . . . You drive your own car, make your own money; you can be the same as a man is, but at the same time you can be feminine. You can play with any kind of doll that you want. You can still look good as a woman. And, like, the toys and the advertisements and all that—you can, like, go to Toys 'R' Us and, like, little girls have the most beautiful wonderful toys to play with. And on top of that, you can go roll in the dirt with your cousin, and climb a tree. . . . Like [my nephew] wants to be playing with his little sister, and he sees all the wonderful toys and the media shows how great it is to be a girl, but he doesn't see how it's great to be a boy. So this is, like, I've been noticing, they show all these great girly things, but then at the same time they show the [animated series] *Powerpuff Girls.* [We can] be anything we want, but a little boy, it's, like, he likes the *Powerpuff Girls,* he likes [the pop singer] Britney Spears, and he likes to play with dolls, and already it's assumed that he's a bit feminine. So it's like, how do we balance this?

Although I may not agree that it is completely "great and wonderful" to be a girl these days, I do think Marina is asking an important question. This question characterizes her own and others' negotiations of gender, ethnicity, nationality, class status, and commercial trends. I imagine she will strike her own balance, as she confronted complex issues of identity and culture before. But how can she help her nephew and other boys and girls be "great and wonderful" while they play with any of the toys they want? I hope educators, scholars, media people, and policymakers can address Marina's concerns. Together we can work out how to help Marina, her nephew, and all young people become "anything [they] want" and make a difference where necessary.

Appendix:
Methodological Notes

Studying Identities and Learning in TV Cultures

A focus on individuals is necessary to examine how diverse people "do" all of their complex identity work, as well as to learn about contemporary social power relations while living in a postmodern world pervaded by commercial media. For although the ideologies of identity groups and power relations are found by examining patterns of social activity, individual persons construct their own configuration of social identities (Erikson 1980 [1959]; Stryker 1987), and learning is found in individuals (Eisenhart 1995; Erickson 1982; Goodenough 1981; Wolcott 1982).

To find and show evidence of individual identity projects, learning about social power relations, and the role television plays in these processes, this study relies on interpretive and semiotic perspectives on locating meaning and learning. For C. Geertz, "ideation . . . is a cultural artifact," to be found in social activities and symbolic interactions, and thought and meaning processes are "trafficking in the symbolic forms available in one or another community" (1983: 152–53). Symbolic forms include languages, social conventions and norms, community rituals, institutional structures and practices, material objects, architecture and design, and different media and technology. All social activities and symbolic interactions represent cultural ideologies, and my research task is to construe and explicate them as they relate to my particular project.

This study also relies on written and spoken language to provide evidence of individual meaning and learning. Drawing on M. Bakhtin's and L. S. Vygotsky's theories of the dialectical relationship among thought, language, and society (see Bruner 1986; Emerson and Holmquist 1981; Wertsch 1985), I assume that talk and writing provide pictures or symbolic outlines of thinking. Likewise, these symbolic outlines are personal and social because of the interactive nature of language processes. Languages that are circulated by cultural and social groups carry and transmit pre-established symbolic outlines that are appropriated by language users. But individual people acquire, value, and use languages idiosyncratically (Dyson 1993; Heath 1983). The talk and writings of the youth in this study are analyzed as they represent the interactive meaning making and learning of distinct individual youth.

However, D. Buckingham (1993) and others warn that the words of youth, or any participant in research, cannot be taken simply at face value. Language is produced in specific social contexts that influence its intent and function, which in turn affects the meaning of the words. Interview contexts may have affected how my participants responded. They may have said things just to impress me or just to be playful, as Buckingham found when working in small groups. And although a measure of trust was established in my research, some participants' responses may have been tempered by the fact that I am an adult. I was seen as a teacher-like figure by these youths, so they may have thought they needed to respond formally and "correctly," not as casually or openly, as they might have with their friends and family. Also, I was sometimes not of the same gender, ethnicity, or class as these youths, which can affect whether and how participants respond (Buckingham 1993). And interview responses are interrelated: No single response on one topic or area can be understood in isolation from the others. Moreover, the participants' responses cannot be understood as separate from the actual situations and circumstances of their existence, which they experience daily, and many of which I participated in and observed over an eighteen-month period.

Age Choice

I chose to study young adolescents for several reasons. I had experience working with students this age on other projects and felt adequately prepared to work with them and to understand their situations. Also, according to R. M. Liebert and J. Sprafkin (1988), youth aged nine to thirteen spend an average of three-and-a-half to four hours per day with television, more than any other age group except the elderly. I thought it would be valuable to learn more about the nature of this statistical fact.

I was also interested in youths on the cusp of becoming sexually active, which means confronting changing body images, dealing with new emotions, and learning new social behaviors and responsibilities. As "pre-teens" they are expected to take on adultlike roles and expectations and give up their childlike ways, at school and at home. I wondered how students this age experience these changes and shifts in identities, and how television culture might figure in to their experiences.

I also chose this age group because they are still young, yet they possess more language and intellectual competencies than younger children, making it easier for me to gain access to what is on their minds. Young adolescents are more able to think and talk about complex, abstract concepts (such as reflecting about themselves and the meaning of television programs) because they have greater experience in the world than do younger children. Mindful of questions about the credibility and rigor of doing in-depth studies of a few individuals, I felt that it was important for the youths to be adept at articulating and expressing their ideas and feelings.

Finding Young Adolescents and Gathering Data

I chose to find young people through a school, as this is where they spend almost a third of their day. Rather than travel around to different schools, I decided to settle into one school so I could come to understand the specific culture created by a school, a neighborhood, and a particular group of peers. Staying in one school, I reasoned, would provide me with a more comprehensive experience of students' everyday lives.

I decided to work with a public school serving a community of families of lower socioeconomic status for two reasons. First, lower-socioeconomic-status populations apparently spend more time watching television than do their more affluent counterparts, generally because their resources are more limited, restricting their access to other kinds of recreational and educational activities and materials (Medrich et al. 1982). I wanted to explore the meaning of television for youth who live with these circumstances. Second, I wanted to give voice to young people whose marginal economic and political status frequently results in their being ignored. Lower-socioeconomic-status youths may be talked about, but they are not often given a chance to be heard (see Weis and Fine 1993).

I gained access to Alternative Middle School (AMS) by contacting a network of agencies and people concerned with the success of education in the public schools. This process was difficult, because most public schools face complex problems. By default, they are in no position to extend themselves to research projects that do not aid the school with funding, services, materials, or guaranteed successes. In traditional schools, I encountered reticence and suspicion when I explained that I wanted to observe classrooms. Although I explained that I would be focusing on students, teachers were wary of having a stranger watching in their rooms.

Eventually, I was fortunate to contact AMS, an alternative school in the public system that had opened five months before I began gathering data. Because of its progressive and innovative philosophy of schooling, AMS welcomed me as a member of the staff (unpaid) on the idea that having another responsible adult around who cared about kids—a much needed resource in public schools—would contribute to its program. AMS included me in faculty meetings and gave me access to the classrooms and any and all activities (see Fisherkeller 1995: appendixes for the permission letters and data-gathering instruments used in this project).

Because I would be staying at one site, it was important that the school population be diverse. AMS included a multicultural group of sixth-, seventh-, and eighth-graders from families with lower-middle and working-class incomes and subsidized incomes. The faculty was diverse, as well (see Chapter 1 for details).

For two and a half months, I went to AMS as an ethnographer, visiting different classrooms strategically to get a sense of what it was like to go to school as a student. The students were grouped in multi-age cohorts that had different schedules for attending language, math, social studies, science, gym, art, and advisory meetings. Following different cohorts on different days of the week, I gained a sense of peer relations, especially by hanging out with different groups during breaks and after school. I took notes on classroom activities and on what was generally going on in the school, including what are considered extracurricular activities and all-school functions at which the parents were sometimes included. I joined in sports and recreational activities. I also gathered artifacts from the school, including the students' autobiographies, other selected writings, and school records.

I surveyed fifty students to find out about household technology and general media habits. I also asked about TV programs the students watched routinely, about movies they liked, and about video games they played to get a sense of their overall media uses and choices. I watched the most popular programs on network TV and asked students to tape cable-based programs they liked for me. I also collected articles and books about television programs and people that were popular with the students and essays that provided critique and commentary about the general context of programming available at the time.

I collaborated with the faculty members to make the questions and format of the survey as clear and simple as possible. Many of the students at AMS struggled with reading and writing, and they would have only forty minutes to complete the form. The students filled out the survey in the context of their language-arts class, and I administered it with the writing teacher's assistance. The students were free to ask questions and talk with others while filling out the survey.

Selecting and Gathering Data with Focal Participants

After spending time at the school as an ethnographer and administering the survey, I started approaching students to see whether they would talk with me individually. The following criteria guided my interest in particular students:

- Their own talk about or references to TV in classroom discussions.
- Their critical comments about social interaction and issues.
- Their participation in TV-associated activities, such as joking, dancing, and singing songs with friends in the gym.
- Teachers' comments about the students' school identity or peer identity.
- Comments in students' autobiographies that referenced TV or other media.

Other questions that guided my taking note of particular students included: Were they approachable? Did they indicate some level of comfort with my presence at the school? Had they talked to me of their own volition? Some of the students were curious to know more about what I was doing at AMS, and I took that as a cue.

These selection criteria—especially the students' level of comfort with me—skewed my focal-participant sample unexpectedly. I showed interest in several students who were considered popular in the school and tried to talk with them casually about television. But popular kids were much more interested in hanging out with their friends than in talking with me. Thus, the students I ultimately selected were considered less popular and were not as involved in large-group peer activities. Yet because they were less popular, the focal participants might have enjoyed my attention and perhaps were choosing me as much as I chose them.

I explained that I wanted to talk with the focal participants about their lives and about television, and that I wanted to meet their families to talk about television. Once the participants understood and gave verbal permission, I contacted the families by phone, then in writing (in a letter constructed in collaboration with the faculty who knew the families) to explain the project and set up time to meet. At the focal participants' homes, I talked casually with their families about their lives and about their TV routines, attitudes, and program preferences. I spent one to three hours with each set of parents, depending on how much time they had, the time of day I visited, and their conversational nature and style. All of the parents allowed me to audiotape our discussions, except one who was embarrassed about her limited skills in English.

The home visits provided information about the focal participants' material conditions and neighborhood situation; the families' talk also provided information about their attitudes, general outlook and beliefs, and their particular sensibilities about television. This provided background for the focal participants' thinking about themselves and their lives and about their interactions with and interpretations of television.

I conducted two audiotaped interviews about one year apart with each of six focal participants. I watched TV with all but two of these focal participants and videotaped what we watched, as well. Two focal participants' household situations did not permit me to be there when they normally watched TV. They did not want to watch just anything with me, nor did I want them to watch within such contrived circumstances.

The talks I had with the focal participants were open-ended, so that they were given free reign to bring up topics and ask questions. I also worked with a list of questions that I checked off but did not follow in a specific order. I asked them to tell me about their lives at home, their lives at school, and their sense of the world at large. I asked them about their sense of their own future. With respect to TV, I asked the following:

- How regularly they watched TV;
- Where and with whom they watched TV;
- Whether they had to follow any rules about watching TV;
- What kinds of programs they liked to watch;
- Why these shows appealed to them;
- Which shows were their favorites;
- What made certain shows good;
- Which characters were their favorites;
- What made favorite characters good;
- Whether they wanted to be like anyone on television;
- Whether they saw their own lives represented on TV;
- Whether television was like real life, and if so, how;
- Why and how television was made, and by whom;
- How they talked to their friends about television.

I tried to check in on the same areas during the second set of interviews. After reviewing the transcripts of the first interviews and coming up with some analyses, I asked the focal participants to tell me whether I was on the right track and whether my speculations and comments about them made sense. For example, with one of my focal participants, I made a list of words that I might use to describe her. After I read the list to her, she said: "Hey, not bad." At the second interview, I also gave each focal participant a copy of the transcript of the first interview, asking them to call me if they wanted to talk about it. Unfortunately, none did. All subsequent interviews were transcribed and mailed to each with the same invitation, eliciting the same response.

Constructing the Individual Portraits

In the introduction to each portrait chapter, I provide details concerning the selection of each focal participant. But in summary, the three I selected for in-depth portrayals were chosen for their diversity in experiences. Unexpectedly, Christopher was the only boy I was able to interview in both years of the study, so he was selected by default. Of the girls in the larger group of participants, Marina and Samantha were most different from each other and from Christopher with respect to race and ethnicity; and Marina was a first-generation immigrant. In addition, the two girls came from families with different structures and socioeconomic standing. Further, their personalities and demeanor contrasted. As I am interested in how individuals negotiate their identities in multiple cultures, choosing portraits that are more variant than similar strengthens my cross-portrait analyses.

To aid in the comparative analyses (found in Chapters 5 and 6), each portrait was organized using the same format.[1] Most young adolescents spend time in three major physical locations: at home, at school, and in the neighborhood. Within and across these physical locations, young adolescents have many different kinds of social experiences with many different kinds of people. But three major social groups structure their experience: family, teachers, and peers. These physical locations and social groups are experienced in an overlapping manner. I organized my descriptions of individual experiences within the following contextual clusters, in which associated physical locations and social situations converged:

- *At Home.* This context included the youth's experience of family and kin, cultural heritage, household arrangements, neighborhood setting, socioeconomic situation, parent's or parents' occupations, and regional circumstances.
- *At School.* This context included the youth's experience of teachers, academic environment, classes, grade status, performance evaluations, and pedagogical modes.
- *With Peers.* This context included the youth's experiences with age- and grade-mates, school friends and rivals, neighborhood acquaintances and friendships, and unofficial school activities and events.

Another major context of experience that is pertinent to constructing these portraits is television. As a context, TV is multidimensional, just like the home, school, and peer contexts. Specifically, on one level, television is an activity that stands in relation to other cultural activities that variously fill people's time and space of existence. On another level, TV is a symbolic form, a collection of cultural codes and conventions particular to its features as a medium and as technology. On a third level, TV tells the stories of culture, whether these narratives are fictional, informational, or both. And finally, TV is an ideological messenger, representing fundamental cultural ideas and values.[2]

The dimensions of television experience are: functional, aesthetic, storytelling, and conceptual. Table 1 shows these dimensions as they are affected by the actualities of audience and media institutions or by the constraints of reception and production.

TABLE 1 *Dimensions of Television Experience*

Level	Audience Aspects	Institutional Aspects
Functional: TV as an activity	• habits, patterns of viewing • family/household situations and schedules • neighborhood circumstances • school schedules • non-school activities and routines • social group camaraderie	• accessibility, convenience • targetting strategies earmark time slots and products for different kinds of audiences • program schedules
Aesthetic: TV as a symbolic form	People's preferences for: • form, craft, art • specific kinds of styles, manners, or presentations [i.e., camera work, acting, special effects, kinds of humor, clothes, language, music, etc.]	• budget constraints • capitalization of popular trends • pace accommodating 'flow' • multiplicity of material to capture target audiences • technical wizardry
Storytelling: TV as a storyteller	People's interests in: • overt narrative elements, character, plot, and genre conventions • explicit topics and messages • program "reality"	• episodic series favored for commercial efficiency • stereotypes and formulas used for expediency • topics and messages need to have broad, non-provocative appeal
Conceptual: TV as an ideologic messenger	People's evaluations of: • issues and ideas • values, norms, beliefs • assumptions and presumptions • philosophies, ideals	• commercialism, consumerism, capitalism • western democratic idealism • racism, sexism, ethnocentrism, classism • cultural and religious "-isms"

The portraits rely on these dimensions to make sense of the focal participants' interactions with TV, primarily illuminating the audience aspects of the chart. Yet when reviewing the participants' comments about television, the aesthetic, storytelling, and conceptual dimensions were so frequently and complexly interrelated that it was impossible to discuss each of the dimensions separately.

Devising "Symbolic Reflections"

I was challenged in this study to discover the nature of each of the participants' most salient identity projects at this point in time and to discover how television plays a role in these projects. To locate the young adolescents' identity projects, I turned to a symbolic meeting point between viewers and TV culture. I focused on each focal participant's choice of and meaningful comments about television people and programs to which he or she was especially attracted. Such comments provided several clues. First, I assumed that a preference for a TV character or a program, in and of itself, revealed something about the nature of the individual viewer. That is, a mainstream decoding of TV material might suggest that viewers identify with such TV material. For example, common readings of Madonna posit that she promotes female strength and independence along with the pleasures of sexuality (Fiske 1992), which young girls find appealing as they confront puberty and patriarchy at the same time.

However, when viewers explain or elaborate on the appeal of their favorite TV personas or programs, they put their values and ideas into their own words. The focal participants' expressions of appeal and admiration yield clues to what each particularly values in terms of qualities and characteristics (for example, "I like her because she's strong"), or what each particularly knows to be familiar and substantive (for example, "She is a female, like me").

But how and why did each focal participant come to value certain qualities and come to understand particular kinds of familiarities and substance? To answer those questions, I used their specific comments about their favorite TV material as a kind of lens and looked through the lens to examine different aspects of their lives, such as:

- Their particular natures and identities;
- Their circumstances and experiences at home, at school, and with peers;

- Their general uses of and regard for television;
- Their other comments about themselves, including their sense of the future.

A sense of the future is an important component of this interpretation process, as it indicates the individuals' goals for their identity projects within their particular realities.

What emerges from this process is a "symbolic reflection," a meaningful explanation of how and why an individual viewer has come to value and understand particular kinds of symbolic materials that embody mainstream cultural values and ideas (television). It is in *how and why* individuals come to admire specific fictional identities (TV material) that identity projects and related learning about power are revealed. And because the "how and why" are based in an individual's complex of interactions with culture, symbolic reflections are "crystallized" representations of identity formation and cultural learning.

The individual portraits as a whole are interpretive, because meanings of symbolic material in television culture and meanings of processes in local cultures are being constructed—an interpretive process, according to C. Geertz (1983). Meanings are being constructed by individual participants, as well as by me. This double layer of meaning construction applies to what is symbolic in the portraits: The participants are individually interpreting the meaning of symbolic material on the TV screen and in their lives, and in turn, I am interpreting the participants' individual meanings as symbolic of their sense of themselves in culture.

Notes

Introduction

1. See the Media Glossary for details about television programs and other media items discussed in this study.

2. The names of the interview participants have been changed to protect confidentiality, as has the name of the educational institution. The focal participants chose their own pseudonyms for the initial study; some later decided to use their real names. The school is identified as "Alternative Middle School" (AMS).

3. These ethnic labels identify the specific backgrounds of the participants. The labels "Black," "Latino," and "White" appear only when the participants used them to refer to themselves and others.

4. Further discussion of postmodern claims can be found in Chapter 1. See also Kellner 1992.

5. For discussions of the history and ownership of the media, see Bagdikian 1992; Barnouw 1978; and Miller 1996. By the time this book is published, of course, the continuing mergers and reorganizations will have changed many specifics of the system and operation of the media.

6. For in-depth discussions and critiques of how sponsors construct the public as consumers, see Barnouw 1978; Gandy 1990; and Kellner 1990.

7. Mergers among media organizations and changes in product-licensing practices have caused mass-media forms to become increasingly interrelated over the years. In today's climate, for example, one form of media (say, a music CD or a Website) can serve as advertising for another (a film or television program). This has accelerated the similarities in content and form among different forms of mass communication. See Gerbner et al. 1980, 1986, 1994; Gitlin 1986.

Chapter One

1. Television was invented in 1927 and used before World War II, but it did not make its way to most of the general public until the 1950s. See Barnouw 1978; 1977 (1975).

167

2. In New York City, certain schools in the public-education system are recognized and promoted as specializing in particular subjects, such as the arts and humanities, math and science, or technology. These magnet schools—unlike neighborhood schools that must admit anyone residing in qualified address locations—are open to all students citywide who meet the admissions criteria. Because they are considered high-quality education centers, the magnet schools have very competitive admissions requirements, which tend to privilege, unwittingly, students from schools that serve higher-income families. Thus, their student bodies tend to be predominately White. See Hansen et al. 1995p; Weis and Fine 1993.

3. The faculty did not try to limit the number of Asian Americans attending the school, but they received few applications from this group. It is beyond the scope of this study to discuss the implications of this situation, which involve issues of race, class, immigration, public policy, and schooling ideologies (Ogbu 1985).

4. Not long after I conducted this study, public-schools budgets in New York City were again tightened at all levels, resulting in layoffs of teachers and staff, overcrowding in the classrooms, closings of libraries, and serious shortages of material (Newman, 1995). The situation was no different while I was at AMS, although the faculty had found ways to support themselves outside the public system's bureaucracy.

5. E. Chin (1993) describes how young girls who live in large and troubled urban locations enjoy going to the mall because it is a safe, clean, weather-protected place to be with friends and it has things to look at in the stores, food to buy, and video arcades to enjoy.

6. I asked Colette whether I could talk with her more and visit her home and family, but she declined.

7. A. H. Dyson shows how young children negotiate identities and re-create symbolic material in their writing and dramatizing stories using *X-Men* cartoons: See Dyson 1994.

Chapter Two

1. Dr. Luis Rayas, personal communication, 1994.

2. Dr. Luis Rayas and Jennifer Pastor, personal communication, 1994. See also Pastor et al. 1996.

3. In *Women Watching Television* (1991), A. L. Press finds working-class women who strongly like a program in which the characters enjoy a higher financial status but still have budgeting concerns. A. L. Press argues that the female viewers "wish that reality might bear a closer resemblance to its television image" (Press 1991: 109).

4. The writing on Madonna is extensive; whole conferences have been dedicated to her and Elvis Presley as popular-culture phenomena. In "Madonna Writes; Academics Explore Her Erotic Semiotics" (1992), M. Kakutani reviews Madonna's book, *Sex* (1992), and Swichtenberg's *The Madonna Connection* (1992). Other books and articles about Madonna include Fiske 1992; Frank and Smith 1993; and Lewis 1990.

5. Marina's admiration of Madonna is somewhat similar to that of the working-class British girls in Fiske's study of television culture; the difference is that those girls saw Madonna as a role model not for achieving corporate, career-oriented success but for achieving sexual liberation in social relations. See Fiske 1992.

Chapter Three

1. For a journalistic comment on the implications of sneakers as status items, see Littwin 1990.

2. For accounts of physical play that work to identify social groupings, see Thorne 1993.

3. In *With the Boys* (1987), G. A. Fine argues that small groups such as sports teams establish an "ideoculture," or a set of practices, beliefs, and interests that are particular to the group and privileged for members only. To identify themselves as members of a unique group, each member has to internalize and maintain ideocultural rules and norms. Fine found that players who joined a team late in the season had difficulty accessing ideocultural knowledge without the support or assistance of an established member. Joining AMS in midseason, then, Christopher would have had difficulty accessing the male basketball ideoculture at AMS. But he did not even attempt to join this high-status group as a team player because of his lack of physical fitness and, perhaps, because of his shoes. His reluctance to learn the male AMS establishment's "rules of the game" might have contributed to his difficulty in finding friendships generally.

4. In *Parents Talking Television* (Simpson 1987), parents describe television as an activity that makes it easier to talk with their older children, who often do not want to interact with their parents. Parents can talk about what is on the screen with their children rather than focus on the children themselves, which some adolescents find annoying and intrusive.

5. Dyson (1994) finds young children using *X-Men* stories and characters to do identity work in the elementary-school classroom.

6. This profiles a "typical" identification process, as described in television research, in which children pick a character they "like" who is the same gender, as well as sometimes the same age or ethnicity. For references and a discussion of factors contributing to identification with TV characters, see Reeves and Miller 1978. For a discussion refuting and complicating the arguments about "typical" identification processes, see Buckingham 1993: chap. 8.

7. See Carter 1992b.

8. See Carter 1992b. Also, Dr. Poissaint, Cosby's consultant, later released a book of advice for Black parents. See Comer and Pouissaint 1993.

9. Saxe 1994 suggests that video-game players get a "power fix" by identifying with superhero characters who can fight and conquer in video games; Saxe also cites Courtney 1992, which argues that young adolescent boys' identification with superhero comic characters provides a fantasy outlet for the frustrations of coping with the adult world.

Chapter Four

1. For illuminating discussions of gendered solidarity in play, see Thorne 1993 and Fine 1987.

2. For a description and discussion of family uses of television, see Lull 1990.

3. It is likely that Beth Gardner was prompted to think more critically about her television attitudes and prior behavior by my asking questions about the family's

TV routines and experiences. Beth was not the only parent who seemed apologetic and felt guilty about television activity in the home, reflecting a common cultural ideology that TV is bad and should be avoided as much as possible. E. Seiter, a mother and author, writes: "As many women commented in response to a survey in *Working Mother* magazine about children and television, merely being asked about my children's consumption patterns is enough to prompt feelings of guilt and uncertainty" (Seiter 1993: 228). See also Berman 1988.

4. This refers to the 1992 case of Rodney King, a Black man who was stopped in a White suburban neighborhood of Los Angeles and whose image was captured on a home video while he was being beaten severely by several White policemen. After the police were acquitted on charges of police brutality, many people in Los Angeles—and around the country—protested.

5. For feminist perspectives and discussions of images of women in media, see Press 1991; Signorielli (1993), "Television, the Portrayal of Women, and Children's Attitudes;" and Tuchman et al. 1978.

Chapter Five

1. M. C. Miller and a collection of authors responded critically to a chart depicting ownership of the news and entertainment media industry that appeared in *The Nation* (see "The National Entertainment State," *The Nation* [June 3, 1996], 9–32). The chart showed that, at that time, four corporate entities owned all major networks, cable and radio stations, and music-recording and print-publishing houses. Although some of the specifics of media ownership would have been different when the data were being gathered for this study, the general situation of media ownership was developing or the same. Of course, since I gathered my data and that issue of *The Nation* was released, mergers have changed the details of ownership further. Indeed, media-industry conglomeration has intensified.

2. Some "inside view" programs appear regularly, such as talk shows and magazine shows such as *Entertainment Tonight*, and some are specials on a particular project or personality. In addition, some programs either reveal or comment on their own construction by showing the background as a set, doing live episodes, having characters talk to the camera, and using special effects that play with the form and style of the work.

Epilogue

1. Ebonics is a dialect of the English language spoken by some African Americans. It is also called Black English. See Dillard 1972 and Smitherman 1977.

Appendix

1. I thank Tom Humphreys for this suggestion.

2. Discussions with Ron Lembo inspired the devising of these dimensions, but I am responsible for the categories and lists in Table 1.

Media Glossary

All My Children
January 5, 1970–
ABC
A daily daytime soap opera that chronicles the trials and tribulations of men and women living in the fictional Pine Valley, New York. The series originally revolved around the lives of the Tyler and Martin families, but after the first decade most of the Martins were written off of the show. The self-centered Erica Kane (Susan Lucci) has become one of the most popular soap-opera characters of all time.

Bamboozled
2000
A motion picture written, directed, and produced by Spike Lee (with John Kilik). This satirical film follows the rise and fall of Pierre Delacroix (Damon Wayans), a young, well-educated television writer, and examines how race, power, and the quest for ratings affects the world of network television. When the fledgling network that employs Delacroix insists that he create a hit series or lose his job, the writer comes up with an outrageous proposal—a blackface minstrel-like show. Surprisingly, the show becomes a hit with audiences of all types, but Delacroix unravels as critics, including his friends and family, attack the show's racial representations. This film about the inner workings of media production combines comedy and social commentary. Lee has written and directed sixteen other films, including *Do the Right Thing* (1989) and *Malcolm X* (1992).

Barney Miller
January 23,1975–September 8, 1982
ABC
A half-hour sitcom set in the 12th Precinct police station in New York City's Greenwich Village. Captain Barney Miller (Hal Linden) led a crew of detectives that included Fish (Abe Vigoda), an aging detective who seemed always to be on his last breath, and Wojo (Maxwell Gail), a young, trusting detective. The cast created laughs as they booked the wacky criminals who came through their doors.

The Beatles
The Beatles are the band known to have revolutionized the music industry, making pop music successful. Consisting of John Lennon, Paul McCartney, Ringo Starr, and George Harrison, the Beatles led the "British invasion" in 1964 and ultimately had twenty number-one singles in the United States. In 1970, Paul McCartney announced that he was leaving the band. All four members pursued successful solo careers but never reunited.

Beverly Hills 90210
October 4, 1990–May 17, 2000
Fox
A weekly drama series and "soap opera" depicting the dilemmas of the wealthy teenagers, beginning in high school and following them beyond college. The show realistically portrayed issues of adolescent development, such as sex and pregnancy, alcohol and drug use, school, growing up, and family relationships. Initially, the central focus of the show was the Walsh family, transplanted from suburban Minneapolis to glamorous Beverly Hills. As the teenagers grew into adults, their parents' roles were minimized, and new cast members replaced old, shifting the story lines and relationships, although the show remained strongly focused on the ideas of friendship and family woven into individual and group development and understanding.

Blossom
January 3, 1991–June 6, 1995
NBC
A half-hour sitcom about the Russo family seen through the eyes of Blossom Russo (Mayim Bialik), a bright adolescent living with her

divorced father and two older brothers. *Blossom* dealt with life's difficulties through fantasy scenes in which the Blossom character conversed with and accepted advice from various celebrities. She also documented her life in a video diary—in effect, talking directly with her audience about her predicaments.

Borge, Victor
1909–2000
Born in Denmark and educated at the Royal Danish Academy of Music, Borge had become one of Denmark's most famous artists by the 1930s. Although he was initially a classical pianist, his penchant for humor worked its way into his performances. Forced to leave Denmark, he moved to New York City in 1940 and began performing on Bing Crosby's radio show in 1941. His radio and television performances, which mixed music and comedy, were extremely popular.

Brokaw, Tom
1940–
Brokaw, born and raised in South Dakota, anchored NBC News's *Today Show* from 1976–1982 and has anchored NBC's *Nightly News* since 1983. He has also appeared in a series of prime-time television specials over the years.

Burnett, Carol
1933–
Burnett, a comedian, actress, and singer, studied theater arts and English at the University of California but left school in her third year to pursue an acting career in New York City. Although she has appeared on Broadway and in films, she is best known for her variety program, *The Carol Burnett Show*, which debuted in 1967 on CBS. In 1972, the show was part of the network's Saturday night lineup, with the highly popular *All in the Family*, *M*A*S*H*, *The Mary Tyler Moore Show*, and *The Bob Newhart Show*.

Cheers
September 30, 1982–May 20, 1993
NBC
A half-hour sitcom set at Cheers, a neighborhood bar in Boston, that revolved around the lives of the bar's employees and regular customers.

The bar was run by the fictional former Boston Red Sox pitcher Sam Malone (Ted Danson), other characters included the aging Coach (Nicholas Colasanto); the naive Woody (Woody Harrelson); Carla (Rhea Perlman), a wise-cracking mother of eight; Diane (Shelley Long), an elitist art student (who later left the show); Rebecca (Kirstie Alley), who joined the cast as the bar's new manager; and regulars Norm (George Wendt), Cliff (John Ratzenberger), and Dr. Frazier Crane (Kelsey Grammer). Throughout the show's run, friendship and camaraderie were its major themes.

Clarissa Explains It All
Produced 1991–1994
Nickelodeon
A syndicated cable-based sitcom that focuses on the adolescent Clarissa Darling (Melissa Joan Hart); her family—younger brother Ferguson (Jason Zimbler); mother Janet (Elizabeth Hess); and father Marshall (Joe O'Connor); and her best friend Sam (Sean O'Neill). The show's episodes open with Clarissa speaking to the camera about a specific issue—friends, love, boys, parents, school—and the plot develops from there. The program also uses special video effects to highlight Clarissa's thoughts and plans. The show deals with adolescent development; at the same time, the focus on Clarissa promotes a positive image of female development.

CNN
June 1980–
Turner Broadcasting's cable-based news network CNN first went on the air in June 1980; although it initially operated at a loss, by 1984 it had earned a reputation as cable-television innovator. The turning point came during CNN's twenty-four-hour coverage of the Democratic and Republican national conventions in that year. In 1991, CNN was the only network to broadcast the Persian Gulf war live, and today, CNN is seen as a basic component of global communications technology.

Coach
February 28, 1989–August 6, 1997
ABC
A half-hour sitcom centered on the life of Hayden Fox (Craig T. Nelson), the head coach of Minnesota State University's football team. The cast also included goofy assistants Luther (Jerry Van Dyke) and Dauber

(Bill Fagerbakke); Hayden's girlfriend (later wife) Christine (Shelley Fabares), a TV newswoman; and Hayden's young adult daughter, Kelly (Clare Casey), a college student.

Cosby, Bill
1937–
The comedian and actor Bill Cosby dropped out of high school, joined the Navy, earned a high-school-equivalency diploma, briefly attended Temple University, and eventually was awarded a doctorate in education from the University of Massachusetts, Amherst. He made his television debut in the 1960s as an undercover CIA agent in *I Spy*, becoming the first African American in a lead role in a dramatic TV series. In 1984, he began his most successful television endeavor, the sitcom *The Cosby Show* (see separate entry). He also created the kids' program *Fat Albert and the Cosby Kids* and the book and television series *Little Bill*, about a young African American boy with a learning disability to educate parents about children and learning disabilities.

The Cosby Show
September 20, 1984–September 17, 1992
NBC
A half-hour sitcom focused on the Huxtables, a large, well-to-do family living in Brooklyn, New York. In the show, patriarch Cliff (Bill Cosby), an obstetrician with an office in the home, and matriarch Clair (Phylicia Ahmad-Rashad), a Legal Aid attorney, raised five children: daughters Sondra (Sabrina Le Beauf), Denise (Lisa Bonet), Vanessa (Tempestt Bledsoe), and Rudy (Keshia Knight Pulliam), and son Theo (Malcolm-Jamal Warner). *The Cosby Show* portrayed a financially comfortable and socially stable Black family, which is rarely depicted on network television. Cosby was both applauded and scorned for the portrayal, caught between arguments that it was important to show that wealthy Black families exist and that such a depiction was unrealistic because the show rarely covered ideas of racial and cultural difficulty.

Dallas
1978–1991
CBS
Dallas, the first prime-time soap opera, was a groundbreaker in establishing many of the features—including stories of feuding families and

moral excesses—that would characterize later dramatic series. In its first year, 1978, *Dallas* earned low ratings and poor reviews, but it soon became popular. The show's central plot dealt with the ongoing feud between the Barneses and the Ewings, two families involved in the oil business in central Texas. *Dallas* was well known for its cliffhanging Friday night episodes and season finales, the most famous of which was titled "Who Shot J. R.?"

A Different World
September 24, 1987–July 9, 1993
NBC
A spin-off of *The Cosby Show* that initially focused on Denise Huxtable's (Lisa Bonet) experiences at the predominantly Black Hillman College (her father's and grandfather's alma mater). The cast also included roommates Jaleesa (Dawnn Lewis), a twenty-six-year-old divorced woman returning to college, and Maggie (Marisa Tomei), one of the few White cast members; Whitley Gilbert (Jasmine Guy), a wealthy and spoiled Southern debutante; Dwayne Wayne (Kadeem Hardison), the romancer; and Dwayne's best friend Ronald Johnson (Darryl Bell). Over the years, the show developed its own identity and shifted to revolve around the nature and development of the college and of the students in the Gilbert Hall dormitory.

Diff'rent Strokes
November 3, 1978–August 30, 1986
NBC
A half-hour sitcom about the White millionaire widower Phillip Drummond (Conrad Bain), who adopts two young Black children, Arnold (Gary Coleman) and Willis (Todd Bridges). Phillip Drummond, who also has a teenage daughter, Kimberly (Dana Plato), raises the boys as his own. Although it was a comedy, *Diff'rent Strokes* also also tackled plot lines about social issues, including racial tension, child molestation, and drug abuse, following the family as it grew and changed.

Don't Just Sit There
1988–1990
Nickelodeon
A skit and variety show hosted by the teenagers Matt Brown, Ali Smith, Bernard J. (B. J.) Schafer, Wendy Douglas, and Will Friedel. The show featured guest stars and the house band Out of Order.

Donahue
1970–1996
Syndicated
Named after its host, the Dayton, Ohio, *Phil Donahue Show* premiered in 1967. The popular, issue-driven talk show's name was shortened to *Donahue* in 1977, when it moved to Chicago and became syndicated. In 1985, *Donahue* relocated again to New York City. Each hour-long show was devoted to a single topic in which Phil Donahue, the studio audience, and phone callers asked questions of the guests. Donahue's reign ended in the 1990s when Oprah Winfrey and other talk-show hosts overtook the lead in ratings. By the time *Donahue* ended in 1996, the show had won twenty Emmy Awards.

Dr. Kildare
September 28, 1961–August 30, 1966
NBC
Inspired by the 1940s movie series of the same title, *Dr. Kildare* told the story of an intern at an urban hospital who was learning how to deal with patients and coworkers. The series, starring Richard Chamberlain as Dr. Kildare, focused on real-life, life-and-death hospital situations. In the course of the show, Dr. Kildare moved from intern to resident, and the plots focused on the relationships between patients and doctor. The show began to take on a serial quality, lengthening stories over several episodes.

Doogie Howser, M.D.
September 19, 1989–July 21, 1993
ABC
A sitcom about a child prodigy, the sixteen-year-old Douglas "Doogie" Howser (Neil Patrick Harris), working as a second-year resident at the fictional Eastman Medical Center. Doogie lived with his father, David (James B. Sikking), who was also a doctor, and his mother, Katherine (Belinda Montgomery). The show focused on both his "adult" life at the hospital and his social life outside the hospital with friends who were typical, academically average high-school students, showing that, although Doogie was intellectually and academically superior to others his age, he still had much to learn about growing up. Each episode closed with Doogie entering the episode's theme into a computer-based diary and pondering the lessons he had learned.

ER
September 19, 1994–
NBC
An hour-long dramatic series that focuses on the emergency-room employees and patients at a Chicago hospital. Created by the best-selling author Michael Crichton, the show depicts the intensity of emergency-room work, often showing graphic details. The show features an ensemble cast, and stories revolve around the tough cases of the emergency room as well as the romances and rivalries that develop among the staff and doctors.

Family Matters
September 22, 1989–May 9, 1997, ABC
1997–1998, CBS
A half-hour spinoff of another sitcom, *Perfect Strangers*, that introduced the family and friends of Harriet Winslow (JoMarie Payton), a newspaper-office elevator operator. *Family Matters* focused on the Winslows, a middle-class African American family that included mother Harriet; father Carl (Reginald Vel Johnson), a Chicago police officer; teenage children Eddie (Darius McCrary), Laura (Kellie Shanygne Williams), and Judy (Jaimee Foxworth); Rachel (Telma Hopkins), Harriet's widowed sister with a young son; and teenage neighbor Steve Urkel (Jaleel White). Urkel, a nerd of comic-book proportions, was introduced halfway through the show's first season, but his crush on daughter Laura and his ability to frustrate father Carl quickly became the focus of the show.

Fresh Prince of Bel Air
September 10, 1990–May 20, 1996
NBC
The rap musician Will Smith starred in this half-hour sitcom about a streetwise youth from Philadelphia sent to live with his wealthy relatives in the Bel Air suburb of Los Angeles after getting into trouble in his urban neighborhood. Smith moves in with his wealthy uncle, Judge Phillip Banks (James Avery), and aunt Vivian (Janet Hubert-Whitten 1990–93; Daphne Maxwell Reid 1993–1996), and their children Carlton (Alfonso Ribeiro), an ultraconservative preppy; Hilary (Karen Parsons), a self-absorbed materialist; and Ashley (Tatyana M. Ali), the youngest and most mature of the children. The Bel Air mansion is

presided over by the liveried, sarcastic butler Geoffrey (Joseph Marcell). In the show, Smith highlighted the clashing cultures of an inner-city youth living in a wealthy suburb and made the difficulties of race and socialization explicit.

Friends
September 22, 1994–
NBC

Half-hour sitcom about six twenty-something friends living in New York City: Monica (Courtney Cox), an assistant chef; Rachel (Jennifer Aniston), Monica's spoiled childhood friend who has moved to New York to try to make it on her own; Ross (David Schwimmer), Monica's paleontologist brother; Chandler (Matthew Perry), Ross's college roommate, a number cruncher at a big firm; Joey (Matt LeBlanc), an aspiring actor and Chandler's roommate; and Phoebe (Lisa Kudrow), their bizarre, New Age pal. The friends hang out in Monica's apartment and at Central Perk, a local coffeehouse, where they talk about work, dating, and families, and over the years, romances develop between different pairs in the group.

Full House
September 22, 1987–August 29, 1995
ABC

A half-hour sitcom centered on Danny Tanner (Bob Saget), a widowed local-television talk-show host in San Francisco who is raising three daughters—D. J. (Candace Cameron), Stephanie (Jodie Sweetin), and Michelle (Mary Kate and Ashley Olsen)— with the help of his brother-in-law, Jesse (John Stamos), and best friend, Joey (David Coulier). They all live together and make up an unlikely family. The show focuses on the relationships among the family members and how they grow together and learn to love one another, despite their differences and unique circumstances.

Get a Life
September 23, 1990–June 14, 1992
FOX

An offbeat comedy about Chris Peterson (Chris Elliot), an infantile thirty-year-old newspaper boy living in an apartment over his parents' garage in a suburb called Greenville. Chris Peterson is an eternal optimist; he is also naive and avoids responsibility at all costs. His parents, Gladys (Elinor Donahue) and Fred (Bob Elliot, Chris Elliot's real-life father), are accustomed to, and somewhat ignorant of, their son's behavior. The Chris Peterson character originated in Chris Elliot's stand-up comedy.

The Golden Girls
September 14, 1985–September 14, 1992
NBC
A half-hour sitcom set in Florida and focused on the lives of four retired women who live together: Dorothy (Bea Arthur), a former teacher with a brash style and a serious sensibility; Blanche (Rue McClanahan), a Southern woman obsessed with sex; Rose (Betty White), an air-brained widow; and Sophia (Estelle Getty), Dorothy's tactless mother.

Growing Pains
September 24, 1985–August 27, 1992
ABC
A half-hour sitcom about the upper-middle-class Seaver family on New York's Long Island in which Jason Seaver (Alan Thicke), the psychiatrist father, works from home so he can be with the kids while wife Maggie (Joanna Kearns) pursues her career as a journalist. The children are Mike (Kirk Cameron), the popular, trouble-making son; Carol (Tracey Gold), the smart, and socially awkward daughter; and Ben (Jeremy Miller), the youngest. The show dealt with light stories while also touching on serious issues such as drunk driving, suicide, racism, and peer pressure.

Hammer, MC
1963–
The rap artist and dancer MC Hammer (Stanley Kirk Burrell), who named himself after the baseball star Henry "Hammerin' Hank" Aaron, had major success in 1990 with the song "U Can't Touch This." The pop dance hit received massive exposure largely through sponsorships by British Knights and Pepsi-Cola. For a time, MC Hammer was praised as a role model for black youth but was criticized for his abuse of music sampling. On the album *Too Legit to Quit*, he asked black youth to give up drugs and find Christianity. Later, he tried to change his image again to that of a gangsta rapper, but poor ticket sales

drove Hammer into financial ruin, and the new image was largely unsuccessful.

Herman's Head
September 8, 1991–April 24, 1994
Fox

Herman's Head was a short-lived sitcom that revolved around Herman (William Ragsdale), an aspiring magazine writer in New York City, whose personal life was monitored by the emotions occupying his mind. The audience watched Herman "think" as his emotions battled for control. He was ruled by Angel (Molly Hagan), the idealist who represented sensitivity; Animal (Ken Hudson Campbell), his socializing, partying side; Genius (Peter Mackenzie), his intellect; and Wimp (Rick Lawless), his nervousness and anxieties. Although the show did not do well and ultimately was cancelled, it was popular with younger age groups.

Herman, Pee Wee (Paul Reubens)
1952–

Paul Reubens created Pee Wee Herman, the gray-suit-and-red-bowtie-wearing, childlike host of *Pee Wee's Playhouse* (1986–1991, CBS), a Saturday morning children's show. The surreal *Pee Wee's Playhouse* mixed live action, animation, puppetry, vintage cartoon clips, and quirky visitors. Reubens developed the character in his stand-up comedy routines and presented himself as Pee Wee at all times. The show celebrated multiculturalism, anti-sexism, and anti-heterosexism and attracted both child and adult audiences. In 1991, Reubens was arrested in an adult movie theater, abruptly ending his career as a child entertainer. He is now rebuilding his acting career as Paul Reubens.

Hey Dude
Produced 1989–1991
Nickelodeon

Shot on location in Tucson, Arizona, *Hey Dude* was a syndicated comedy set at the Bar None Ranch, which was staffed by a group of teenagers: Ted (David Lascher), Melody (Christine Taylor), Brad (Kelly Brown), and Danny (Joe Torres). Although the teenagers sometimes interacted with and helped the ranch's guests, the show focused mostly on their interactions with one another.

In Living Color
April 15, 1990–August 25, 1994
Fox
A weekly half-hour comedy and variety show similar to the late-night program *Saturday Night Live*, featuring a regular cast of predominantly African American comedians performing short comical skits. Headed by Keenan Ivory Wayans, the show's writer and producer, *In Living Color* featured satirical parodies of popular culture fare, icons, and stereotypes. At its height of popularity, the show offered a wide variety of skits and recurring sketches; performances by the Fly Girls, a group of hip-hop dancers; and guest performances by popular musicians.

Just the Ten of Us
April 26, 1988–September 27, 1990
ABC
A sitcom spin-off of *Growing Pains* (see entry) in which Coach Graham Lubbock (Bill Kirchbauer), Mike Seaver's high-school teacher, leaves Long Island to take a job in California, taking wife and eight children with him. By special arrangement, the four oldest daughters are allowed to attend the all-boys academy, causing their father much dismay. The show focused mostly on issues of family relationships, faith, and love.

LA Law
October 3,1986–May 19, 1994
NBC
An hour-long, prime-time dramatic series/soap opera that featured the office politics and adventures of a high-powered Los Angeles law firm. The series combined stories about the stars' professional and romantic lives, often contrasting their powerful positions with their human frailties.

Living Single
August 22, 1993–January 1, 1998
Fox
A half-hour sitcom focusing on the lives of four African American friends living in Brooklyn: Khadijah (Queen Latifah), the editor of *Flavor* magazine for Black women; her cousin Synclaire (Kim Coles), who was also her secretary; her gold-digging childhood friend Regine (Kim Fields Freeman), who worked in a fashion boutique; and her college

friend Maxine (Erika Alexander), a divorce attorney. The show revolved around the professional and dating lives of these four single women.

M*A*S*H
September 17, 1972–September 23, 1983
CBS

An antiwar comedy based on the lives of the men and women of the 4077th Mobile Army Surgical Hospital during the Korean War in the 1950s. The ensemble cast included, among others, Hawkeye Pierce (Alan Alda), Trapper John McIntyre (Wayne Rogers), B.J. Hunnicut (Mike Farrell), Frank Burns (Larry Linville), Margaret "Hot Lips" Houlihan (Loretta Swit), Henry Blake (McLean Stevenson), Colonel Potter (Harry Morgan), "Radar" O'Reilly (Gary Burghoff), and Max Klinger (Jamie Farr). M*A*S*H was based on a motion picture of the same name that, in turn, was based on a novel written by the pseudonymous Richard Hooker, a doctor who served in the Korean War.

Madonna
1958–

Madonna, who has become one of the most popular pop-music icons of the times, moved to New York in 1977 to become a dancer; she started her career performing club and dance music in the 1980s. At the same time, she pursued a film career. She made a documentary of her "Blond Ambition" concert tour. Madonna is known for her controversial lyrics, highly sexualized public persona, and various identity transformations. She has two children, one with her husband, the British film director Guy Ritchie.

Married . . . with Children
April 5, 1987–May 5, 1997
Fox

A very popular half-hour sitcom that ran for ten years, featuring the exaggerated and almost cartoonlike dysfunctional middle-class Bundy family: Al (Ed O'Neill), a beer-swilling, chauvinistic shoe salesman; Peg (Katey Sagal), the spandex-clad, gum-cracking stay-at-home wife; Kelly (Christina Applegate), the sexually promiscuous teenage daughter; and Bud (David Faustino), the sex-starved, "loser" son. The show, set primarily in the Bundy's living room, parodied and commented on typical family sitcoms through exchanges of insults.

Martin
August 27, 1992–August 28, 1997
Fox
A half-hour sitcom that centered on the lives of the young African American professionals Martin (Martin Lawrence), an egotistical talk-show host at a Detroit radio station, and Gina (Tisha Campbell), his girlfriend and later wife, a marketing executive who put up with his antics. Episodes often depicted Martin's resistance to being in a relationship, though he always came around in the end.

The Mary Tyler Moore Show
September 19, 1970–September 3, 1977
CBS
Drawing on the second-wave feminist movement, *The Mary Tyler Moore Show* focused on Mary Richards (Mary Tyler Moore), a single woman who moved to Minneapolis after breaking up with her boyfriend. Initially, the character was to be divorced, but the producers decided that was too risky for 1970s viewers. Mary worked as an assistant producer at a television news station and was interested in getting married and raising a family, but that was not her main focus. Throughout the seasons, the show focused on Mary and her work and personal associates. Despite high ratings, Moore, the show's producer, and her business partner and husband, Grant Tinker, decided to end the show in 1977.

Monroe, Marilyn
1926–1962
Born Norma Jean Mortenson and raised in orphanages and foster homes, Marilyn Monroe became a model in 1946, then moved to Hollywood to become an actor. Her career took off in 1950, and she was promoted by the studios as a highly sexualized blonde. Monroe had a difficult time with her emotional stability and developed a drug addiction. She was dropped from several films because of irresponsibility and ultimately died of a drug overdose in 1962.

Murphy Brown
November 14, 1988–August 10, 1998
CBS
A half-hour sitcom that focused on the activities and personalities at *FYI*, a fictitious TV newsmagazine show based in Washington, D.C. Most

of the action took place at the news studio, where Murphy (Candice Bergen), a high-strung, veteran star reporter, and her coworkers had to contend with breaking stories in the nation's capital. It is evident that, outside of official office titles, Murphy is the ringleader of her coworkers: Miles Silverberg (Grant Shaud), the young producer who, though Murphy's boss, always concedes to her power; Corky Sherwood (Faith Ford), the ditsy but earnest new reporter and former Miss America; Frank Regalbuto), the old-school field reporter; and Jim Dial (Charles Kimbrough), the vapid anchorman. Rounding out the office set are Phil's, the bar where the crew often has lunch or drinks, and Murphy's Georgetown townhouse, also occupied by her permanent housepainter Eldin (Robert Pastorelli), who has trouble finishing his work but is always available as confidant for Murphy. In 1992, the show—and Bergen's character, in particular—were catapulted into the limelight when Vice President Dan Quayle singled her out as an example of America's lack of "family values" for her decision to raise a child as a single parent.

Night Court
January 4, 1984–July 1, 1992
NBC
A half-hour sitcom in which Judge Harry Stone (Harry Anderson) presided over the night court using a bizarre approach to law that was met by an equally bizarre staff. Despite a lot of turnover in the supporting roles in later seasons, Judge Stone continued to deliver unconventional sentences that sometimes worked for the cast of characters who appeared before his bench.

The Outer Limits
September 16, 1963–January 16, 1965
ABC (1963–1965)
Showtime Cable Network (1995–)
A science-fiction anthology series that relies on special effects, costuming, and intriguing plots to make viewers feel uneasy. The show's major theme is that control of the television set lies within the show, not in the viewer—that is, one must relinquish power to participate in the story line. Several well-known actors had guest roles on the original show; Showtime revived the show in syndication in 1995.

Parker Lewis Can't Lose
September 2, 1990–August 22, 1993
Fox
A half-hour youth comedy chronicling the exploits of Parker Lewis (Corin Nemec), a well-connected and resourceful student at suburban Santo-Domingo High School, and his one-dimensional friends. Parker seemed able to do almost anything—and never got caught. His trademark line was that, whatever the situation, it was "not a problem" for Parker Lewis. Unusual camera angles, special visual effects, and a high-school set with television screens in the hallways and classrooms gave the sitcom a surreal, cartoonlike character.

Party of Five
September 12, 1994–May 3, 2000
Fox
An hour-long drama about five siblings growing up together in San Francisco after their parents die in a car accident. The oldest brother, Charlie Salinger (Matthew Fox), managed the family restaurant and raised siblings Julia (Neve Campbell), Bailey (Scott Wolf), Claudia (Lacey Chabert), and Owen (Brandon and Taylor Porter, 1995–98; Jacob Smith, 1998–2000). Over the show's six-year run, the Salinger family dealt with various "real-life" issues, such as teen pregnancy, drug abuse, the college-application process, dating, breakups, marriage, and sibling rivalry.

Pasionara
Venevision
The Venezuelan "tele-novella" *Pasionara* ran for 254 episodes on the Spanish cable station UniVision. The plot revolved around an affair between the independent, free-willed Barbara Santana (Catherine Fullop) and the traditional, methodical, married Jesus Alberto (Fernando Carrillo). The show touched on themes of conflicting social classes and the struggle between living standards and the human social and economic condition in a Latin American country. Despite its popular themes, *Pasionara* was not a highly successful soap opera and was terminated after its initial run.

Powerpuff Girls
November 19, 1998–
Cartoon Network
Created by the cartoonist Craig McCracken, this animated series featured three flying girls—Blossom, Buttercup, and Bubbles—who, under the mentorship of Professor Utonium, worked to keep the town of Townsville free of danger. According to the show's premise, Professor Utonium was trying to create three perfect little girls but accidentally added the powerful Chemical X. Instead of sweet, girly-girls, he got three cute but tough superheroes.

Pryor, Richard
1940–
The comedian, actor, screenwriter, and producer Pryor, the only child of a prostitute mother, dropped out of school at fourteen and began working on his comedy at community centers. A guest spot on *The Ed Sullivan Show* in 1966 introduced him to a national audience; his act included commentary on racial injustice. In the late 1960s, Pryor became a heavy drug and alcohol abuser, which lasted for twenty years. Despite his addiction, he had tremendous professional success. In 1986, he acknowledged that he has multiple sclerosis and no longer performs publicly.

Quantum Leap
March 26, 1989–August 15, 1993
Fox
In this hour-long dramatic series, Sam Beckett (Scott Bakula) traveled through time with the ability to "leap" in and out of other bodies. In his travels, Beckett assumed the identities of others in order to influence history. (In the show, the course of an individual's life could be altered, but major historical events could not.) Beckett was aided by Al (Dean Stockwell), a holographic sidekick who was visible only to Sam. Because Sam was ignorant of his duties on arrival, Al guided him with the aid of a computer, giving him clues about his new identity as well as about the others around him. Once inside a body, Beckett appeared as that individual, but to the TV viewing audience he still looked like himself. The series dealt with a range of topics, including racism, prejudice against the handicapped, Vietnam, single parenthood, and prostitution, via the perspective of seeing life through someone else's eyes.

Rather, Dan
1931–
Dan Rather, born in 1931 in Texas and educated at Sam Houston State Teachers College, where he also taught. He began his journalism career in 1950 and joined the CBS News organization in 1962. Since then, he has covered many national and international news stories. He anchors the *CBS Evening News* and the news program *48 Hours*. He is also a correspondent for *60 Minutes II*.

Roc
August 24, 1991–May 10, 1994
Fox
The short-lived sitcom *Roc* told the story of the lives of the working-class Emerson family in Baltimore. The cast included Roc Emerson (Charles Dutton), his wife (Ella Joyce), his brother (Rocky Carroll), and his father (Carl Gordon). The show was known for its strong writing, directing, and acting, especially in its portrayal of the Emerson family as a normal, hardworking African American family, but nevertheless lasted only a short while on TV.

Roseanne
October 18, 1988–May 20, 1997
ABC
A half-hour sitcom that focused on the blue-collar Connor family firmly run by the matriarch Roseanne (Roseanne). The cast also included husband Dan (John Goodman), a sometimes employed home contractor, and children Becky (Lecy Goranson 1988–92 and 1995–97; Sarah Chalke 1993–95), the smart, well-behaved oldest daughter; Darlene (Sara Gilbert), the tomboy middle child; and D. J. (Michael Fishman), the youngest. Jackie (Laurie Metcalf), Roseanne's younger sister, also lived in the area and spent most of her time with the Connors. As the series developed, it focused on the precarious employment of the Connor parents and the growth of the children, dealing realistically with the difficulties of a working-class family and how they relied on one another for love and support no matter what the rest of the world tossed their way.

Rowan and Martin's Laugh-In
January 22, 1968–May 14, 1973
NBC
An hour-long, free-form comedy show that was known for its vaudeville-style shtick and fast-paced humor. It was hosted by the comedians Dick Rowan and Dan Martin, and regular guest performers included the now famous Richard Dawson, Goldie Hawn, and Lily Tomlin. Guest stars such as Johnny Carson; Sammy Davis, Jr.; Zsa Zsa Gabor; and John Wayne also appeared on the show. President Richard Nixon also made a cameo appearance, speaking the line that the show made famous: "Sock it to me!" *Laugh-In* had high ratings throughout its tenure on TV and continued to be aired in syndication after it ended in 1973.

Saved By the Bell
August 20, 1989–September 4, 1993
NBC
A Saturday-morning sitcom that focused on the daily lives of a group of high-school students in California that, over time, gained a regular following and was shown in syndication as well as an occasional prime-time special. The cast included Zack Morris (Mark-Paul Gosselaar), the leader and a crafty but essentially good kid; A. C. Slater (Mario Lopez), a jock; Kelly Kapowski (Tiffani-Amber Thiessen), a cheerleader; Jessie Spano (Elizabeth Berkeley), a smart feminist; Lisa Turtle (Lark Voorhies), a "shopaholic"; and "Screech" (Dustin Diamond), a stereotypical geek who earned his nickname from his annoying voice. The show rarely focused on the characters' lives outside school; instead, it took place mostly in the hallways of the high school and at a nearby diner.

Seinfeld
May 31, 1990–September 10, 1998
NBC
A half-hour sitcom based on the lives of four self-centered friends living in New York City: Jerry (Jerry Seinfeld), a standup comedian; Elaine (Julia Louis-Dreyfus), Jerry's former girlfriend; George (Jason Alexander), Jerry's neurotic best friend; and Kramer (Michael Richards), the wacky neighbor. Frequently called a "show about nothing," *Seinfeld* focused on the humor and triviality of everyday life: episodes dealt with subjects such as the frustration involved in waiting for a table at a crowded restaurant or losing a car in a mall's parking lot.

The Simpsons
December 17, 1989–
Fox
Created by the cartoonist Matt Groening, the long-running, half-hour prime-time comedy *The Simpsons* focuses on the working-class cartoon Simpson family: Homer, the bumbling father; Marge, the blue-haired, well-meaning mother; Bart, the fourth-grade troublemaker and proud underachiever; Lisa, the prodigy middle child; and Maggie, the permanently pacifier-sucking infant. Homer works at a nearby nuclear-power plant but prefers guzzling beer with his buddies to his job. Although Homer rarely takes responsibility for his actions, or even tries to accomplish much, his family is renowned and the recipient of many awards and honors based mostly on dumb luck and coincidental accidents. The show manages to get away with its sarcastic humor and anarchic message largely because it is a cartoon that children enjoy but is intellectually appreciated by adults.

The Supremes
1961–
The Supremes rose out of Detroit poverty to become one of the most successful Motown groups of the 1960s. Diana Ross, Florence Ballard, and Mary Wilson made The Supremes the most popular female group of their time. In June 1965, they set the record for the most consecutive number-one hits with "Back in My Arms." By 1965, the group was known as Diana Ross and the Supremes. In 1969, Ross left the group to pursue a solo career, but on occasion the trio still worked together.

Tales from the Crypt
June 10, 1989–January 3, 1996
Fox/HBO
Hosted by the Cryptkeeper (John Kassir), *Tales from the Crypt* was a horror anthology series featuring a wide range of made-for-television ghoul stories. The show was based on stories that originally appeared in a 1950s magazine of the same title. The Cryptkeeper, a talking skeleton who appeared to enjoy the horror, introduced each episode. The show originated as an HBO cable program in 1991; Fox began to broadcast reruns in 1994. Cast members were generally unknown actors, but well-known personalities sometimes played small roles.

The Temptations
1961–
The Temptations began as a quintet in 1961 in the Detroit Motown scene but did not receive critical and popular success until 1964. Between 1964 and 1968, the group released a lineup of classic Motown hits. In the late 1960s, the Temptations began making psychedelic music. The group underwent several lineup and style changes from the 1970s to the 1990s, but the Temptations continue to make music.

3rd Rock from the Sun
January 9, 1996–May 22, 2001
NBC
A bizarre half-hour sitcom about four aliens sent to Earth (the "3rd Rock") to investigate its life forms. The aliens take the form of members of the eccentric Solomon family during their stay on Earth, with the "High Commander" becoming Dick (John Lithgow), a physics professor who falls in love with fellow professor (and real-life human) Dr. Albright (Jane Curtain). The second in command, a male lieutenant, becomes Sally, a sexy and self-determined woman; the two other aliens become Harry (French Stewart) and Tommy (Joseph Gordon-Levitt). As the aliens learn about the ways of life on Earth, the constructed nature of morality, tradition, and convention in everyday life are brought to light.

Tiny Toons Adventures
1990–1992
Syndicated
An afternoon cartoon series that featured classic Warner Brothers cartoon characters in smaller, younger versions. The characters included Buster and Babs Bunny and Plucky Duck.

True Colors
September 2, 1990–August 23, 1992
Fox
A half-hour sitcom about the marriage between Ron (Frankie Faison, 1990–91; Cleavon Little, 1991–92), a widowed African American dentist with two sons, and Ellen (Stephanie Faracy), a divorced, Caucasian teacher with a daughter. Joining them in their new life together was Ellen's mother, Sara (Nancy Walker), an opinionated woman who did not think highly of Ron but softened toward her new grandchildren.

21 Jump Street
April 12, 1987–September 17, 1990
Fox
An hour-long police drama that revolved around four young Los Angeles police officers working in a special unit to fight crime in schools. In this capacity, the main characters—Officers Hanson (Johnny Depp), Penhall (Peter DeLuise), Hoffs (Holly Robinson), and Truman (Dustin Nguyen)—went undercover each week as high-school students to arrest criminals involved in school-based crimes such as drug dealing, gangs, and prostitution. They were led by Captain Adam Fuller (Steven Williams), who met the undercover officers in an abandoned church at 21 Jump Street.

The Twilight Zone
1959–1965; 1985–1987
CBS
The playwright Rod Serling started, and originally hosted and wrote, this science-fiction anthology series. The surreal outer-world or moral tales usually usually contained a moral or ironic twist. Although well-known actors appeared on the show, it was the stories' focus on the "fifth dimension beyond that which is known to man" that made *The Twilight Zone* popular. The show initially ran from 1959 to 1965; it was remade in 1985, following the 1983 release of the *Twilight Zone* movie. The 1980s' *Twilight Zone* series remade many of the original episodes and created new stories in color and using elaborate special effects.

Welcome Freshman
1991–93
Nickelodeon
The show began as a sketch comedy focusing on the typical lives of five freshmen who used humor to deal being first-years students. The show shifted as the characters moved to the next grade. As a situation comedy, the show covered all the years of school at Hawthorne High in Anytown, USA.

Who's the Boss?
September 20, 1984–September 10, 1992
ABC
A half-hour sitcom about a widower, Tony Micelli (Tony Danza), and his young daughter, Samantha (Alyssa Milano), who leave the congestion of

New York City to move to Connecticut, where Tony finds work as a housekeeper for the advertising executive Angela Bower (Judith Glass) and her son, Jonathan (Danny Pintauro). The Bowers live in a large suburban house, and Angela's mother, Mona (Katherine Helman), a wildly liberal contrast to her practical, conservative daughter, lives nearby. The show focused on the mid-1980s' acceptance of gender-role reversal, with Tony staying at home, cleaning and cooking, while Angela worked.

Winfrey, Oprah
1954–
Born in 1954 in Kosciusko, Mississippi, Oprah Winfrey became the first African American news anchor in Nashville, Tennessee, in 1972. In 1984, she began hosting WLS-TV's *AM Chicago;* within a month, it had become the top-rated talk show in its market. Less than a year later, the show expanded to a one-hour format and was renamed *The Oprah Winfrey Show.* In 1986, *The Oprah Winfrey Show* went into syndication, and it held the number-one spot nationally for fourteen seasons. Winfrey also has starred in movies and television specials; launched a book club, magazine, and Website; and publicly speaks out for healthy lifestyles and against child abuse, among other social-justice movements. She recently renewed the contract for *The Oprah Winfrey Show* as host and producer through 2004.

The Wizard of Oz
1939
Based on the story by Frank Baum (1900), the movie *The Wizard of Oz* tells the fantastical tale of Dorothy (Judy Garland), who gets caught up in a Kansas tornado and lands in the world of Oz. To return to Kansas, Dorothy must ask the Wizard's permission and sets off on her quest with her dog Toto, the Scarecrow (Ray Bolger), the Tin Man (Jack Haley), and the Cowardly Lion (Bert Lauer), battling the Wicked Witch of the West (Margaret Hamilton) in the process. The film was nominated in 1939 for an Academy Award for Best Picture and was first broadcast on television in November 1956. *The Wizard of Oz* is believed to be the most watched film of all times.

The Wonder Years
March 15, 1988–September 1, 1993
ABC
A half-hour series that looked nostalgically at suburban life in the late 1960s through the eyes of the twelve-year-old protagonist, Kevin

Arnold (Fred Savage), with an off-camera voice (Daniel Stern) providing narration as Kevin in middle age. Kevin lived with his earnest but distant father (Dan Lauria); stay-at-home, politically innocent mother (Alley Mills); and two siblings, Wayne (Jason Hervey), the terrorizing older brother, and Karen (Olivia d'Abo), the hippie older sister. Although the show explicitly followed Kevin's growth and development through junior high and high school, it also touched on influential historical events.

The X-Files
September 10, 1993–
Fox
An hour-long science-fiction drama that follows Agents Mulder (David Duchovny) and Scully (Gillian Anderson) as they investigate the FBI's "X-Files"—cases that deal with unnatural phenomena. Scully and Mulder investigate oddities such as alien abduction, UFO sightings, cloned and genetically altered beings, and life-size parasites. Underlying the show is the theme that a hidden extraterrestrial world exists that is being kept secret by the government.

X-Men
October 31, 1992–
Fox
A half-hour cartoon series that features typical good-versus-evil tales with a twist: the superheroes are mutant adolescents. Based on the Marvel comic books of the same name, the television show centers on eight students—the Beast, Cyclops, Gambit, Jean Grey, Jubilee, Rogue, Storm, and Wolverine—who attend a school for mutants and are taught by Professor Charles Xavier, who named the octet "the X-Men." Together, they battle arch-villain Magneto.

Sources

The information for this section was drawn from a range of sources, from published books to fan-created Websites. As of December 2001, all of the Web sources were active. Although fan-based sites often move or cease to exist, some of the information, particular about older, short-lived television shows, was found only on such sites.

Websites

<http://www.johnsrealmonline.com/classicnick.index.html>
<http://bamboozledmovie.com>
<http://www.biography.com>
<http://www.cbsnews.com>
<http://geocities.com/Vienna/1864/borge.htm>
<http://lcweb.loc.gov/exhibits/oz>
<http://members.aol.com/rexfelis>
<http://msnbc.com/onair/bios/t_brokaw.asp>
<http://www.oprah.com>
<http://pbs.org/newshour/bb/entertainment/donahue.html>
<http://www.rockhall.com>
<http://www.rollingstone.com>
<http://sitcomsonline.com>
<http://yahoo.com> (see music pages)
<http://zianet.com/jjohnson/oz.htm>

Texts

Brooks, T., and E. Marsh. 1995. *The Complete Directory to Prime Time Network and Cable TV Shows*, 6th ed. New York: Ballantine Books.

Newcomb, Harris, ed. 1997. *Encyclopedia of Television, Volume 1*. Chicago: Fitzroy Dearborn Publishers, s.v. "CNN" (pp. 271–72); s.v. *"Dallas"* (pp. 453–55); s.v. *"Pee Wee's Playhouse"* (pp. 1237–39);

Hands, Cynthia. 2000. *The Powerpuff Girls: Girl Power.* New York: Golden Book.

"Herman's Head." 1991. *TV Guide* (September 14), 19.

Jarvis, Jeff. 1992. "The Couch Critic." *TV Guide* (December 5), 10.

McNeil, A. 1996. *Total Television: The Comprehensive Guide to Programming for 1948 to the Present*, 4th ed. New York: Penguin Books.

"Roc." 1991. *TV Guide* (September 14), 18.

"Save Our Shows!" 1992. *TV Guide* (April 11), 8–15

Programming Departments

ABC Programming Department
CBS Programming Department
Fox Programming Department
NBC Programming Department
Nickelodeon Series Descriptions, *Welcome Freshmen*
Venevision Series Descriptions, *Pasionara*

Works Cited

Alexander, A., and M. A. Morrison. 1995. "Electronic Toyland and the Structures of Power: An Analysis of Critical Studies on Children as Consumers." *Critical Studies in Mass Communication* 12, no. 3 (September): 344–53.

Amit-Talai, V. 1995. "Conclusion: The Multi-cultural of Youth." In *Youth Cultures: A Cross-Cultural Perspective*, ed. V. Amit-Talai and H. Wulff. London: Routledge.

Anderson, D. R., and P. A Collins. 1988. "The Impact on Children's Education: Television's Influence on Cognitive Development." Working paper no. 2, U.S. Department of Education, Office of Educational Research and Improvement (April).

Ang, I. 1990. "The Nature of the Audience." Pp. 207–20 in *Questioning the Media*, ed. J. Downing, A. Mohammadi, and A. S. Mohammadi. Thousand Oaks, Calif.: Sage Publications.

Bagdikian, B. H. 1992. *The Media Monopoly*, 4th ed. Boston: Beacon Press.

Barker, M. 1984. *A Haunt of Fears*. London: Pluto.

Barnouw, E. 1977 (1975). *Tube of Plenty: The Evolution of American Television*. London: Oxford University Press.

———. 1978. *The Sponsor*. Oxford: Oxford University Press.

Bazelgette, C. 1997. "An Agenda for the Second Phase of Media Literacy Development." Pp. 69–78 in *Media Literacy in the Information Age: Current Perspectives*, ed. R. Kubey. New Brunswick, N.J.: Transaction Publishers.

Benhabib, S. 1992. *Situating the Self: Gender, Community and Postmodernism in Contemporary Ethics*. Cambridge: Polity Press.

Berger, P. L., and T. Luckman. 1967 (1966). *The Social Construction of Reality*. New York: Anchor Books.

Berman, E. 1988. "Survey on Children and Television." *Working Mother* (November), 126.

Blumer, Herbert. 1933. *Movies and Conduct*. New York: Macmillan.

Brown, B. B. 1990. "Peer Groups and Peer Cultures." Pp. 171–96 in *At the Threshold: The Developing Adolescent*, ed. S. S. Feldman and G. R. Elliott. Cambridge, Mass.: Harvard University Press.

Brown, J. D., C. R. Dykers, J. R. Steele, and A. B. White. 1994. "Teenage Room Culture: Where Media and Identities Intersect." *Communication Research* 21, no. 6 (December): 813–27.

Bruner, J. 1986. *Actual Minds, Possible Worlds.* Cambridge, Mass.: Harvard University Press.

Buckingham, D. 1993. *Children Talking Television: The Making of Television Literacy.* London: Falmer Press.

———. 2000. *After the Death of Childhood: Growing Up in the Age of Electronic Media.* Cambridge: Polity Press.

Buckingham, D., and J. Sefton-Greene. 1994. "'Hardcore Rappin': Popular Music, Identity and Critical Discourse." Pp. 60–83 in *Cultural Studies Goes to School.* London: Taylor and Francis.

Carter, B. 1992a. "CBS in First Place of Ratings Race for Year." *New York Times* (April 15), C22.

———. 1992b. "In the Huxtable World, Parents Knew Best." *New York Times* (April 26), H1, H33.

Chin, E. 1993. "Not of Whole Cloth Made: The Consumer Environment of Children," *Children's Environments* 10, no. 1: 72–84.

Clark, L. 1998. "Dating on the Net: Teens and the Rise of 'Pure' Relationships." Pp. 159–83 in *Cybersociety 2.0: Revisiting Computer Mediated Communication and Community,* ed. S. Jones. Thousand Oaks, Calif.: Sage Publications.

Cole, M., and S. R. Cole. 1993. *The Development of Children,* 2nd ed. New York: Scientific American Books.

Comer, J. P., and A. F. Pouissaint. 1993. *Raising Black Children.* New York: Plume.

Comstock, G. 1980. *Television in America.* Beverly Hills, Calif.: Sage Publications.

———. 1993. "The Medium and the Society: The Role of Television in American Life." Pp. 117–31 in *Children and Television: Images in a Changing Sociocultural World,* ed. G. L. Berry and J. K. Asamen. Newbury Park, Calif.: Sage Publications.

Courtney, T. 1992. "Early Adolescent Males' Use of Comic Book Super Heroes as Ego Ideals." Master's thesis, Smith College School of Social Work, Northampton, Mass.

Csikszentmihalyi, M., and R. Larson. 1984. *Being Adolescent: Conflict and Growth in the Teenage Years.* New York: Basic Books.

D'Andrade, R. G. 1992. "Schemas and Motivation." Pp. 23–44 in *Human Motives and Cultural Models,* ed. R. D'Andrade and C. Strauss. Cambridge, Mass.: Cambridge University Press.

Davies, M. M. 1996. *Fake Fact and Fantasy: Children's Interpretations of Television Reality.* Mahwah, N.J.: Lawrence Erlbaum Associates.

Dillard, J. L. 1972. *Black English.* New York: Random House.

DiMaggio, P. 1991. "Cultural Entrepreneurship in Nineteenth-Century Boston: The Creation of an Organizational Base for High Culture in America." Pp. 374–97 in *Rethinking Popular Culture: Contemporary Perspectives in Cultural Studies,* ed. C. Mukerji and M. Schudson. Berkeley: University of California Press.

Dyson, A. H. 1993. *Social Worlds of Children Learning to Write in an Urban Primary School.* New York: Teachers College Press.

————. 1994. "The Ninjas, the X-Men, and the Ladies: Playing with Power and Identity in an Urban Primary School." *Teachers College Record* 96, no. 2 (Winter): 219–39.

————. 1997. *Writing Superheroes: The Social and Ideological Dynamics of Child Writing.* New York: Teachers College Press.

Eisenhart, M. 1995. "The Fax, the Jazz Player, and the Self-Story Teller: How Do People Organize Culture?" *Anthropology and Education Quarterly* 26, no. 1: 3–26.

Emerson, C., and M. Holquist, eds. 1981. *The Dialogic Imagination: Four Essays by M. Bakhtin.* Austin: University of Texas Press.

Erenberg, L. A. 1981. *Steppin' Out: New York Nightlife and the Transformation of American Culture, 1890–1930.* Chicago: University of Chicago Press.

Erickson, F. 1982. "Taught Cognitive Learning in Its Immediate Environments: A Neglected Topic in the Anthropology of Education." *Anthropology and Education Quarterly* 13, no. 2: 149–80.

Erikson, E. H. 1980 (1959). *Identity and the Life Cycle.* New York: W. W. Norton.

Fabrikant, G. 1996. "The Young and the Restless Audience." *New York Times* (April 8), D1, D8.

Faludi, S. 1991. *Backlash: The Undeclared War Against American Women.* New York: Crown Publishers.

Feldman, S. S., and G. R. Elliott, eds. 1990. *At the Threshold: The Developing Adolescent.* Cambridge, Mass.: Harvard University Press.

Fine, G. A. 1987. *With the Boys: Little League Baseball and Preadolescent Culture.* Chicago: University of Chicago Press.

Fine, G. A., J. T. Mortimer, and D. F. Roberts. 1990. "Leisure, Work, and the Mass Media." Pp. 225–52 in *At the Threshold: The Developing Adolescent,* ed. S. S. Feldman and G. R. Elliott. Cambridge, Mass.: Harvard University Press.

Fisherkeller, J. 1995. "Identity Work and Television: Young Adolescents Learning in Local and Mediated Cultures." Ph.D. diss., University of California, Berkeley.

————. 1997. "Everyday Learning About Identities Among Young Adolescents in TV Culture." *Anthropology and Education Quarterly* 28, no. 4 (December): 467–92.

————. 1999. "Learning About Power and Success: Young Adolescents Interpret TV Culture." *Communication Review* 3, no. 3 (Summer): 187–212.

————. 2000. "'The Writers Are Getting Kind of Desperate': Young Adolescents, Television, and Literacy." *Journal of Adolescent and Adult Literacy* 43, no. 7 (April): 596–606.

Fiske, J. 1987. *Television Culture.* London: Routledge.

————. 1992. "British Cultural Studies." Pp. 284–326 in *Channels of Discourse, Reassembled: Television and Contemporary Criticism,* ed. R. C. Allen. Chapel Hill: University of North Carolina Press.

Frank, L., and P. Smith, eds. 1993. *Madonnarama: Essays on Sex and Popular Culture.* Pittsburgh: Cleis Press.

Frith, S. 1981."Youth and Music." Pp. 202–34 in *Sound Effects: Youth, Leisure, and the Politics of Rock 'n' Roll.* New York: Pantheon Books.

Gandy, O. H., Jr. 1990. "Tracking the Audience: Personal Information and Privacy." Pp. 166–79 in *Questioning the Media,* ed. J. Downing, A. Mohammadi, and A. S. Mohammadi. Thousand Oaks, Calif.: Sage Publications.

Geertz, C. 1973. *The Interpretation of Cultures.* New York: Basic Books.

———. 1983. *Local Knowledge: Further Essays in Interpretive Anthropology.* New York: Basic Books.

Gerbner, G., L. Gross, M. Morgan, and N. Signorielli. 1980. "The Mainstreaming of America." *Journal of Communication* 30, no. 3: 12–29.

———. 1986. "Living with Television: The Dynamics of the Cultivation Process." Pp. 17–40 in *Perspectives on Media Effects,* ed. D. Zillman and J. Bryant. Hillsdale, N.J.: Lawrence Erlbaum Associates.

———. 1994. "Growing Up with Television: The Cultivation Perspective." Pp. 17–42 in *Media Effects: Advances in Theory and Research,* ed. J. Bryant and D. Zillman. Hillsdale, N.J.: Lawrence Erlbaum Associates.

Gergen, K. J. 1991.*The Saturated Self: Dilemmas of Identity in Contemporary Life.* New York: Basic Books.

Gilligan, C. 1993. *In a Different Voice: Psychological Theory and Women's Development,* 2nd ed. Cambridge, Mass.: Harvard University Press.

Giddens, A. 1991. *Modernity and Self-Identity: Self and Society in the Late Modern Age.* Stanford, Calif.: Stanford University Press.

Giroux, H. A., and R. I. Simon. 1989. *Popular Culture, Schooling, and Everyday Life.* Granby, Mass: Bergin and Garvey Publishers.

Gitlin, T. 1985 (1983). *Inside Prime Time,* 2nd ed. New York: Pantheon Books.

Gitlin, T., ed. 1986. "Introduction: Looking Through the Screen." Pp. 3–8 in *Watching Television.* New York: Pantheon Books.

Goffman, E. 1959. *The Presentation of Self in Everyday Life.* New York: Anchor.

Goodenough, W. 1981. *Culture, Language, and Society,* 2nd ed. Menlo Park, Calif.: Benjamin Cummings Publishing.

Gray, H. 1995. *Watching Race: Television and the Struggle for "Blackness."* Minneapolis: University of Minnesota Press.

Hall, S. 1980. *Culture, Media, Language.* Working Papers in Cultural Studies, 1972–79, Centre for Contemporary Cultural Studies. London: Hutchinson and Company.

Hansen, D. A. 1986. "Family–School Articulations: The Effects of Interaction Rule Mismatch." *American Educational Research Journal* 23, no. 4 (Winter): 643–59.

———. 1993. "The Child in Family and School: Agency and the Workings of Time." Pp. 69–102 in *Family, Self and Society: Towards a New Agenda for Family Research,* ed. P. Cowan, D. Field, D. A. Hansen, A. Skolnick, and G. Swanson. Hillsdale, NJ: Lawrence Erlbaum Press.

Hansen, D. A., J. E. Fisherkeller, and V. Johnson. 1995. "The Hidden Persistence of Immigrant 'Drop Outs': Distortions, Blank Spots and Blind Spots in Research on Schooling Careers." *International Journal of Educational Research* 23, no. 1: 83–105.

Hartley, J. 1983. "Television and the Power of Dirt." *Australian Journal of Cultural Studies* 1, no. 2: 62–82.

Heath, S. B. 1983.*Ways with Words: Language, Life and Work in Communities and Classrooms.* Cambridge, Mass.: Cambridge University Press.

Heath, S. B., and M. W. McLaughlin, eds. 1993. *Identity and Inner-City Youth: Beyond Ethnicity and Gender.* New York: Teachers College Press.

Hebdige, D. 1979. *Subculture: The Meaning of Style*. London: Methuen.

Honess, T., and K. Yardley. 1987. *Self and Identity: Perspectives Across the Lifespan*. London: Routledge and Kegan Paul.

Jagtenberg, T. 1994. "Lost and Found: Dialectics of Self and Identity." Paper presented at the Annual Conference of the International Communication Association, Sydney, July 11–15.

Jameson, F. 1991 (1983). "Postmodernism and Consumer Society." Pp. 111–25 in *The Anti-Aesthetic: Essays on Postmodern Culture*, ed. H. Foster. Seattle: Bay Press.

Jenkins, H. 1992. *Textual Poachers: Television Fans and Participatory Culture*. New York and London: Routledge.

Kakutani, M. 1992. "Madonna Writes; Academics Explore Her Erotic Semiotics." *New York Times* (October 21), C21.

Kellner, D. 1990. "Advertising and Consumer Culture." Pp. 242–54 in *Questioning the Media*, ed. J. Downing, A. Mohammadi, and A. S. Mohammadi. Thousand Oaks, Calif.: Sage Publications.

———. 1992. "Popular Culture and the Construction of Postmodern Identities." Pp. 141–77 in *Modernity and Identity*, ed. S. Lash and J. Friedman. Oxford: Blackwell.

Kinder, M., ed. 1999. *Kids' Media Culture*. Durham, N.C.: Duke University Press.

Klapper, J. T. 1960. *The Effects of Mass Communication*. Glencoe, Ill.: Free Press.

Kline, S. 1993. *Out of the Garden: Toys and Children's Culture in the Age of TV Marketing*. London: Verso.

Kubey, R., and M. Csikszentmihalyi. 1990. *Television and the Quality of Life: How Viewing Shapes Everyday Experience*. Hillsdale, N.J.: Lawrence Erlbaum Associates.

Lees, S. 1993. *Sugar and Spice: Sexuality and Adolescent Girls*. London: Penguin Books.

Leichter, H. J., ed. 1979. *Families and Communites as Educators*. New York: Teachers College Press.

Lembo, R. 1997. "Situating Television in Everyday Life: Reformulating a Cultural Studies Approach to the Study of Television Use." Pp. 203–33 in *From Sociology to Cultural Studies: New Perspectives*, ed. E. Long. Oxford: Blackwell Publishers.

———. 2000. *Thinking Through Television: Viewing Culture and the Social Limits to Power*. Cambridge: Cambridge University Press.

Lewis, L. 1990. *Gender Politics and MTV: Voicing the Difference*. Philadelphia: Temple University Press.

Liebert, R. M., and J. Sprafkin. 1988. *The Early Window: Effects of Television on Children and Youth*, 3rd ed. New York: Pergamon Press.

Liebes, T., and E. Katz. 1990. *The Export of Meaning: Cross Cultural Readings of Dallas*. Oxford: Oxford University Press.

Lipsitz, G. 1990. *Time Passages: Collective Memory and American Popular Culture*. Minneapolis: University of Minnesota Press.

Littwin, M. 1990. "Pumping Up Trouble: Sports Stars Shouldn't Promote Sneakers Kids Can't Afford." *San Francisco Chronicle* (February 26), D1, D7.

Livingstone, S. 1994. "Watching Talk: Gender and Engagement in the Viewing of Audience Discussion Programmes." *Media, Culture, and Society* 16, no. 3: 429–47.

Lull, J. 1982, "How Families Select Television Programs: A Mass-Observational Study." *Journal of Broadcasting* 26: 801–12.

———. 1990. *Inside Family Viewing: Ethnographic Research on Television's Audiences.* London: Comedia and Routledge.

Madonna. 1992. *Sex.* New York: Warner Books.

Markus, H., and P. Nurius. 1987. "Possible Selves: The Interface Between Motivation and Self-Concept." Pp. 157–72 in *Self and Identity: Psychosocial Perspectives,* ed. K. Yardley and T. Honess. Chichester, U.K.: John Wiley and Sons.

McRobbie, A. 1992. "Post-Marxism and Cultural Studies." Pp. 719–30 in *Cultural Studies,* ed. L. Grossberg, C. Nelson, and P. Treichler. New York: Routledge.

———. 1994. *Postmodernism and Popular Culture.* London: Routledge.

Mead, G. H. 1962 (1934). *Mind, Self, and Society,* ed. Charles W. Morris. Chicago: University of Chicago Press.

Means Coleman, R. 2000. *African American Viewers and the Black Situation Comedy: Situating Racial Humor.* New York: Garland.

Medrich, E. A., J. A. Roizen, V. Rubin, and S. Buckley. 1982. *The Serious Business of Growing Up: A Study of Children's Lives Outside School.* Berkeley: University of Californa Press.

Meyrowitz, J. 1985. *No Sense of Place: The Impact of Electronic Media on Social Behavior.* New York: Oxford University Press.

Miller, M. C. 1988. *Boxed In: The Culture of TV.* Evanston, Ill.: Northwestern University Press.

———. 1996. "The National Entertainment State." *The Nation* (June 3), 9–32.

Morley, D. 1988 (1986). *Family Television: Cultural Power and Domestic Leisure.* London: Comedia and Routledge.

———. 1989. "Changing Paradigms in Audience Studies." Pp. 16–43 in *Remote Control: Television, Audiences, and Cultural Power,* ed. E. Seiter, H. Borchers, G. Kreutzner, and E. Warth. London: Routledge.

———. 1992. *Television, Audiences and Cultural Studies.* London: Routledge.

Murdock, G., and G. Phelps. 1973. *Mass Media and the Secondary School.* London: Macmillan.

Nava, M., and O. Nava. 1990. "Discriminating or Duped? Young People as Consumers of Advertising/Art." *Magazine of Cultural Studies,* no. 1: 15–21.

Newman, M. 1995. "Essentials Become Luxuries as Schools Cope with Budget Cuts." *New York Times* (January 16), B1–B2.

Ogbu, J. U. 1985. "Research Currents: Cultural–Ecological Influences on Minority School Learning." *Language Arts* 62, no. 8: 860–68.

Paley, V. G. 1992. *You Can't Say You Can't Play.* Cambridge, Mass.: Harvard University Press.

Palmer, P. 1986. *The Lively Audience.* Sydney: Allen and Unwin.

Pastor, J., J. McCormick, and M. Fine. 1996. "Makin' Homes: An Urban Girl Thing." Pp. 15–34 in *Urban Adolescent Girls,* ed. B. Leadbetter and N. Way. Philadelphia: Temple University Press.

Pitman, M. A., R. A. Eisikovits, and M. L. Dobbert. 1989. *Culture Acquisition: A Holistic Approach to Human Learning.* New York: Praeger.

Postman, N. 1985. *Amusing Ourselves to Death: Public Discourse in the Age of Show Business.* New York: Penguin Books.

Press, A. L. 1991. *Women Watching Television: Gender, Class, and Generation in the American Television Experience.* Philadelphia: University of Pennsylvania Press.

Provenzo, E. F., Jr. 1991. *Video Kids: Making Sense of Nintendo.* Cambridge, Mass.: Harvard University Press.

Reeves, B., and M. M. Miller. 1978. "A Multidimensional Measure of Children's Identification with Television Characters." *Journal of Broadcasting* 22, no. 1 (Winter): 71–86.

Roberts, D. F. 2000. "Media and Youth: Access, Exposure, and Privatization." *Journal of Adolescent Health* 27S, no. 2:8–14.

Savin-Williams, R. C., and T. J. Berndt. 1990. "Friendships and Peer Relations." Pp. 277–307 in *At the Threshold: The Developing Adolescent,* ed. S. S. Feldman and G. R. Elliott. Cambridge, Mass.: Harvard University Press.

Saxe, J. 1994. "Violence in Video Games: What Are the Pleasures?" Paper presented at the International Conference on Violence in the Media, St. John's University, New York, October 3.

Schiller, H. I. 1989. *Culture, Inc.: The Corporate Takeover of Public Expression.* New York: Oxford University Press.

Schwichtenberg, C., ed. 1992. *The Madonna Connection: Representational Politics, Subcultural Identities and Cultural Theory.* Boulder, Colo.: Westview Press.

Seiter, E. 1993. *Sold Separately: Parents and Children in Consumer Culture,* New Brunswick, N.J.: Rutgers University Press.

———. 1999. *Television and New Media Audiences.* Oxford: Clarendon Press.

Sefton-Green, J., ed. 1998. *Digital Diversions: Youth Culture in the Age of Multimedia.* London: UCL Press.

Sennet, R., and J. Cobb. 1973. *The Hidden Injuries of Class.* New York: Vintage Books.

Signorielli, N. 1993. "Television, the Portrayal of Women, and Children's Attitudes." Pp. 229–42 in *Children and Television: Images in a Changing Sociocultural World,* ed. G. L. Berry and J. K. Asamen. Newbury Park, Calif.: Sage Publications.

Simpson, P., ed. 1987. *Parents Talking Television: Television in the Home.* London: Comedia Publishing Group.

Smitherman, G. 1977. *Talkin and Testifyin.* Boston: Houghton Mifflin.

Steinberg, L. 1990. "Autonomy, Conflict, and Harmony in the Family Relationship." Pp. 255–76 in *At the Threshold: The Developing Adolescent,* ed. S.S. Feldman and G. R. Elliott. Cambridge, Mass.: Harvard University Press.

Steinberg, S. R., and J. L. Kincheloe. 1997. *Kinderculture: The Corporate Construction of Childhood.* Boulder, Colo.: Westview Press.

Strauss, C. 1992. "Models and Motives." Pp. 1–20 in *Human Motives and Cultural Models,* ed. R. D'Andrade and C. Strauss. Cambridge: Cambridge University Press.

Stryker, S. 1987. "Identity Theory: Developments and Extensions." Pp. 89–104 in *Self and Identity: Psychosocial Perspectives,* ed. K. Yardley and T. Honess. New York: John Wiley and Sons.

Suarez-Orozco, M. 1989. *Central American Refugees and U.S. High Schools.* Stanford, Calif.: Stanford University Press.

Thorne, B. 1993. *Gender Play: Girls and Boys at School.* New Brunswick, N.J.: Rutgers University Press.

Tuchman, G. 1978. "The Symbolic Annihilation of Women by the Mass Media." In *Hearth and Home: Images of Women in the Mass Media*, ed. G. Tuchman, A. K. Daniels, and J. Benet. New York: Oxford University Press.

Turkle, S. 1995. *Life on the Screen: Identity in the Age of the Internet.* New York: Simon and Schuster.

Tyner, K. 1998. *Literacy in a Digital World: Teaching and Learning in the Age of Information.* Mahwah, N.J.: Lawrence Erlbaum Associates.

Way, N. 1998. *Everyday Courage: The Lives and Stories of Urban Teenagers.* New York: New York University Press.

Weis, L., and M. Fine, eds. 1993. *Beyond Silenced Voices: Class, Race and Gender in United States Schools.* Albany: State University of New York Press.

Wertsch, J. V. 1985. *Vygotsky and the Social Formation of Mind.* Cambridge, Mass.: Harvard University Press.

Williams, T. M., and M. C. Boyes. 1986. "Television-Viewing Patterns and Use of the Media." Pp. 215–64 in *The Impact of Television: A Natural Experiment in Three Communities*, ed. T. M. Williams. Orlando, Fla.: Academic Press.

Willis, P. 1977. *Learning to Labour: How Working Class Kids Get Working Class Jobs.* Farnborough, U.K.: Saxon House.

———. 1990. *Common Culture: Symbolic Work at Play in the Everyday Cultures of the Young.* Boulder, Colo.: Westview Press.

Wines, M. 1992. "Views on Single Motherhood Are Multiple at White House." *New York Times* (May 21), A1, B16.

Winnicott, D. W. 1990 (1971). *Playing and Reality.* London: Tavistock Publications.

Wolcott, H. 1982. "The Anthropology of Learning." *Anthropology and Education Quarterly* 13, no. 2: 83–108.

Index

Acting, before peers, 57–58, 69, 122; in identity formation, 100; and Murphy Brown, 95

Adolescents: identity projects, 14–15; media imagery of, 119; media influence on, 2; and peer groups, 22, 23, 30; perspective on New York City, 16–17; reasons for study of, 156–57; social experiences of, 162; social spaces for, 18–19; in television culture, 3; and TV activity, 26–32

Adults, perception of television, 13, 31, 119–20, 170n 3

Adventure genre, reality judgment for, 66

Advertising, and audience ratings, 12; fulfilling human needs, 15–16, 129; and gender identity, 153; social responsibility in, 48–49; young people's awareness of, 112, 117–118, 123, 127, 130

All My Children: compared to talk shows, 138; description of, 171

Alternative Middle School (AMS): diversity of, 19–20, 158; location of, 19; methodology for study of, 158–59; philosophy of, 20; reasons for choice of, 157–58

American dream, television in promotion of, 11, 104, 131

Apartments, urban, 18

The Arsenio Hall Show, in identity work, 69

Audience, programming power of, 12–13

Bakhtin, M., thought, language and society, 16, 156

Bamboozled: cultural tension in, 152; description of, 171

Barney Miller, 84, 172

Basketball: sexism in, 81–82; social importance of, 63, 75, 169n 3; on television, 64–65

The Beatles, 6, 172

Beauty standards, on television, 97–98

Benhabib, S., private and public spheres, 89

Bergen, Candice: as celebrity, 124–25; in media institutions, 112. *See also Murphy Brown*

Beverly Hills 90210, 1, 13–14, 151, 172

Blossom, 45, 172–73

Borge, Victor, 6, 173

Brokaw, Tom, 140, 173

Buckingham, D., youth language, 156; youth, media, and education, ix

Burnett, Carol, 6, 173

Career, social responsibility in, 48–49

Cartoons, preferences for, 28

Cheers, 66, 150, 173–74

Clarissa Explains It All, 174

Class identity, in power relations, 110

Clothing: in peer acceptance, 62, 75; sexual boundaries for, 37, 50–51

CNN, 1, 174

Coach, 45, 174–75; romantic relationships in, 150

College, role of, in success, 46–47, 54, 81, 142

Commercialism: entertainment used for, 12–13; in identity work, 15–16, 112–13; in image play, 123–24; television used for, 10–11, 31